DAS KAPITAL

DAS KAPITAL

A CRITIQUE OF
POLITICAL ECONOMY

BY KARL MARX

Gateway Editions

Gateway Editions™ is a trademark of Salem Communications Holding Corporation; Regnery® is a registered trademark of Salem Communications Holding Corporation

Cataloging-in-Publication data on file with the Library of Congress

ISBN 978-0-89526-711-5

Published in the United States by
Gateway Editions
An imprint of Regnery Publishing
A Division of Salem Media Group
Washington, DC 20001
www.Regnery.com

Manufactured in the United States of America

2021 printing

Books are available in quantity for promotional or premium use. For information on discounts and terms, please visit our website: www.Regnery.com.

CONTENTS

PART II
The Transformation of Money into Capital

PART III
The Production of Absolute Surplus-Value

PART VI
Wages

PART VII
The Accumulation of Capital

PART VIII
The So-Called Primitive Accumulation

INTRODUCTION

D*as Kapital*, it has been said, is the bible of Communism, while the *Communist Manifesto* is its creed. Few can boast that they have read all three volumes of *Das Kapital*; fewer still, that they have understood its tortuous prose. Yet millions have passionately defended or attacked it, and revolutions have been made in its name. *Sua fata habent libelli*. *Das Kapital* acquired the significance of a symbol. Even today, while many of the theories developed in *Das Kapital* tend to be obsolete, and most the arguments used in support of these theories are no longer relevant, one-fifth of the globe is governed by a system which traces its political ethos to the writings of Karl Marx. *Das Kapital* remains, in retrospect, an important milestone in the history of nineteenth-century European social thought.

It is necessary to say *in retrospect*, because Volume I of *Das Kapital*, the only one to have appeared during Marx's lifetime, found no immediate acceptance. The book was so ignored that Friedrich Engels was forced to write numerous reviews of it under assumed names, some laudatory and some critical, to bring it to public attention. Under this impetus and with the growing notoriety of Marx's movement, *Das Kapital* was read and studied by an increasingly important circle of intellectuals who, rather than the workers to whom its central message was directed, were responsible for establishing the book's reputation.

Volume I of *Das Kapital* was published in 1867 (almost two decades after the *Manifesto*) by combining two chapters of an earlier study (*Critique of Political Economy*) with the mass of material which Marx had accumulated during his long sessions in the British Museum in London. When Marx died in 1883, Volumes II and III were no more than a confused mass of notes, references, and outlines. It was Engels' lot to put them into final form and prepare them for publication. They appeared in 1885 and 1894, respectively. However, they remained considerably inferior, both intellectually and from the point of view of vigor and impact, to Volume I, which became a classic. It is this volume that is condensed in the present edition.

Having in the *Communist Manifesto* assured the workers that capitalism was doomed and that the future belonged to them, Marx owed the world a more solid proof of his assertions. *Das Kapital* claims to do just that. The task which Marx set himself was an ambitious one. His goal was nothing less than the discovery of the economic laws of motion of modern society, and to show that these laws assured the eventual triumph of the proletariat. He sought to do this through a historical correlation of the rise of the modern proletariat with the general development of the technical means of production—to demonstrate that the processes of production, exchange, and distribution as they actually occur proved his thesis.

The result was a curious amalgamation of economic and political theory, history, sociology, and utopia. Marx, in effect, attempted to unite all the philosophical, scientific, and moral strands of the Victorian age into one vast system of a universal scope. His dialectical philosophy was borrowed from German classical philosophy (Hegel in particular), and transformed into historical materialism. With it went a concept of state and revolution that was borrowed from French revolutionary tradition. His system of political economy was built on notions of labor theory of value and the theory of surplus value which he derived from classical (particularly British) economic doctrine.

Marx's method was not that of observation and scientific deduction. It was rather that of an *a priori* conceptual scheme, supplemented by a wealth of documentary material selected to fit the main tenets of the scheme.

He takes as the point of departure the assertion that *production* is the primordial fact to which all other facts without exception must be subordinated if they are to be understood correctly. By production, Marx meant specifically man's production of his means of subsistence. He defines production as the appropriation of nature by the individual within and through a certain form of society. Thus production, for Marx, is always a social activity, not an individual one.

Marx pictures a social class (the "workers" or proletariat) which is capable of, and does, produce more wealth ("value") than it actually enjoys, and another class (the "bourgeoisie" or the "capitalists") which appropriates the residue ("surplus value") by virtue of its possession of the means of production (i.e., machinery, natural resources, transports, financial credit, etc.). It is Marx's contention that this system is doomed, for the vested interests on which it rests depend for survival on an absolute freedom of competition which the mechanism of capitalist society tends to eliminate. Why? Here Marx introduces, without apparent necessity, the notion of value to explain the process as he sees it.

Marx argues that the capitalist who owns the means of production also appropriates the product, while the worker who produces it is given a fixed wage. Thus human labor itself is turned into a commodity. According to Marx, the wage does not correspond to the value created by the worker, but is lower. For while the wage (i.e., the market value of labor) is equivalent to the minimum sum necessary to keep the worker in a state enabling him to continue to produce (subsistence wage), the worker is capable of producing more than what he needs for his subsistence. This "surplus value" is the capitalist's profit derived from unpaid labor time. Thus, if $x represents the wage, and $y the price at which the capitalist sells the value produced by the worker, $y-x is the surplus value pocketed by the capitalist.

Now, Marx maintains that only those members of society who contribute to the actual production of commodities create value; those who merely carry on the process of circulation needed to keep the capitalist system functioning (including supervision of labor) do not. Nor do the means of production detained by the capitalists (so-called "constant capital," such as machinery, mineral deposits, raw materials, etc.) have any other than stored-up value (i.e., value already produced) or potential value (i.e., before labor is applied to them). Under these conditions, Marx says, labor alone (which he calls "variable capital") is entitled to the full value produced. Indeed, when the capitalist society is overthrown, the worker will retain the full value produced by him, and at the same time have access to the "constant capital" which all workers will own in common.

In the meanwhile, the capitalists' profits grow, Marx complains. The rate of profit depends on the proportion of variable capital to constant capital employed in a given enterprise—that is, the more labor and the less machinery is employed, the greater will be the rate of profit. But competition forces the capitalist to install more and more machinery and labor-saving devices, because labor is more productive if applied on a larger scale of organization and if expensive machinery is applied. The ensuing losses in the capitalist's profits are offset by him by intensifying the exploitation of labor (i.e., by forcing the workers to produce more unpaid-for surplus value). The capitalist's task is facilitated by the growing unemployment brought about by the process automation. As competition between capitalists becomes ever keener, the misery of the proletariat (i.e., of the workers) grows correspondingly (a theory Marx apparently borrowed from Genovesi, Ortes, and the Utopian Socialists). This process, according to Marx, is an inevitable aspect of the mechanism of capitalist society, just as the exploitation urge is an inescapable phenomenon in the presence of competition. He maintains that this urge is not necessarily inherent in human nature but is dictated by the class structure of a society which compels individuals and groups to act according to their narrow self-interest.

Competition, in Marx's analysis, gradually leads to the concentration of accumulated capital in fewer and fewer hands, since the largest, and therefore the most efficient, of the competing groups are bound to absorb and eliminate the smaller ones. The owners of most smaller businesses are reduced to the status of proletarians.

However, while the number of exploited workers swells and eventually embraces almost the entire population, and while the degree of their poverty increases, so does the intensity of their wrath against their oppressors. The proletarian class is organized and disciplined by the very mechanism of capitalist production. The violent intervention by this class, together with the growing contradictions inherent in the capitalist system, will spell the doom of capitalism. Private property will be abolished by the expropriation of the few remaining super-usurpers by the mass of the working people. The dictatorship of the proletariat will replace capitalist society, together with its super-structure of state, culture, and ethics.

Now, it may be argued that Marx's thesis, that the employment of labor by private capitalists necessarily leads to exploitation (with the implication that all means of production should be socialized), derives from considerations that have nothing to do with economic theory. And, indeed, this is basically an ethical, not economic doctrine. Exploitation is not a scientific phenomenon but one of the moral order. The old-fashioned law of supply and demand (assuming that labor is in greater supply than demand for it) suffices to explain Marx's theory of the "increasing misery" of the workers without bringing into it the theory of value at all. Even Marx's distinction between "bourgeois" and "proletarian" has a distinctly axiological connotation.

However, it was this ethical and messianic character of Marx's theory which gave *Das Kapital* a power capable of driving to the barricades. It was a doctrine of deliverance of the proletariat, a myth of a class with which Marx himself had no direct bonds or contacts, a bible of technological messianism. Marx endowed his theories with the double attribute of *universality* and *inevitability*. He made his observations in mid-nineteenth-century capitalist Europe. His analyses were often correct, although they did not reveal anything that was not general knowledge, and to an extent constitute valid contributions to the history of social relations. His great error was to ascribe to his observations a static, permanent, as well as general, character. He did not believe capitalism capable of evolution, and what he saw in the society of his time, he regarded as the basis for all society, everywhere and at all times. Moreover, in keeping with the laws of dialectics which Marx formulated in the preface to his *Critique of Political Economy* inasmuch as they applied to the growth of society, Marx insisted that the laws governing capitalist society, as well as those leading to that society's final destruction, were "natural laws" working independently of human volition toward "inevitable" results. Once society has entered upon a given economic system, it must go through with it to the end. It may only hasten the transition from one stage of this evolution to another. Incidentally, neither is this idea original with Marx. Indeed, all of the concepts which he claimed as the "scientific" basis of his theories were formulated long before him by Condorcet, Saint-Simon, Auguste Comte, and others.

A century has passed since Marx first developed his theses on the mechanism of capitalist society. A great deal has happened during those years, but precious little to confirm the validity of his allegations. Most of his theses have failed to withstand the test of time. He was right when he predicted that capitalism as he knew it would not survive; but he did not foresee the significant evolution of capitalist society which took place after *Das Kapital* was published. The "inevitable" collapse of capitalism did not occur. Instead, capitalism in its new form flourishes as never before.

(1) The rapid growth and extension of joint-stock companies have all but eliminated the individual capitalist-owner who was the prime target of Marx's attacks. The tycoon has been replaced by the professional manager who does not own the capital, but is himself a salaried employee of the company which owns the capital. Accumulated capital is redistributed as profit among the shareholders, a turn which is nowhere anticipated in Marx's writings.

(2) The workers themselves, the "proletarians" as Marx liked to call them, stand no longer helplessly facing the all-powerful capitalist. They established unions of their own, just as Marx said they would, but these unions are powerful enough to impose the workers' demands on the "capitalists" without having to resort to violent revolution. Nor are the labor unions anxious to seize ownership of the means of production or, more often than not, even to take part in the management. The unions have also been quite successful in obtaining a steady rise in real wages and working conditions, thus belying Marx's thesis about the growing pauperization of the masses. In addition, scientific progress itself has increased production and ended the type of poverty for which socialism to many thinking people of the late nineteenth century seemed to be the only remedy.

(3) Marx could not conceive of a state in terms other than as the power of one class organized for the exploitation of other classes. He would have found the modern "capitalist" state, which sets itself social goals and intervenes to protect the interests of the "proletariat," utterly unbelievable. The degree of such intervention varies today greatly from country to country. It ranges anywhere from the setting of minimum wages, grants of housing and schooling subsidies, social security programs, government-supported

cultural facilities, and progressive-tax systems, to the institution of profit-sharing by workers, the acquisition of certain means of production by public bodies, and the establishment of the welfare state. The aim of this intervention, whatever the degree, is always to establish a balance between private control, on the one hand, and public control, on the other, over the functioning of the economic system so as to prevent the exploitation of labor which Marx believed to be an iron law of capitalism.

(4) Nor did Marx foresee that the middle class, far from being reduced to the status of the proletariat by the operation of the law of capitalist competition, would actually enjoy a remarkable consolidation of its position and broadening of its bases. Today, because of the increased prosperity of the workers, there is a steady influx of laboring people into the middle class. This new middle class is acquiring shares in the capital and thus has a vested interest in the perpetuation of the modern capitalist system, not in its downfall.

(5) As prosperity grows, "class-consciousness" tends to disappear. Modern capitalist society is in the process of establishing a common denominator for all men irrespective of their social origin, by the standardization of living conditions and of ways of life and by the creation of equal opportunities for all. Marx's theory of the "struggle of classes" is fast becoming obsolete with the equally rapid disappearance of the "proletariat."

(6) As prosperity grows, government intervention becomes increasingly unnecessary and even odious to an increasing majority of people. Thus in Great Britain in 1959, a country which Marx regarded as a model of the capitalist society he was describing in *Das Kapital*, the electorate has clearly rejected further nationalization of the means of production and any increased control of the economy. In general, there is a remarkable coincidence between, on the one hand, unprecedented economic prosperity, and, on the other hand, a decline of social democracy, in mid-twentieth-century Western "capitalist" society. It is equally significant that the oldest and most

powerful large-scale Marxist organization, the German Social Democratic party, felt itself compelled to revise its program in 1959 by departing from all the economic principles of Marxian socialism. It called for "free competition in a free economy" and denounced "totalitarian controlled economy." It declared that "private ownership of the means of production may justly claim the protection of society," and asked for modification of the *laissez faire* approach only from fear that cartels might render sound competition impossible. Characteristically, the modification suggested is not nationalization, but "effective public controls to prevent misuse of the economy by the powerful."

(7) Marx proved equally wrong in his assumption that (a) the proletariat is eagerly awaiting opportune moment to establish its dictatorship over the defeated property-owning classes; and that (b) the establishment of socialism must by necessity be effected by violent means.

In fact, all governments which today claim to embody the teachings of Marx and to have carried out successfully the transition to the dictatorship of the proletariat owe their position to the action of minority groups which was neither supported nor ratified by the vast majority of the "proletarians." On the other hand, even Soviet rulers are loath today to claim that violence is absolutely necessary for the establishment of socialism. It has already been pointed out that many modern "capitalist" states have adopted certain of the Marxist remedies without the compulsion of the struggle of classes and violent overthrow of the existing order.

The planned economy made its appearance in "Socialist" and "capitalist" countries alike under the pressure of national emergencies either during or after war. It owed nothing to Marx's ideas. At best it was justified by vague references to Utopian-Socialist concepts of "equitable distribution." Marx himself did not have a clear idea about the mechanics of a planned economy after the passing of capitalist society.

What then, is the meaning of *Das Kapital* for the modern reader? Erich Ollenhauer, the chairman of the German Social Democratic party declared on November 13, 1959, "The demand that the political programs of Karl Marx and Friedrich Engels be made the basis of a Social Democratic program in the year 1959 is so un-Marxist as to be unthinkable." Modern Marxists, except in Communist-ruled countries, today tend to relegate Marx's writings to the rank of outstanding historic documents, no longer in step with modern times. And even the term "capitalism," which Marx used as the basis of all his analyses, has no longer any generic meaning applicable to modern society.

However, *Das Kapital* should continue to be read and studied by the modern reader, not because it contains a set of interesting but erroneous economic doctrines, but because these economic doctrines are presented in the context of a philosophy which subordinates the problems of human freedom and human dignity to the issues of who should own the means of production and how wealth should be distributed.

The economic theories of *Das Kapital* are no longer an active challenge to us. But its philosophy, which elevates the triumph of matter over spirit to the category of a historical necessity, continues to haunt the world like a spectre, just as in 1848 Marx said it would. It is to understand the nature of the challenge that we must return to this ominous classic.

—SERGE L. LEVITSKY

PART I

Commodities and Money

CHAPTER I

COMMODITIES

SECTION 1—THE TWO FACTORS OF A COMMODITY: USE-VALUE AND VALUE (THE SUBSTANCE OF VALUE AND THE MAGNITUDE OF VALUE)

The wealth of those societies in which the capitalist mode of production prevails, presents itself as "an immense accumulation of commodities," its unit being a single commodity.

A commodity is, in the first place, an object outside us, a thing that by its properties satisfies human wants of some sort or another. The nature of such wants, whether, for instance, they spring from the stomach or from fancy, makes no difference. Neither are we here concerned to know how the object satisfies these wants, whether directly as means of subsistence, or indirectly as means of production.

★ ★ ★

The utility of a thing makes it a use-value. But this utility is not a thing of air. Being limited by the physical properties of the commodity, it has no existence apart from that commodity. A commodity, such as iron, corn, or a diamond, is therefore, so far as it is a material thing, a use-value, something useful. This property of a commodity is independent of the amount of labor required to appropriate its useful qualities. When treating of use-value, we always assume to be dealing with definite quantities, such as dozens of watches, yards of linen, or tons of iron. The use-values of commodities furnish the material for a special study, that of the commercial knowledge commodities. Use-values become a reality only by use or consumption: they also constitute the substance of all wealth, whatever may be the social form of that wealth. In the form of society we are about to consider, they are, in addition, the material depositories of exchange value.

Exchange value, at first sight, presents itself as a quantitative relation, as the proportion in which values in use of one sort are exchanged for those of another sort, a relation constantly changing with time and place. Hence exchange value appears to be something accidental and purely relative, and consequently an intrinsic value, i.e., an exchange value that is inseparably connected with, inherent in commodities, seems a contradiction in terms.

★ ★ ★

Let us take two commodities, e.g., corn and iron. The proportions in which they are exchangeable, whatever those proportions may be, can always be represented by an equation in which a given quantity of corn is equated to some quantity of iron: e.g., 1 quarter corn=x cwt. iron. What does this equation tell us? It tells us that in two different things—in 1 quarter of corn and x cwt. of iron, there exists in equal quantities something common to both. The two things must therefore be equal to a third, which in itself is neither the one nor the other. Each of them, so far as it is exchange value, must therefore be reducible to this third.

★ ★ ★

This common "something" cannot be either a geometrical, a chemical, or any other natural property of commodities. Such properties claim our attention only insofar as they affect the utility of those commodities, make them use-values. But the exchange of commodities is evidently an act characterized by a total abstraction from use-value.

★ ★ ★

If then we leave out of consideration the use-value of commodities, they have only one common property left, that of being products of labor. But even the product of labor itself has undergone a change in our hands. If we make abstraction from its use-value, we make abstraction at the same time from the material elements and shapes that make the product a use-value; we see in it no longer a table, a house, yarn, or any other useful thing. Its existence as a material thing is put out of sight. Neither can it any longer be regarded as the product of the labor of the joiner, the mason, the spinner, or of any other definite kind of productive labor. Along with the useful qualities of the products themselves, we put out of sight both the useful character of the various kinds of labor embodied in them, and the concrete forms of that labor; there is nothing left but what is common to them all; all are reduced to one and the same sort of labor, human labor in the abstract.

Let us now consider the residue of each of these products; it consists of the same unsubstantial reality in each, a mere congelation of homogeneous human labor, of labor-power expended without regard to the mode of its expenditure. All that these things now tell us is, that human labor-power has been expended in their production, that human labor is embodied in them. When looked at as crystals of this social substance, common to them all, they are—Values.

We have seen that when commodities are exchanged, their exchange value manifests itself as something totally independent of their use-value. But if we abstract from their use-value, there remains their Value as defined above. Therefore, the common substance that manifests itself in the exchange value of commodities, whenever they are exchanged, is their value.

★ ★ ★

A use-value, or useful article, therefore, has value only because human labor in the abstract has been embodied or materialized in it. How, then, is the magnitude of this value to be measured? Plainly, by the quantity of the value-creating substance, the labor, contained in the article. The quantity of labor, however, is measured by its duration, and labor-time in its turn finds its standard in weeks, days, and hours.

Some people might think that if the value of a commodity is determined by the quantity of labor spent on it, the more idle and unskilful the laborer, the more valuable would his commodity be, because more time would be required in its production. The labor, however, that forms the substance of value, is homogeneous human labor, expenditure of one uniform labor-power. The total labor-power of society, which is embodied in the sum total of the values of all commodities produced by that society, counts here as one homogeneous mass of human labor-power, composed though it be of innumerable individual units. Each of these units is the same as any other, so far as it has the character of the average labor-power of society, and takes effect as such; that is, so far as it requires for producing a commodity, no more time than is needed on an average, no more than is socially necessary. The labor-time socially necessary is that required to produce an article under the normal conditions of production, and with the average degree of skill and intensity prevalent at the time.

★ ★ ★

We see then that that which determines the magnitude of the value of any article is the amount of labor socially necessary, or the labor-time socially necessary for its production. Each individual commodity, in this connection, is to be considered as an average sample of its class. Commodities, therefore, in which equal quantities of labor are embodied, or which can be produced in the same time, have the same value. The value of one commodity is to the value of any other, as the labor-time necessary for the production of the one is to that necessary for the production of the other.

★ ★ ★

The value of a commodity would therefore remain constant, if the labor-time required for its production also remained constant. But the latter changes with every variation in the productiveness of labor. This productiveness is determined by various circumstances, among others, by the average amount of skill of the workmen, the state of science and the degree of its practical application, the social organization of production, the extent and capabilities of the means of production, and by physical conditions. For example, the same amount of labor in favorable seasons is embodied in eight bushels of corn, and in unfavourable, only in four. The same labor extracts from rich mines more metal than from poor mines. Diamonds are of very rare occurrence on the earth's surface, and hence their discovery costs, on average, a great deal of labor-time. Consequently much labor is represented in a small compass. In general, the greater the productiveness of labor, the less is the labor-time required for the production of an article, the less is the amount of labor crystallised in that article, and the less is its value; and *vice versa*, the less the productiveness of labor, the greater is the labor-time required for the production of an article, and the greater is its value. The value of a commodity, therefore, varies directly as the quantity, and inversely as the productiveness, of the labor incorporated in it.

A thing can be a use-value, without having value. This is the case whenever its utility to man is not due to labor. Such are air, virgin soil, natural meadows, etc. A thing can be useful, and the product of human labor, without being a commodity. Whoever directly satisfies his wants with the produce of his own labor, creates, indeed, use-values, but not commodities. In order to produce the latter, he must not only produce use-values, but use-values for others, social use-values. Lastly, nothing can have value without being an object of utility. If the thing is useless, so is the labor contained in it; the labor does not count as labor, and therefore creates no value.

SECTION 2—THE TWOFOLD CHARACTER OF THE LABOR EMBODIED IN COMMODITIES

At first sight a commodity presented itself to us as a complex of two things—use-value and exchange-value. Later on, we saw also that labor, too, possesses the same two-fold nature; for, so far as it finds expression in value, it does not possess the same characteristics that belong to it as a creator of use-values. I was the first to point out and to examine critically this two-fold nature of the labor contained in commodities. As this point is the pivot on which a clear comprehension of political economy turns, we must go more into detail.

Let us take two commodities such as a coat and 10 yards of linen, and let the former be double the value of the latter, so that, if 10 yards of linen=W, the coat=2W.

The coat is a use-value that satisfies a particular want. Its existence is the result of a special sort of productive activity, the nature of which is determined by its aim, mode of operation, subject, means, and result. The labor, whose utility is thus represented by the value in use of its product, or which manifests itself by making its product a use-value, we call useful labor. In this connection we consider only its useful effect.

As the coat and the linen are two qualitatively different use-values, so also are the two forms of labor that produce them, tailoring and weaving. Were these two objects not qualitatively different, not produced respectively by labor of different quality, they could not stand to each other in the relation of commodities. Coats are not exchanged for coats, one use-value is not exchange for another of the same kind.

To all the different varieties of values in use there correspond as many different kinds of useful labor, classified according to the order, genus, species, and variety to which they belong in the social division of labor. This division of labor is a necessary condition for the production of commodities, but it does not follow conversely that the production of commodities is a necessary condition for the division of labor.

★ ★ ★

To resume, then: In the use-value of each commodity there is contained useful labor, i.e., productive activity of a definite kind and exercised with a definite aim. Use-values cannot confront each other as commodities unless the useful labor embodied in them is qualitatively different in each of them. In a community, the produce of which in general takes the form of commodities, i.e., in a community of commodity producers, this qualitative difference between the useful forms of labor that are carried on independently by individual producers, each on their own account, develops into a complex system, a social division of labor.

Anyhow, whether the coat be worn by the tailor or by his customer, in either case it operates as a use-value. Nor is the relation between the coat and the labor that produced it altered by the circumstance that tailoring may have become a trade, an independent branch of the social division of labor. Wherever the want of clothing forced them to it, the human race made clothes for thousands of years, without a single man becoming a tailor. But coats and linen, like every other element of material wealth that is not the spontaneous product of nature, must invariably owe their existence to a special productive activity, exercised with a definite aim, an activity that appropriates particular nature-given materials to particular human wants. So far therefore as labor is a creator of use-value, it is useful labor, and it is a necessary condition, independent of all forms of society, for the existence of the human race; it is an eternal nature-imposed necessity, without which there can be no material exchanges between man and nature, and therefore no life.

The use-values, coat, linen, etc., i.e., the bodies of commodities, are combinations of two elements—matter and labor. If we take away the useful labor expended upon them, a material substratum is always left, which is furnished by nature without the help of man. The latter can work only as nature does, that is, by changing the form of matter. Nay more, in this work of changing the form he is constantly helped by natural forces. We see, then, that labor is not the only source of material wealth, of use-values produced by labor.

Let us now pass from the commodity considered as a use-value to the value of commodities.

By our assumption, the coat is worth twice as much as the linen. But this is a mere quantitative difference, which for the present does not concern us. We bear in mind, however, that if the value of the coat is double that of 10 yds. of linen, 20 yds. of linen must have the same value as one coat. So far as they are values, the coat and the linen are things of a like substance, objective expressions of essentially identical labor. But tailoring and weaving are, qualitatively, different kinds of labor. There are, however, states of society in which one and the same man does tailoring and weaving alternately, in which case these two forms of labor are mere modifications of the labor of the same individual, and not special and fixed functions of different persons; just as the coat which our tailor makes one day, and the trousers which he makes another day, imply only a variation in the labor of one and the same individual. Moreover, we see at a glance that, in our capitalist society, a given portion of human labor is, in accordance with the varying demand, at one time supplied in the form of tailoring, at another in the form of weaving. This change may possibly cause friction, but take place it must.

Productive activity, if we leave out of sight its special form, viz., the useful character of the labor, is nothing but the expenditure of human labor-power. Tailoring and weaving, though qualitatively different productive activities, are each a productive expenditure of human brains, nerves, and muscles, and in this sense are human labor. They are but two different modes of expending human labor-power. Of course, this labor-power, which remains the same under all its modifications, must have attained a certain pitch of development before it can be expended in a multiplicity of modes. But the value of a commodity represents human labor in the abstract, the expenditure of human labor in general. And just as in society, a general or a banker plays a great part, but mere man, on the other hand, a very shabby part, so here with mere human labor. It is the expenditure of simple labor-power, i.e., of the labor-power which, on average, apart from any special development, exists in the organism of every ordinary individual. Simple average labor, it is true, varies in character in different countries and at different times, but in a particular society it is given. Skilled labor counts only as simple labor intensified, or rather, as multiplied simple labor, a given quantity of skilled labor being considered equal to a greater quantity of simple labor. Experience shows that this reduction is constantly being made. A commodity may be the product of the most skilled labor, but its value, by equating it to the product of simple unskilled labor, represents a definite quality of the latter labor alone.★ The different proportions in which different sorts of labor are reduced to unskilled labor as their standard, are established by a social process that goes on behind the backs of the producers, and, consequently, appear to be fixed by custom. For simplicity's sake we shall henceforth account every kind of labor to be unskilled, simple labor; by this we do no more than save ourselves the trouble of making the reduction.

★The reader must note that we are not speaking here of the wages or value that the laborer gets for a given labor time, but of the value of the commodity in which that labor time is materialized. Wages is a category that, as yet, has no existence at the present stage of our investigation.

Just as, therefore, in viewing the coat and linen as values, we abstract from their different use-values, so it is with the labor represented by those values: we disregard the difference between its useful forms, weaving and tailoring. As the use-values, coat and linen, are combinations of special productive activities with cloth and yarn, while the values, coat and linen, are, on the other hand, mere homogeneous congelations of indifferentiated labor, so the labor embodied in these latter values does not count by virtue of its productive relation to cloth and yarn, but only as being an expenditure of human labor-power. Tailoring and weaving are neccessary factors in the creation of the use-values, coat and linen, precisely because these two kinds of labor are of different qualities; but only insofar as abstraction is made from their special qualities, only insofar as both possess the same quality of being human labor, do tailoring and weaving form the substance of the values of the same articles.

Coats and linen, however, are not merely values, but values of definite magnitude, and according to our assumption, the coat is worth twice as much as the ten yards of linen. Whence this difference in their values? It is owing to the fact that the linen contains only half as much labor as the coat, and consequently, that in the production of the latter, labor-power must have been expended during twice the time necessary for the production of the former.

While, therefore, with reference to use-value, the labor contained in a commodity counts only qualitatively, with reference to value it counts only quantitively, and must first be reduced to human labor pure and simple. In the former case, it is a question of how and what, in the latter of how much? How long a time? Since the magnitude of the value of a commodity represents only the quantity of labor embodied in it, it follows that all commodities, when taken in certain proportions, must be equal in value.

If the productive power of all the different sorts of useful labor required for the production of a coat remains unchanged, the sum of the values of the coat produced increases with their number. If one coat represents x days' labor, two coats represent 2x days' labor, and so on. But assume that the duration of the labor necessary for the production of a coat becomes doubled or halved. In the first case, one coat is worth as much as two coats were before; in the second case, two coats are only worth as much as one was before, although in both cases one coat renders the same service as before, and the useful labor embodied in it remains of the same quality. But the quantity of labor spent on its production has altered.

An increase in the quantity of use-values is an increase of material wealth. With two coats two men can be clothed, with one coat only one man. Nevertheless, an increased quantity of material wealth may correspond to a simultaneous fall in the magnitude of its value. This antagonistic movement has its origin in the two-fold character of labor. Productive power has reference, of course, only to labor of some useful concrete form, the efficacy of any special productive activity during a given time being dependent on its productiveness. Useful labor becomes, therefore, a more or less abundant source of products, in proportion to the rise or fall of its productiveness. On the other hand, no change in this productiveness affects the labor represented by value. Since productive power is an attribute of the concrete useful forms of labor, of course it can no longer have any bearing on that labor as soon as we make abstraction from those concrete useful forms. However then productive power may vary, the same labor, exercised during equal periods of time, always yields equal amounts of value. But it will yield, during equal periods of time, different quantities of values in use; more, if the productive power rises, fewer if it falls. The same change in productive power, which increases the fruitfulness of labor, and, in consequence, the quantity of use-values produced by that labor, will diminish the total value of this increased quantity of use-values, provided such shorten the total labor-time necessary for their production, and vice versa.

On the one hand all labor is, speaking physiologically, an expenditure of human labor-power, and in its character of identical abstract human labor, it creates and forms the value of commodities. On the other hand, all labor is the expenditure of human labor-power in a special form and with a definite aim, and in this, its character of concrete useful labor, it produces use-values.

SECTION 3—THE FORM OF VALUE OR EXCHANGE VALUE

Commodities come into the world in the shape of use-values, articles, or goods, such as iron, linen, corn, etc. This is their plain, homely, bodily form. They are, however, commodities, because they are something twofold, both objects of utility, and, at the same time, depositories of value. They manifest themselves therefore as commodities, or have the form of commodities, only insofar as they have two forms, a physical or natural form, and a value form.

★ ★ ★

Everyone knows, if he knows nothing else, that commodities have a value form common to them all, presenting a marked contrast with the varied bodily forms of their use-values. I mean their money form. Here, however, a task is set for us, the performance of which has not yet even been attempted by *bourgeois* economy— the task of tracing the genesis of this money form, of developing the expression of value implied in the value relation of commodities, from its simplest, almost imperceptible outline, to the dazzling money form. By doing this we shall, at the same time, solve the riddle presented by money.

The simplest value relation is evidently that of one commodity to some other commodity of a different kind. Hence the relation between the values of two commodities supplies us with the expression of the value of a single commodity.

A. Elementary or Accidental Form of Value.

x commodity A=y commodity B, or
x commodity A is worth y commodity B.
20 yards of linen=1 coat, or
20 yards of linen are worth 1 coat.

1. *The two poles of the expression of value:*
relative form and equivalent form.

The whole mystery of the form of value lies hidden in this elementary form.

Here two different kinds of commodities (in our example the linen and the coat) evidently play two different parts. The linen expresses its value in the coat; the coat serves as the material in which that value is expressed. The former plays an active, the latter a passive, part. The value of the linen is represented as relative value, or appears in relative form. The coat officiates as equivalent, or appears in equivalent form.

The relative form and the equivalent form are two intimately connected, mutually dependent and inseparable elements of the expression of value; but, at the same time, are mutually exclusive, antagonistic extremes—i.e., poles of the same expression. They are allotted to the two different commodities brought into relation by that expression. It is not possible to express the value of linen in linen. Twenty yards of linen=20 yards of linen is no expression of value. On the contrary, such an equation merely says that 20 yards of linen are nothing else than 20 yards of linen, a definite quantity of the use-value linen. The value of the linen can therefore be expressed only relatively—i.e., in some other commodity. The relative form of the value of the linen presupposes, therefore, the presence of some other commodity—here the coat—under the form of an equivalent. On the other hand, the commodity that figures as the equivalent cannot at the same time assume the relative form. That second commodity is not the one whose value is expressed. Its function is merely to serve as the material in which the value of the first commodity is expressed.

No doubt, the expression 20 yards of linen=1 coat, or 20 yards of linen are worth 1 coat, implies the opposite relation: 1 coat=20 yards of linen, or 1 coat is worth 20 yards of linen. But, in that case, I must reverse the equation in order to express the value of the coat relatively; and as soon as I do that the linen becomes the equivalent instead of the coat. A single commodity cannot, therefore, simultaneously assume, in the same expression of value, both forms. The very polarity of these forms makes them mutually exclusive.

Whether, then, a commodity assumes the relative form, or the opposite equivalent form, depends entirely upon its accidental position in the expression of value—that is, upon whether it is the commodity whose value is being expressed or the commodity in which value is being expressed.

2. The Relative form of value:
(a.) The nature and importance of this form

In order to discover how the elementary expression of the value of a commodity lies hidden in the value relation of two commodities, we must, in the first place, consider the latter entirely apart from its quantitative aspect. The usual mode of procedure is generally the reverse, and in the value relation nothing is seen but the proportion between definite quantities of two different sorts of commodities that are considered equal to each other. It is apt to be forgotten that the magnitudes of different things can be compared quantitatively only when those magnitudes are expressed in terms of the same unit. It is only as expressions of such a unit that they are of the same denomination, and therefore commensurable.

Whether 20 yards of linen=1 coat, or equals 20 coats, or equals x coats—that is, whether a given quantity of linen is worth few or many coats, every such statement implies that the linen and coats, as magnitudes of value, are expressions of the same unit, things of the same kind. Linen=coat is the basis of the equation.

But the two commodities, whose identity of quality is thus assumed, do not play the same part. It is only the value of the linen that is expressed. And how? By its reference to the coat as its equivalent, as something that can be exchanged for it. In this relation the coat is the mode of existence of value, is value embodied, for only as such is it the same as the linen. On the other hand, the linen's own value comes to the front, receives independent expression, for it is only as being value that it is comparable with the coat as a thing of equal value, or exchangeable with the coat. To borrow an illustration from chemistry, butyric acid is a different substance from propyl formate. Yet both are made up of the same chemical substances, carbon (C), hydrogen (H), and oxygen (O), and that, too, in like proportions—namely, $C_4H_8O_2$. If now we equate butyric acid to propyl formate, then, in the first place, propyl formate would be, in this relation, merely a form of existence of $C_4H_8O_2$; and in the second place, we should be stating that butyric acid also consists of $C_4H_8O_2$. Therefore, by thus equating the two substances, expression would be given to their chemical composition, while their different physical forms would be neglected.

If we say that, as values, commodities are mere congelations of human labor, we reduce them by our analysis, it is true, to the abstraction, value; but we ascribe to this value no form apart from their bodily form. It is otherwise in the value relation of one commodity to another. Here, the one stands forth in its character of value by reason of its relation to the other.

By making the coat the equivalent of the linen, we equate the labor embodied in the former to that in the latter. Now, it is true that the tailoring, which makes the coat, is concrete labor of a different sort from the weaving which makes the linen. But the act of equating it to the weaving reduces the tailoring to that which is really equal in the two kinds of labor, to their common character of human labor. In this roundabout way, then, the fact is expressed that weaving also, insofar as it weaves value, has nothing to distinguish it from tailoring, and, consequently, is abstract human labor. It is the expression of equivalence between different sorts of commodities that alone brings into relief the specific character of value-creating labor, and this it does by actually reducing the different varieties of labor embodied in the different kinds of commodities to their common quality of human labor in the abstract.

There is, however, something else required beyond the expression of the specific character of the labor of which the value of the linen consists. Human labor-power in motion, or human labor, creates value, but is not itself value. It becomes value only in its congealed state when embodied in the form of some object. In order to express the value of the linen as a congelation of human labor, that value must be expressed as having objective existence, as being something materially different from the linen itself, and yet something common to the linen and all other commodities. The problem is already solved.

When occupying the position of equivalent in the equation of value, the coat ranks qualitatively as the equal of the linen, as something of the same kind, because it is value. In this position it is a thing in which we see nothing but value, or whose palpable bodily form represents value. Yet the coat itself, the body of the commodity, coat, is a mere use-value. A coat as such no more tells us it is value than does the first piece of linen we take hold of. This shows that when placed in value relation to the linen, the coat signifies more than when it is out of that relation, just as many a man strutting about in a gorgeous uniform counts for more than when dressed as a civilian.

In the production of the coat, human labor-power, in the shape of tailoring, must have been actually expended. Human labor is therefore accumulated in it. In this aspect the coat is a depository of value, but though worn to a thread, it does not let this fact show through. And as the equivalent of the linen in the value equation, it exists under this aspect alone, and counts therefore as embodied value, as a body that is value. *A*, for instance, cannot be "your majesty" to *B*, unless at the same time majesty in B's eyes assumes the bodily form of A, and, what is more, with every new father of the people, changes its features, hair, and many other things.

Hence, in the value equation in which the coat is the equivalent of the linen, the coat officiates as the form of value. The value of the commodity linen is expressed by the bodily form of the commodity coat, the value of one by the use-value of the other. As a use-value, the linen is something palpably different from the coat; as value, it is the same as the coat, and now has the appearance of a coat. Thus the linen acquires a value form different from its physical form. The fact that it is value is made manifest by its equality with the coat.

We see, then, all that our analysis of the value of commodities has already told us is told us by the linen itself, as soon as it comes into communication with another commodity, the coat. Only it betrays its thoughts in that language with which it alone is familiar, the language of commodities. In order to tell us that its own value is created by labor in its abstract character of human labor, it says that the coat, insofar as it is worth as much as the linen, and therefore is value, consists of the same labor as the linen. In order to inform us that its sublime reality as value is not the same as its cheap body, it says that value has the appearance of a coat, and consequently that so far as the linen is value, it and the coat are as alike as two peas.

★ ★ ★

By means, therefore, of the value relation expressed in our equation, the bodily form of commodity B becomes the value form of commodity A, or the body of commodity B acts as a mirror to the value of commodity A.★ By putting itself in relation with commodity B, as value in *propriâ personâ*, as the matter of which human labor is made up, the commodity A converts the value in use, B, into the substance in which to express its, A's, own use-value. The value of A, thus expressed in the use-value of B, has taken the form of relative value.

(b.) Quantitative determination of relative value

Every commodity, whose value it is intended to express, is a useful object of given quantity, as 15 bushels of corn, or 100 lbs. of coffee. And a given quantity of any commodity contains a definite quantity of human labor. The value-form must therefore not only express value generally, but also value in definite quantity. Therefore, in the value relation of A to commodity B, of the linen to the coat, not only is the latter, as value in general, made the equal in quality of the linen, but a definite quantity of coat (1 coat) is made the equivalent of a definite quantity (20 yards) of linen.

The equation 20 yards of linen=1 coat, or 20 yards of linen are worth one coat, implies that the same quantity of value-substance (congealed labor) is embodied in both; that the two commodities have each cost the same amount of labor or the same quantity of labor time. But the labor time necessary for the production of 20 yards of linen or 1 coat varies with every change in the productiveness of weaving or tailoring. We have now to consider the in-

---

★ In a way, it is with man as with commodities. Since he comes into the world neither with a looking glass in his hand, nor as a Fichtian philosopher, to whom "I am I" is sufficient, man first sees and recognizes himself in other men. Peter only establishes his own identity as a man by first comparing himself with Paul as being of like kind. And thereby Paul, just as he stands in his Pauline personality, becomes to Peter the type of the genus homo.

fluence of such changes on the quantitative aspect of the relative expression of value.

I. Let the value of the linen vary,* that of the coat remaining constant. If, say, in consequence of exhaustion of flax-growing soil, the labor time necessary for the production of the linen is doubled, the value of the linen will also be doubled. Instead of the equation 20 yards of linen=1 coat, we should have 20 yards of linen=2 coats, since 1 coat would now contain only half the labor time embodied in 20 yards of linen. If, on the other hand, in consequence, say, of improved looms, this labor time were reduced by one-half, the value of the linen would fall one-half. Consequently, we should have 20 yards of linen=1/2 coat. The relative value of commodity A, i.e., its value expressed in commodity B, rises and falls directly as the value of A, the value of B being supposed constant.

II. Let the value of the linen remain constant, while the value of the coat varies. If, under these circumstances, in consequence, for instance, of a poor crop of wool, the labor time necessary for the production of a coat becomes doubled, we have instead of 20 yards of linen=1 coat, 20 yards of linen=1/2 coat. If, on the other hand, the value of the coat sinks by one half, then 20 yards of linen=2 coats. Hence, if the value of commodity A remain constant, its relative value expressed in commodity B rises and falls inversely as the value of B.

If we compare the different cases in I. and II., we see that the same change of magnitude in relative value may arise from totally opposite causes. Thus, the equation 20 yards of linen=1 coat, becomes 20 yards of linen=2 coats, either because the

---

* Value is here, as occasionally in the preceding pages, used in the sense of value determined as to quantity, or of magnitude of value.

value of the linen has doubled, or because the value of the coat has fallen by one-half; and it becomes 20 yards of linen=1/2 coat, either because the value of the linen has fallen by one-half, or because the value of the coat has doubled.

III. Let the quantities of labor time respectively necessary for the production of the linen and the coat vary simultaneously in the same direction and in the same proportion. In this case 20 yards of linen continue to equal 1 coat, however much their values may have altered. Their change of value is seen as soon as they are compared with a third commodity whose value has remained constant. If the values of all commodities rose or fell simultaneously, and in the same proportion, their relative values would remain unaltered. Their real change of value would appear from the diminished or increased quantity of commodities produced in a given time.

IV. The labor time respectively necessary for the production of the linen and the coat, and therefore the value of these commodities, may simultaneously vary in the same direction, but at unequal rates, or in opposite directions, or in other ways. The effect of all these possible different variations on the relative value of a commodity may be deduced from the results of I., II., and III.

Thus real changes in the magnitude of value are neither unequivocally nor exhaustively reflected in their relative expression, that is, in the equation expressing the magnitude of relative value. The relative value of a commodity may vary, although its value remains constant. Its relative value may remain constant, although its value varies; and finally, simultaneous variations in the magnitude of value and in that of its relative expression by no means necessarily correspond in amount.

3. The equivalent form of value.

We have seen that commodity A (the linen), by expressing its value in the use-value of a commodity differing in kind (the coat), at the same time impresses upon the latter a specific form of value, namely that of the equivalent. The commodity linen manifests its quality of having a value by the fact that the coat, without having assumed a value form different from its bodily form, is equated to the linen. The fact that the latter therefore has a value is expressed by saying that the coat is directly exchangeable with it. Therefore, when we say that a commodity is in the equivalent form, we express the fact that it is directly exchangeable with other commodities.

When one commodity, such as a coat, serves as the equivalent of another, such as linen, and coats consequently acquire the characteristic property of being directly exchangeable with linen, we are far from knowing in what proportion the two are exchangeable. The value of the linen being given in magnitude, that proportion depends on the value of the coat. Whether the coat serves as the equivalent and the linen as relative value, or the linen as the equivalent and the coat as relative value, the magnitude of the coat's value is determined, independently of its value form, by the labor time necessary for its production. But whenever the coat assumes the position of equivalent in the equation of value, its value acquires no quantitative expression; on the contrary, the commodity coat now figures only as a definite quantity of some article.

For instance, 40 yards of linen are worth—what? Two coats. Because the commodity coat here plays the part of equivalent, because the use-value coat, as opposed to the linen, figures as an embodiment of value, therefore a definite number of coats suffices to express the definite quantity of value in the linen. Two coats may therefore express the quantity of value of 40 yards of linen, but they can never express the quantity of their own value. A superficial observation of this fact, namely, that in the equation of value, the equivalent figures exclusively as a simple quantity of some article, of some use-value, has misled Bailey, and also many others both before and after him, into seeing, in the expression of value, merely a quantitative relation. The truth is that when a commodity acts as equivalent, no quantitative determination of its value is expressed.

The first peculiarity that strikes us, in considering the form of equivalent, is this: use-value becomes the form of manifestation, the phenomenal form of its opposite, value.

The bodily form of the commodity becomes its value form. But, mark well, that this quid pro quo exists in the case of any commodity B only when some other commodity A enters into a value relation with it, and then only within the limits of this relation. Since no commodity can stand in the relation of equivalent to itself, and thus turn its own bodily shape into the expression of its own value, every commodity is compelled to choose some other commodity for its equivalent and to accept the use-value, that is to say, the bodily shape of that other commodity as the form of its own value.

One of the measures that we apply to commodities as material substances, as use-values, will serve to illustrate this point. A sugar-loaf, being a body, is heavy, and therefore has weight: but we can neither see nor touch this weight. We then take various pieces of iron, whose weight has been determined beforehand. The iron, as iron, is no more the form of manifestation of weight than is the sugar-loaf. Nevertheless, in order to express the sugar-loaf as so much weight, we put it into a weight-relation with the iron. In this relation, the iron officiates as a body representing nothing but weight. A certain quantity of iron therefore serves as the measure of the weight of the sugar, and represents, in relation to the sugar-loaf, weight embodied, the form of manifestation of weight. This part is played by the iron only within this relation, into which the sugar or any other body, whose weight has to be determined, enters with the iron. Were they not both heavy, they could not enter into this relation, and the one could therefore not serve as the expression of the weight of the other. When we throw both into the scales, we see in reality that as weight they are both the same, and that, therefore, when taken in proper proportions, they have the same weight. Just as the substance iron, as a measure of weight, represents in relation to the sugar-loaf weight alone, so, in our expression of value, the material object, coat, in relation to the linen represents value alone.

Here, however, the analogy ceases. The iron, in the expression of the weight of the sugar-loaf, represents a natural property common to both bodies, namely their weight; but the coat, in the expression of value of the linen, represents a non-natural property of both, something purely social, namely, their value.

Since the relative form of value of a commodity—the linen, for example—expresses the value of that commodity as being something wholly different from its substance and properties, as being, for instance, coat-like, we see that this expression itself indicates that some social relation lies at the bottom of it. With the equivalent form it is just the contrary. The very essence of this form is that the material commodity itself—the coat—just as it is, expresses value, and is endowed with the form of value by nature itself. Of course this holds good only so long as the value relation exists in which the coat stands in the position of equivalent to the linen. Since, however, the properties of a thing are not the result of its relations to other things but only manifest themselves in such relations, the coat seems to be endowed with its equivalent form, its property of being directly exchangeable, just as much by nature as it is endowed with the property of being heavy, or the capacity to keep us warm. Hence the enigmatic character of the equivalent form escapes the notice of the bourgeois political economist until this form, completely developed, confronts him in the shape of money. He then seeks to explain away the mystical character of gold and silver by substituting for them less dazzling commodities and by reciting, with ever renewed satisfaction, the catalogue of all possible commodities which at one time or another have the part of equivalent. He has not the least suspicion that the most simple expression of value, such as 20 yds. of linen=1 coat, already propounds the riddle of the equivalent form for our solution.

The body of the commodity that serves as the equivalent figures as the materialization of human labor in the abstract and is at the same time the product of some specifically useful concrete labor. This concrete labor becomes, therefore, the medium for expressing abstract human labor. If on the one hand the coat ranks as nothing but the embodiment of abstract human labor, so, on the other hand, the tailoring which is actually embodied in it counts as nothing but the form under which that abstract labor is realized. In the expression of value of the linen, the utility of the tailoring consists, not in making clothes, but in making an object, which we at once recognize to be value, and therefore to be a congelation of labor, but of labor indistinguishable from that realized in the value of the linen. In order to act as such a mirror of value, the labor of tailoring must reflect nothing besides its own abstract quality of being human labor generally.

In tailoring, as well as in weaving, human labor-power is expended. Both, therefore, possess the general property of being human labor, and may, therefore, in certain cases, such as in the production of value, have to be considered under this aspect alone. There is nothing mysterious in this. But in the expression of value there is a complete turning of the tables. For instance, how is the fact to be expressed that weaving creates the value of the linen, not by virtue of being weaving as such, but by reason of its general property of being human labor? Simply by opposing to weaving that other particular form of concrete labor (in this instance tailoring), which produces the equivalent of the product of weaving. Just as the coat in its bodily form became a direct expression of value, so now does tailoring, a concrete form of labor, appear as the direct and palpable embodiment of human labor generally.

Hence, the second peculiarity of the equivalent form is that concrete labor becomes the form under which its opposite, abstract human labor, manifests itself.

But because this concrete labor, tailoring in our case, ranks as, and is directly identified with, undifferentiated human labor, it also ranks as identical with any other sort of labor, and therefore with that embodied in linen. Consequently, although, like all other commodity-producing labor, it is the labor of private individuals, at the same time, it ranks as labor directly social in its character. This is the reason why it results in a product directly exchangeable with other commodities. We have then a third peculiarity of the equivalent form, namely, that the labor of private individuals takes the form of its opposite, labor directly social in its form.

★ ★ ★

To attribute value to commodities is merely a mode of expressing all labor as equal human labor, and consequently as labor of equal quality. Greek society was founded upon slavery and had, therefore, for its natural basis, the inequality of men and of their labor powers. The secret of the expression of value is that all kinds of labor are equal and equivalent, because, insofar as they are human labor in general, they cannot be deciphered until the notion of human equality has already become fixed as a popular prejudice. This, however, is possible only in a society in which the great mass of the product of labor takes the form of commodities in which, consequently, the dominant relation between man and man is that of owners of commodities.

4. The elementary form of value considered as a whole

The elementary form of value of a commodity is contained in the equation, expressing its value relation to another commodity of a different kind, or in its exchange relation to the same. The value of commodity A is qualitatively expressed by the fact that commodity B is exchangeable with it. Its value is quantitively expressed by the fact that a definite quantity of B is exchangeable with a definite quantity of A. In other words, the value of a commodity obtains independent and definite expression by taking the form of exchange value. When, at the beginning of this chapter, we said, in common parlance, that a commodity is both a use-value and an exchange value, we were, strictly speaking, wrong. A commodity is a use-value or object of utility, and a value. It manifests itself as this two-fold thing, that it is, as soon as its value assumes an independent form—viz., the form exchange value. It never assumes this form when isolated, but only when placed in a value or exchange relation with another commodity of a different kind. When once we know this, such a mode of expression does no harm; it simply serves as an abbreviation.

Our analysis has shown that the form or expression of the value of a commodity originates in the nature of value, and not that value and its magnitude originate in the mode of their expression as exchange value.

★ ★ ★

A close scrutiny of the expression of the value of A in terms of B, contained in the equation expressing the value relation of A to B, has shown us that within that relation, the bodily form of A figures only as a use-value, the bodily form of B only as the form or aspect of value. The opposition or contrast existing internally in each commodity between use-value and value is, therefore, made evident externally by two commodities being placed in such relation to each other that the commodity whose value it is sought to express figures directly as a mere use-value, while the commodity in which that value is to be expressed figures directly as mere exchange value. Hence the elementary form of value of a commodity is the elementary form in which the contrast contained in that commodity, between use-value and value, becomes apparent.

Every product of labor is, in all states of society, a use-value; but it is only at a definite historical epoch in a society's development that such a product becomes a commodity, viz., at the epoch when the labor spent on the production of a useful article becomes expressed as one of the objective qualities of that article, i.e., as its value. It therefore follows that the elementary value-form is also the primitive form under which a product of labor appears historically as a commodity, and that the gradual transformation of such products into commodities proceeds *pari passu* with the development of the value-form.

We perceive, at first sight, the deficiencies of the elementary form of value: it is a mere germ, which must undergo a series of metamorphoses before it can ripen into the price-form.

The expression of the value of commodity A in terms of any other commodity B merely distinguishes the value from the use-value of A, and therefore places A merely in a relation of exchange with a single different commodity, B; but it is still far from expressing A's qualitative equality, and quantitative proportionality, to all commodities. To the elementary relative value-form of a commodity, there corresponds the single equivalent form of one other commodity. Thus, in the relative expression of value of the linen, the coat assumes the form of equivalent, or of being directly exchangeable, only in relation to a single commodity, the linen.

Nevertheless, the elementary form of value passes by an easy transition into a more complete form. It is true that by means of the elementary form, the value of a commodity A becomes expressed in terms of one, and only one, other commodity. But that one may be a commodity of any kind, coat, iron, corn, or anything else. There-fore, as A is placed in relation with one or the other, we get differ-ent elementary expressions of value for one and the same commodity. The number of such possible expressions is limited only by the number of the different kinds of commodities distinct from it. The isolated expression of A's value is therefore convert-ible into a series, prolonged to any length, of the different elemen-tary expressions of that value.

B. Total or Expanded form of value

z Com. A equals u Com. B, or equals v Com. C, or equals w Com. D, or equals x Com. E.

(20 yards of linen equals 1 coat, or equals 10 lbs. tea, or equals 40 lbs. coffee, or equals 1 quarter corn, or equals 2 ounces of gold, or equals 1/2 ton iron)

1. *The expanded relative form of value*

The value of a single commodity, the linen for example, is now expressed in terms of numberless other elements of the world of commodities. Every other commodity now becomes a mirror of the linen's value.[*] Thus, for the first time this value shows itself in its true light as a congelation of undifferentiated human labor. For the labor that creates it now stands expressly revealed as labor that ranks equally with every other sort of human labor, no matter what its form, whether tailoring, ploughing, mining, etc. and no matter, therefore, whether it is realized in coats, corn, iron, or gold. The linen, by virtue of the form of its value, now stands in a social rela-

[*] For this reason, we can speak of the coat-value of the linen when its value is ex-pressed in coats, or of its corn-value when expressed in corn, and so on. Every such expression tells us that what appears in the use-values, coat, corn, etc., is the value of the linen.

tion, no longer with only one other kind of commodity, but with the whole world of commodities. As a commodity, it is a citizen of that world. At the same time, the interminable series of value equations implies that it doesn't matter under what particular form, or kind, of use-value a commodity appears.

In the first form, 20 yds. of linen=1 coat, it might appear that these two commodities are exchangeable in definite quantities. In the second form, on the contrary, we perceive at once the background that determines, and is essentially different from, this accidental appearance. The value of the linen remains unaltered in magnitude, whether expressed in coats, coffee, or iron, or in numberless different commodities, the property of as many different owners. The accidental relation between two individual commodity-owners disappears. It becomes clear that it is not the exchange of commodities which regulates the magnitude of their value but, on the contrary, that it is the magnitude of their value which controls their exchange proportions.

2. The particular equivalent form

Each commodity, such as coat, tea, corn, iron, etc., figures in the expression of value of the linen as an equivalent, and consequently as a thing that is value. The bodily form of each of these commodities figures now as a particular equivalent form, one out of many. In the same way, the manifold concrete useful kinds of labor embodied in these different commodities rank now as so many different forms of the realization, or manifestation, of undifferentiated human labor.

3. Defects of the total or expanded form of value

In the first place, the relative expression of value is incomplete because the series representing it is interminable. The chain, of which each equation of value is a link, is liable at any moment to be lengthened by each new kind of commodity that comes into existence and furnishes the material for a fresh expression of value. In the second place, it is a many-coloured mosaic of disparate and independent expressions of value. And lastly, if, as must be the case, the relative value of each commodity in turn becomes expressed in this expanded form, we get for each of them a relative value-form, different in every case and consisting of an interminable series of expressions of value. The defects of the expanded relative-value form are reflected in the corresponding equivalent form. Since the bodily form of each single commodity is one particular equivalent form among numberless others, we have, on the whole, nothing but fragmentary equivalent forms, each excluding the others. In the same way, the special, concrete, useful kind of labor embodied in each particular equivalent is presented only as a particular kind of labor, and therefore not as an exhaustive representative of human labor generally. The latter, indeed, gains adequate manifestation in the totality of its manifold, particular, concrete forms. But, in that case, its expression in an infinite series is ever incomplete and deficient in unity.

The expanded relative value form is, however, nothing but the sum of the elementary relative expressions or equations of the first kind, such as:

20 yards of linen=1 coat

20 yards of linen=10 lbs. of tea, etc.

Each of these implies the corresponding inverted equation:

1 coat=20 yards of linen

10 lbs. of tea=20 yards of linen, etc.

In fact, when a person exchanges his linen for many other commodities, and thus expresses its value in a series of other commodities, it necessarily follows that the various owners of the latter exchange them for the linen, and consequently express the value of their various commodities in one and the same third commodity, the linen. If then, we reverse the series, 20 yards of linen=1 coat or equals 10 lbs. of tea, etc., that is to say, if we give expression to the converse relation already implied in the series, we get:

C. THE GENERAL FORM OF VALUE

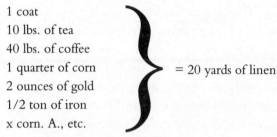

1 coat
10 lbs. of tea
40 lbs. of coffee
1 quarter of corn   = 20 yards of linen
2 ounces of gold
1/2 ton of iron
x corn. A., etc.

1. The altered character of the form of value

All commodities now express their value (1) in an elementary form, because they are in a single commodity; (2) with unity, because they are in one and the same commodity. This form of value is elementary and the same for all, and is therefore general.

The forms A and B were fit only to express the value of a commodity as something distinct from its use-value or material form.

The first form, A, furnishes such equations as the following: 1 coat=20 yards of linen, 10 lbs. of tea=1/2 ton of iron. The value of the coat is equated to linen, that of the tea to iron. But to be equated to linen, and again to iron, is to be as different as are linen and iron. This form, it is plain, occurs practically only in the beginning, when the products of labor are converted into commodities by accidental and occasional exchanges.

The second form, B, distinguishes, in a more adequate manner than the first, the value of a commodity from its use-value; for the value of the coat is placed in contrast under all possible shapes with the bodily form of the coat; it is equated to linen, to iron, to tea, in short, to everything else, only not to itself, the coat. On the other hand, any general expression of value common to all is directly excluded; for, in the equation of value of each commodity, all other commodities now appear only under the form of equivalents. The expanded form of value comes into actual existence for the first time as soon as a particular product of labor, such as cattle, is no longer exceptionally, but habitually, exchanged for various other commodities.

The third and last developed form expresses the values of the whole world of commodities in terms of a single commodity set apart for the purpose, namely, the linen, and thus represents to us their values by means of their equality with linen. The value of every commodity is now, by being equated to linen, not only differentiated from its own use-value, but from all other use-values generally, and is, by that very fact, expressed as that which is common to all commodities. By this form, commodities are, for the first time, effectively brought into relation with one another as values, or made to appear as exchange values.

The two earlier forms either express the value of each commodity in terms of a single commodity of a different kind, or in a series of many such commodities. In both cases, it is, so to say, the special business of each single commodity to find an expression for its value, and this it does without the help of the others. These others, with respect to the former, play the passive parts of equivalents. The general form of value C results from the joint action of the whole world of commodities, and from that alone. A commodity can acquire a general expression of its value only by all other commodities, simultaneously with it, expressing their values in the same equivalent; and every new commodity must follow suit. It thus becomes evident that, since the existence of commodities as values is purely social, this social existence can be expressed by the totality of their social relations alone, and consequently that the form of their value must be a socially recognized form.

All commodities being equated to linen now appear not only qualitatively equal as values generally, but also as values whose magnitudes are capable of comparison. By expressing the magnitudes of their values in one and the same material, the linen, those magnitudes are also compared with each other. For instance, 10 lbs. of tea=20 yards of linen, and 40 lbs. of coffee=20 yards of linen. Therefore, 10 lbs. of tea=40 lbs. of coffee. In other words, there is contained in 1 lb. of coffee only one-forth as much substance of value—labor—as is contained in 1 lb. of tea.

The general form of relative value, embracing the whole world of commodities, converts the commodity that is excluded from the rest and made to play the part of equivalent—here the linen—into the universal equivalent. The bodily form of the linen is now the form assumed in common by the value of all commodities; it therefore becomes directly exchangeable with each of them. The substance linen becomes the visible incarnation, the social chrysalis state of every kind of human labor. Weaving, which is the labor of certain private individuals producing a particular article, linen, acquires in consequence a social character, the character of equality with all other kinds of labor. The innumerable equations of which the general form of value is composed equate in turn the labor embodied in the linen to that embodied in every other commodity, and they thus convert weaving into the general form of manifestation of undifferentiated human labor. In this manner the labor realized in the values of commodities is presented not only under its negative aspect, under which abstraction is made from every concrete form and useful property of actual work, but its own positive nature is made to reveal itself expressly. The general value-form is the reduction of all kinds of actual labor to their common character of being human labor generally, of being the expenditure of human labor power.

The general value form, which represents all products of labor as mere congelations of undifferentiated human labor, shows by its very structure that it is the social resumé of the world of commodities. That form consequently makes it indisputably evident that in the world of commodities the character possessed by all labor—that it is *human* labor—constitutes its specific social character.

2. The interdependent development of the relative form of value, and of the equivalent form

The degree of development of the relative form of value corresponds to that of the equivalent form. But we must bear in mind that the development of the latter is only the expression and result of the development of the former.

The primary or isolated relative form of value of one commodity converts some other commodity into an isolated equivalent. The expanded form of relative value, which is the expression of the value of one commodity in terms of all other commodities, endows those other commodities with the character of particular equivalents differing in kind. And lastly, a particular kind of commodity acquires the character of universal equivalent, because all other commodities make it the material in which they uniformly express their value.

The antagonism between the relative form of value and the equivalent form, the two poles of the value form, is developed concurrently with that form itself.

The first form, 20 yds. of linen=one coat, already contains this antagonism, without as yet fixing it. Depending on whether we read this equation forwards or backwards, the parts played by the linen and the coat are different. In the one case the relative value of the linen is expressed in the coat, in the other case the relative value of the coat is expressed in the linen. In this first form of value, therefore, it is difficult to grasp the polar contrast.

Form B shows that only one single commodity at a time can completely expand its relative value, and that it acquires this expanded form only because, and insofar as all other commodities are, with respect to it, equivalents. Here we cannot reverse the equation, as we can the equation 20 yds. of linen=1 coat, without altering its general character, and converting it from the expanded form of value into the general form of value.

Finally, the form C gives to the world of commodities a general social relative form of value, because all commodities with one exception are excluded from the equivalent form. A single commodity, the linen, appears therefore to have acquired the character of direct exchangeability with every other commodity because this character is denied to every other commodity.

The commodity that figures as the universal equivalent is, on the other hand, excluded from the relative value form. If the linen, or any other commodity serving as universal equivalent, were at the same time to share in the relative form of value, it would have to serve as its own equivalent. We should then have 20 yds. of linen=20 yds. of linen; this tautology expresses neither value nor magnitude of value. In order to express the relative value of the universal equivalent, we must rather reverse the form C. This equivalent has no relative form of value in common with other commodities, but its value is relatively expressed by a never ending series of other commodities. Thus, the expanded form of relative value, or form B, now shows itself as the specific form of relative value for the equivalent commodity.

3. Transition from the general form to the money form

The universal equivalent form is a form of value in general. It can, therefore, be assumed by any commodity. On the other hand, if a commodity is found to have assumed the universal equivalent form (form C), this is only because it has been excluded from the rest of all other commodities as their equivalent, and that by their own act. And from the moment that this exclusion becomes finally restricted to one particular commodity, from that moment only, the general form of relative value of the world of commodities obtains real consistence and general social validity.

The particular commodity with whose bodily form the equivalent form is thus socially identified now becomes the money commodity, or serves as money. It becomes the special social function of that commodity, and consequently its social monopoly, to play within the world of commodities the part of the universal equivalent.

Among the commodities which, in form B, figure as particular equivalents of the linen, and in form C, express in common their relative values in linen, this foremost place has been attained by one in particular—namely, gold. If, then, in form C we replace the linen by gold, we get:

D. The Money form

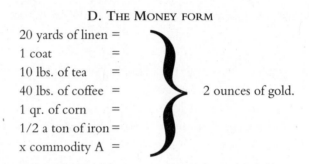

20 yards of linen =
1 coat   =
10 lbs. of tea   =
40 lbs. of coffee =   2 ounces of gold.
1 qr. of corn   =
1/2 a ton of iron =
x commodity A =

In passing from form A to form B, and from the latter to form C, the changes are fundamental. On the other hand, there is no difference between forms C and D, except that in the latter, gold has assumed the equivalent form in the place of linen. Gold is in form D what linen was in form C—the universal equivalent. The progress consists in this alone, that the character of direct and universal exchangeability—in other words, that the universal equivalent form—has now, by social custom, become finally identified with the substance, gold.

Gold is now money with reference to all other commodities only because it was previously, with reference to them, a simple commodity. Like all other commodities, it was also capable of serving as an equivalent, either as a simple equivalent in isolated exchanges, or as a particular equivalent by the side of others. Gradually it began to serve, within varying limits, as the universal equivalent. As soon as it monopolizes this position in the expression of value for the world of commodities, it becomes the money commodity, and then, and not till then, does form D become distinct from form C, and the general form of value become changed into the money form.

The elementary expression of the relative value of a single commodity, such as linen, in terms of the commodity, such as gold, that plays the part of money, is the price form of that commodity. The price form of the linen is therefore:

20 yards of linen=2 ounces of gold, or if 2 ounces of gold when coined are £2, 20 yards of linen=£2.

The difficulty in forming a concept of the money form consists in clearly comprehending the universal equivalent form, and as a necessary corollary, the general form of value, form C. The latter is deducible from form B, the expanded form of value, the essential component element of which, we saw, is form A, 20 yards of linen=1 coat, or x commodity A=y commodity B. The simple commodity form is therefore the germ of the money form.

SECTION 4—THE FETISHISM OF COMMODITIES AND THE SECRET THEREOF

A commodity appears, at first sight, a very trivial thing and easily understood. Its analysis shows that it is, in reality, a very strange thing, abounding in metaphysical subtleties and theological niceties. So far as it is a value in use, there is nothing mysterious about it, whether we consider it from the point of view that by its properties it is capable satisfying human wants, or from the standpoint that those properties are the product of human labor. It is as clear as day that man, by his industry, changes the forms of the materials furnished by nature, in such a way as to make them useful to him. The form of wood, for instance, is altered by making a table out of it. Yet, the table continues to be that common, everyday thing, wood.

But, as soon as it steps forth as a commodity, it is changed into something transcendent. It not only stands with its feet on the ground, but, in relation to all other commodities, it stands on its head, and evolves out of its wooden brain grotesque ideas, far more wonderful than "table turning" ever was.

The mystical character of commodities does not originate, therefore, in their use-value, and neither does it proceed from the nature of the determining factors of value. For, in the first place, however varied the useful kinds of labor or productive activities may be, it is a physiological fact that they are functions of the human organism, and that each such function, whatever may be its nature or form, is essentially the expenditure of human brain, nerves, muscles, etc. Secondly, with regard to that which forms the ground-work for the quantitative determination of value, namely, the duration of that expenditure or the quantity of labor, it is quite clear that there is a palpable difference between its quantity and quality. In all states of society, the labor-time that it costs to produce the means of subsistence must necessarily be an object of interest to mankind, though not of equal interest in different stages of development. And lastly, from the moment that men in any way work for one another, their labor assumes a social form.

Whence, then, arises the enigmatical character of the product of labor, as soon as it assumes the form of commodities? Clearly from this form itself. The equality of all sorts of human labor is expressed objectively by their products all being of equal value; the measure of the expenditure of labor-power by the duration of that expenditure takes the form of the quantity of value of the products of labor; and finally, the mutual relations of the producers, within which the social character of their labor affirms itself, take the form of a social relation between the products.

A commodity is therefore a mysterious thing, simply because in it the social character of men's labor appears to them as an objective character stamped upon the product of that labor; because the relation of the producers to the sum total of their own labor is presented to them as a social relation, existing not between themselves, but between the products of their labor. This is the reason why the products of labor become commodities, social things whose qualities are at the same time perceptible and imperceptible by the senses. In the same way the light from an object is perceived by us not as the subjective excitation of our optic nerve, but as the objective form of something outside the eye itself. But, in the act of seeing, there is always an actual passage of light from one thing to another, from the external object to the eye. There is a physical relation between physical things. But it is different with commodities. There, the existence of the things *qua* commodities, and the value relation between the products of labor which stamps them as commodities, have absolutely no connection with their physical properties and with the material relations arising therefrom. There, it is a definite social relation between men that assumes, in their eyes, the fantastic form of a relation between things. In order, therefore, to find an analogy, we must have recourse to the mist-enveloped regions of the religious world. In that world the productions of the human brain appear as independent beings endowed with life, and entering into relation both with one another and the human race. So it is in the world of commodities with the products of men's hands. This I call the fetishism which attaches itself to the products of labor as soon as they are produced as commodities, and which is therefore inseparable from the production of commodities.

This fetishism of commodities has its origin, as the foregoing analysis has already shown, in the peculiar social character of the labor that produces them.

As a general rule, articles of utility become commodities only because they are products of the labor of private individuals or groups of individuals who carry on their work independently of each other. The sum total of the labor of all these private individuals forms the aggregate labor of society. Since the producers do not come into social contact with each other until they exchange their products, the specific social character of each producer's labor does not show itself except in the act of exchange. In other words, the labor of the individual asserts itself as a part of the labor of society only by means of the relations which the act of exchange establishes directly between the products, and indirectly through them, between the producers. To the latter, therefore, the relations connecting the labor of one individual with that of the rest appear not as direct social relations between individuals at work, but as what they really are, material relations between persons and social relations between things. It is only by being exchanged that the products of labor acquire, as values, one uniform social status, distinct from their varied forms of existence as objects of utility. This division of a product into a useful thing and a value becomes practically important only when exchange has acquired such an extension that useful articles are produced for the purpose of being exchanged, and their character as values has therefore to be taken into account beforehand, during production. From this moment the labor of the individual producer acquires socially a two-fold character. On the one hand, it must, as a definite useful kind of labor, satisfy a definite social want, and thus hold its place as part and parcel of the collective labor of all, as a branch of a social division of labor that has sprung up spontaneously. On the other hand, it can satisfy the manifold wants of the individual producer himself only insofar as the mutual exchangeability of all kinds of useful private labor is an established social fact, and therefore the private useful labor of each producer ranks equally with that of all others. The equalization of the most different kinds of labor can be the result only of an abstraction from their inequalities, or of reducing them to their common denominator, viz., expenditure of human labor power or human labor in the abstract. The two-fold social character of the labor of the individual appears to him, when reflected in his brain, only under those forms which are impressed upon that labor in everyday practice by the exchange of products. In this way, the character that his own labor possesses of being socially useful takes the form of the condition that the product must be not only useful, but useful for others. And the social character that his particular labor has of being the equal of all other particular kinds of labor takes the form of all the physically different articles that are the products of labor, having one common quality, viz, that of having value.

Hence, when we bring the products of our labor into relation with each other as values, it is not because we see in these articles the material receptacles of human labor. Quite the contrary; whenever, by an exchange, we equate as values our different products, by that very act, we also equate, as human labor, the different kinds of labor expended upon them. We are not aware of this, nevertheless we do it. Value, therefore, does not stalk about with a label describing what it is. It is value, rather, that converts every product into a social hieroglyphic. Later on we try to decipher the hieroglyphic, to get behind the secret our own social products; for to stamp an object of utility as a value is just as much a social product as language. The recent scientific discovery that the products of labor, so far as they are values, are but material expression of the human labor spent in their production, indeed marks an epoch in the history of the development of the human race, but by no means dissipates the mist through which the social character of labor appears to us to be an objective character of the products themselves. The fact that in the particular form of production with which we are dealing, viz., the production of commodities, the specific social character of private labor carried on independently consists in the equality of every kind of that labor, by virtue of its being human labor whose character, therefore, assumes in the product the form of value—this fact appears to the producers, notwithstanding the discovery mentioned above, to be just as real and final as the fact that after the discovery by science of the component gases of air, the atmosphere itself remained unaltered.

What most of all practically concerns producers when they make an exchange is the question of how much of some other product they get for their own, and in what proportions are the products exchangeable? When these proportions have, by custom, attained a certain stability, they appear to result from the nature of the products so that, for instance, one ton of iron and two ounces of gold appear as naturally to be of equal value as a pound of gold and a pound of iron in spite of their different physical and chemical qualities appearing to be of equal weight. The character of having value, when once impressed upon products, is fixed only by reason of their acting and re-acting upon each other as quantities of value. These quantities vary continually, independently of the will, foresight, and action of the producers. To them, their own social action takes the form of the action of objects, which rule the producers instead of being ruled by them. It requires a fully developed production of commodities before, from accumulated experience alone, the scientific conviction springs up that all the different kinds of private labor—which are carried on independently of each other, and yet as spontaneously developed branches of the social division of labor—are continually being reduced to the quantitative proportions in which society requires them. And why? Because in the midst of all the accidental and ever fluctuating exchange-relations between the products, the labor-time socially necessary for their production forcibly asserts itself like an over-riding law of nature. The law of gravity thus asserts itself when a house falls about our ears. The determination of the magnitude of value by labor-time is therefore a secret, hidden under the apparent fluctuations in the relative values of commodities. Its discovery, while removing all appearance of mere accident from the determination of the magnitude of the values of products, in no way alters the mode in which that determination takes place.

Man's reflections on the forms of social life, and consequently, also his scientific analysis of those forms, take a course directly opposite to that of their actual historical development. He begins, *post festum*, with the results of the process of development at hand before him. The characters that stamp products as commodities, and whose establishment is a necessary preliminary to the circulation of commodities, have already acquired the stability of natural, self-understood forms of social life before man seeks to decipher not their historical character, for in his eyes they are immutable, but their meaning. Consequently it was the analysis of the prices of commodities that alone led to the determination of the magnitude of value, and it was the common expression of all commodities in money that alone led to the establishment of their characters as values. It is, however, just this ultimate money form of the world of commodities that actually conceals, instead of disclosing, the social character of private labor and the social relations between individual producers. When I state that coats or boots stand in a relation to linen because it is the universal incarnation of abstract human labor, the absurdity of the statement is self-evident. Nevertheless, when the producers of coats and boots compare those articles with linen or with gold or silver as the universal equivalent, they express the relation between their own private labor and the collective labor of society in the same absurd form.

The categories of bourgeois economy consist of such like forms. They are forms of thought expressing with social validity the conditions and relations of a definite, historically determined mode of production, viz., the production of commodities. The whole mystery of commodities, all the magic and necromancy that surrounds the products of labor as long as they take the form of commodities, therefore vanishes as soon as we come to other forms of production.

★ ★ ★

Let us imagine a community of free individuals, carrying on their work with the means of production in common, in which the labor-power of all the different individuals is consciously applied as the combined labor-power of the community. All the characteristics of

Robinson's labor are here repeated, but with this difference: that they are social, instead of individual. Everything produced by him was exclusively the result of his own personal labor, and therefore simply an object of use for himself. The total product of our community is a social product. One portion serves as fresh means of production and remains social. But another portion is consumed by the members as means of subsistence. A distribution of this portion among them is consequently necessary. The mode of this distribution will vary with the productive organization of the community and the degree of historical development attained by the producers. We will assume, but merely for the sake of a parallel with the production of commodities, that the share of each individual producer in the means of subsistence is determined by his labor-time. Labor-time would, in that case, play a double part. Its apportionment in accordance with a definite social plan maintains the proper proportion between the different kinds of work to be done and the various wants of the community. On the other hand, it also serves as a measure of the portion of the common labor borne by each individual and of his share in the part of the total product destined for individual consumption. The social relations of the individual producers, with regard both to their labor and to its products, are in this case perfectly simple and intelligible with regard not only to production but also to distribution.

The religious world is but the reflex of the real world. And for a society based upon the production of commodities in which the producers in general enter into social relations with one another by treating their products as commodities and values—whereby they reduce their individual private labor to the standard of homogeneous human labor—for such a society Christianity, with its *cultus* of abstract man, and more especially in its bourgeois developments—Protestantism, Deism, etc.—is the most fitting form of religion. In the ancient Asiatic and other ancient modes of production, we find that the conversion of products into commodities, and therefore the conversion of men into producers of commodities, holds a subordinate place which, however, increases in importance as the primitive communities approach nearer and nearer to their dissolution. Trading nations, properly so called, exist in the ancient world only in its gaps, like the gods of Epicurus in Intermundia, or like Jews in the crevices of Polish society. Those ancient social organisms of production are, as compared with bourgeois society, extremely simple and transparent. But they are founded either on the immature development of man individually, who has not yet severed the umbilical cord that unites him with his fellow men in a primitive tribal community, or upon direct relations of subjection. They can arise and exist only when the development of the productive power of labor has not risen beyond a low stage and when, therefore, the social relations within the sphere of material life between man and man, and between man and nature are correspondingly narrow. This narrowness is reflected in the ancient worship of nature, and in the other elements of the popular religions. The religious reflex of the real world can, in any case, only finally vanish when the practical relations of everyday life offer to man perfectly intelligible and reasonable relations with regard to his fellow men and to nature.

The life-process of society, which is based on the process of material production, does not strip off its mystical veil until it is treated as production by freely associated men and is consciously regulated by them in accordance with a settled plan. This, however, demands for society a certain material groundwork or set of conditions of existence which in their turn are the spontaneous product of a long and painful proccess of development.

Political economy has indeed analyzed, however incompletely, value and its magnitude, and has discovered what lies beneath these forms. But it has never once asked the question why labor is represented by the value of its product and labor time by the magnitude of that value. These formulae, which bear stamped upon them in unmistakable letters that they belong to a state of society in which the process of production has the mastery over man, instead of being controlled by him, appear to the bourgeois intellect to be as much a self-evident thing imposed by nature as productive labor itself. Hence, forms of social production that preceded the bourgeois form are treated by the bourgeoisie in much the same way as the Fathers of the Church treated pre-Christian religions.

★ ★ ★

The mode of production in which the product takes the form of a commodity or is produced directly for exchange is the most general and most embryonic form of bourgeois production. It therefore makes its appearance at an early date in history, though not in the same predominating and characteristic manner as today. Hence, its fetish character is comparatively easy to be seen through. But when we come to more concrete forms, even this appearance of simplicity vanishes. Whence arose the illusions of the monetary system? To it gold and silver, when serving as money, did not represent a social relation between producers, but were natural objects with strange social properties. And as for the modern economy, which looks down with such disdain on the monetary system, does not its superstition come out as clear as day whenever it deals with capital? How long is it since the economy discarded the physiocratic illusion that income grows out of the soil and not out of society?

CHAPTER II

EXCHANGE

I T IS CLEAR that commodities cannot go to market and make exchanges of their own accord. We must, therefore, have recourse to their guardians, who are also their owners. Commodities are things, and therefore without the power to resist man. If they are not docile enough he can use force; in other words, he can take possession of them. In order that these objects may enter into relation with each other as commodities, their guardians must place themselves in relation to one another as persons whose will resides in those objects, and must behave in such a way that each does not appropriate the commodity of the other and part with his own except by means of an act done by mutual consent. They must, therefore, mutually recognize in each other the right of private proprietors. This juridical relation, which thus expresses itself in a contract, whether such contract be part of a developed legal system or not, is a relation between two wills and is but the reflex of the real economic relation between the two. It is this economic relation that determines the subject matter comprised in each such juridical act. The persons exist for one another merely as representatives of, and therefore as owners of, commodities. In the course of our investigation we shall find in general that the characters who appear on the economic stage are but the personifications of the economic relations that exist between them.

What chiefly distinguishes a commodity from its owner is the fact that it looks upon every other commodity as the form of appearance of its own value.

★ ★ ★

All commodities are non-use-values for their owners and use-values for their non-owners. Consequently, they must all change hands. But this change of hands is what constitutes their exchange, and the latter puts them in relation with each other as values and realizes them as values. Hence commodities must be realized as values before they can be realized as use-values.

On the other hand, they must show that they are use-values before they can be realized as values. For the labor spent upon them counts effectively only insofar as it is spent in a form that is useful for others. Whether that labor is useful for others and its product consequently capable of satisfying the wants of others can be proved only by the act of exchange.

Every owner of a commodity wishes to part with it in exchange only for those commodities whose use-value satisfies some want of his. Looked at in this way, exchange is for him simply a private transaction. On the other hand, he desires to realise the value of his commodity, to convert it into any other suitable commodity of equal value, irrespective of whether his own commodity has or has not any use-value for the owner of the other. From this point of view, exchange is for him a social transaction of a general character. But for all owners of commodities, one and the same set of transactions cannot be simultaneously both exclusively private and exclusively social and general.

★ ★ ★

Money is a crystal formed of necessity in the course of exchanges whereby different products of labor are practically equated to one another and thus by practice converted into commodities. The historical progress and extension of exchanges develops the contrast, latent in commodities, between use-value and value. The necessity of giving an external expression to this contrast for the purposes of commercial intercourse urges on the establishment of an independent form of value, and finds no rest until it is once and for all satisfied by the differentiation of commodities into commodities and money. At the same rate, then, as the conversion of products into commodities is being accomplished, so also is the conversion of one special commodity into money.

The direct barter of products attains the elementary form of the relative expression of value in one respect, but not in another. That form is x Commodity A=y Commodity B. The form of direct barter is x use-value A=y use-value B. The articles A and B in this case are not as yet commodities, but become so only by the act of barter. The first step made by an object of utility towards acquiring exchange-value is when it forms a non-use-value for its owner, and that happens when it forms a superfluous portion of some article required for his immediate wants. Objects in themselves are external to man, and consequently alienable by him. In order that this alienation may be reciprocal, it is only necessary for men, by a tacit understanding, to treat each other as private owners of those alienable objects, and by implication as independent individuals. But such a state of reciprocal independence has no existence in a primitive society based on communal property, whether such a society takes the form of a patriarchal family, an ancient Indian community, or a Peruvian Inca State. The exchange of commodities, therefore, first begins on the boundaries of such communities, at their points of contact with other similar communities, or with members of the latter. As soon, however, as products once become commodities in the external relations of a community, they also, by reaction, become so in its internal intercourse. The proportions in which they are exchangeable are at first quite a matter of chance. What makes them exchangeable is the mutual desire of their owners to alienate them. Meantime the need for foreign objects of utility gradually establishes itself. The constant repetition of exchange makes it a normal social act. In the course of time, therefore, some portion at least of the products of labor must be produced with a special view to exchange. From that moment the distinction becomes firmly established between the utility of an object for the purposes of consumption, and its utility for the purposes of exchange. Its use-value becomes distinguished from its exchange value. On the other hand, the quantitative proportion in which the articles are exchangeable becomes dependent on their production itself. Custom stamps them as values with definite magnitudes.

In the direct barter of products, each commodity is directly a means of exchange to its owner, and to all other persons an equivalent, but only insofar as it has use-value for them. At this stage, therefore, the articles exchanged do not acquire a value-form independent of their own use-value, or of the individual needs of the exchangers. The necessity for a value-form grows with the increasing number and variety of the commodities exchanged. The problem and the means of solution arise simultaneously. Commodity-owners never equate their own commodities to those of others, and exchange them on a large scale without different kinds of commodities belonging to different owners being exchangeable for, and equated as values to, one and the same special article. Such an article, by becoming the equivalent of various other commodities, acquires at once, though within narrow limits, the character of a general social equivalent. This character comes and goes with the momentary social acts that called it into life. It attaches itself first to this and then to that commodity. But with the development of exchange it fixes itself firmly and exclusively to particular sorts of commodities and becomes crystallised by assuming the money-form. The particular kind of commodity to which it sticks is at first a matter of accident. Nevertheless there are two circumstances whose influence is decisive. The money-form attaches itself either to the most important articles of exchange from outside, and these in fact are primitive and natural forms in which the exchange-value of home products finds expression; or else it attaches itself to the object of utility that forms, like cattle, the chief portion of indigenous alienable wealth. Nomad races are the first to develop the money-form, because all their worldly goods consist of movable objects and are therefore directly alienable, and because their mode of life, by continually bringing them into contact with foreign communities, solicits the exchange of products. Man has often made man himself, under the form of slaves, serve as the primitive material of money, but has never used land for that purpose. Such an idea could only spring up in a bourgeois society already well developed. It dates from the last third of the seventeenth century, and the first attempt to put it in practice on a national scale was made a century afterwards, during the French bourgeois revolution.

In proportion as exchange bursts its local bonds, and the value of commodities increasingly expands into an embodiment of human labor in the abstract, in the same proportion the character of money attaches itself to commodities that are by nature fitted to perform the social function of a universal equivalent. Those commodities are the precious metals.

★ ★ ★

Up to this point, however, we are acquainted only with one function of money, namely, to serve as the form of manifestation of the value of commodities, or as the material in which the magnitudes of their values are socially expressed. Only that material, whose every sample exhibits the same uniform qualities, can be an adequate form of manifestation of value, a fit embodiment of abstract, undifferentiated, and therefore equal human labor. On the other hand, since the difference between the magnitudes of value is purely quantitative, the money commodity must be susceptible to merely quantitative differences, and must therefore be divisible at will, and equally capable of being reunited. Gold and silver possess these properties by nature.

The use-value of the money commodity becomes twofold. In addition to its special use-value as a commodity (gold, for instance, serving to fix teeth, to form the raw material of articles of luxury, etc.), it acquires a formal use-value, originating in its specific social function.

Since all commodities are merely particular equivalents of money, the latter being their universal equivalent, they, with regard to the latter as the universal commodity, play the parts of particular commodities.

We have seen that the money-form is but the reflection, thrown upon one single commodity, of the value relations between all the rest. That money is a commodity is therefore a new discovery only for those who, when they analyse it, start from its fully developed shape. The act of exchange gives to the commodity converted into money not its value, but its specific value-form.

★ ★ ★

Money, like every other commodity, cannot express the magnitude of its value except relatively in other commodities. This value is determined by the labor-time required for its production, and is expressed by the quantity of any other commodity that costs the same amount of labor-time. Such quantitative determination of its relative value takes place at the source of its production by means of barter. When it steps into circulation as money, its value is already given.

★ ★ ★

What appears to happen is, not that gold becomes money as a consequence of all commodities expressing their values in it, but on the contrary, that all other commodities universally express their values in gold because it is money. The intermediate steps of the process vanish in the result and leave no trace behind. Commodities find their own value already completely represented, without any initiative on their part, in another commodity existing in company with them. These objects, gold and silver, just as they come out of the bowels of the earth, are forthwith the direct incarnation of all human labor. Hence the magic of money. In the form of society now under consideration, the behavior of men in the social process of production is purely instinctive. Hence their relations to each other in production assume a material character independent of their control and conscious individual action. These facts manifest themselves at first by products as a general rule taking the form of commodities. Hence the riddle presented by money is but the riddle presented by commodities; only now it strikes us in its most glaring form.

CHAPTER III

MONEY, OR THE CIRCULATION OF COMMODITIES

SECTION 1—THE MEASURE OF VALUES

Throughout this work I assume, for the sake of simplicity, gold as the money-commodity.

The first chief function of money is to supply commodities with the material for the expression of their values, or to represent their values as magnitudes of the same denomination, qualitatively equal and quantitatively comparable. It thus serves as a *universal measure of value*. And only by virtue of this function does gold, the equivalent commodity *par excellence*, become money.

It is not money that renders commodities commensurable. Just the contrary. It is because all commodities, as values, are realized human labor and therefore commensurable, that their values can be measured by one and the same special commodity, and the latter be converted into the common measure of their values, i.e., into money. Money, as a measure of value, is the phenomenal form that must of necessity be assumed by that measure of value which is immanent in commodities—labor-time.[*]

---

[*] The question "Why does not money directly represent labor-time, so that a piece of paper may represent, for instance, x hour's labor?" is at bottom the same as the question "Why, given the production of commodities, must products take the form of commodities?" This is evident, since their taking the form of commodities implies their differentiation into commodities and money.

The expression of the value of a commodity in gold—x commodity A=y money-commodity—is its money-form or price. A single equation, such as 1 ton of iron=2 ounces of gold, now suffices to express the value of the iron in a socially valid manner. The general form of relative value has resumed its original shape of simple or isolated relative value. On the other hand, the expanded expression of relative value, the endless series of equations, has now become the form peculiar to the relative value of the money-commodity. The series itself, too, is now given, and has social recognition in the prices of actual commodities. We have only to read the quotations of a price-list backwards to find the magnitude of the value of money expressed in all sorts of commodities. But money itself has no price. In order to put it on an equal footing with all other commodities in this respect, we should be obliged to equate it to itself as its own equivalent.

The price or money-form of commodities is, like their form of value generally, a form quite distinct from their palpable bodily form; it is, therefore, a purely ideal or mental form. Although invisible, the value of iron, linen and corn has actual existence in these very articles: it is ideally made perceptible by their equality with gold, a relation that, so to say, exists only in their own heads. Their owner must, therefore, lend them his tongue, or hang a ticket on them, before their prices can be communicated to the outside world. Since the expression of the value of commodities in gold is a merely ideal act, we may use for this purpose imaginary or ideal money. Every trader knows that he is far from having turned his goods into money when he has expressed their value in a price or in imaginary money, and that it does not require the least bit of real gold to estimate in that metal millions of pounds' worth of goods. When, therefore, money serves as a measure of value, it is employed only as imaginary or ideal money. This circumstance has given rise to the wildest theories. But, although the money that performs the functions of a measure of value is only ideal money, price depends entirely upon the actual substance that is money. The value, or in other words, the quantity of human labor contained in a ton of iron, is expressed in the imagination by such a quantity of the money-commodity as contains the same amount of labor as the iron. Therefore, as the measure of value is gold, silver, or copper, the value of the ton of iron will be expressed by very different prices, or will be represented by very different quantities of those metals respectively.

If, therefore, two different commodities such as gold and silver are simultaneously measures of value, all commodities have two prices—one a gold-price, the other a silver-price. These exist quietly side by side, so long as the ratio of the value of silver to that of gold remains unchanged, say, at 15:1. Every change in their ratio disturbs the ratio which exists between the gold-prices and the silver-prices of commodities, and thus proves by facts that a double standard of value is inconsistent with the functions of a standard.

Commodities with definite prices present themselves under the form: a commodity A=x gold; b commodity B=z gold; c commodity C=y gold, etc., where a, b, and c represent definite quantities of the commodities A, B, C, and x, z, and y definite quantities of gold. The values of these commodities are, therefore, changed in the imagination into so many different quantities of gold. Hence, in spite of the confusing variety of the commodities themselves, their values become magnitudes of the same denomination—gold-magnitudes. They are now capable of being compared with each other and measured, and the desire becomes felt to compare them with some fixed quantity of gold as a unit measure. This unit, by subsequent division into aliquot parts, becomes itself the standard or scale. Before they become money, gold, silver, and copper already possess such standard measures in their standards of weight so that, for example, a pound weight, while serving as the unit, is, on the one hand, divisible into ounces, and on the other, may be combined to make up hundredweights.

As a *measure of value* and as a *standard of price*, money has two entirely distinct functions to perform. It is the measure of value inasmuch as it is the socially recognized incarnation of human labor; it is the standard of price inasmuch as it is a fixed weight of metal. As the measure of value it serves to convert the values of all the manifold commodities into prices, into imaginary quantities of gold; as the standard of price it measures those quantities of gold. The measure of values measures commodities considered as values; the standard of price measures, on the contrary, quantities of gold by a unit quantity of gold, not the value of one quantity of gold by the weight of another. In order to make gold a standard of price, a certain weight must be fixed upon as the unit. In this case, as in all cases of measuring quantities of the same denomination, the establishment of an unvarying unit of measure is all-important. Hence, the less the unit is subject to variation, the better the standard of price fulfills its office. But only insofar as it is itself a product of labor, and therefore potentially variable in value, can gold serve as a measure of value.

It is, in the first place, quite clear that a change in the value of gold does not, in any way, affect its function as a standard of price. No matter how this value varies, the proportions between the values of different quantities of the metal remain constant. However great the fall in its value, 12 ounces of gold still have 12 times the value of 1 ounce; and in prices, the only thing considered is the relation between different quantities of gold. Since, on the other hand, no rise or fall in the value of an ounce of gold can alter its weight, no alteration can take place in the weight of its aliquot parts. Thus gold always renders the same service as an invariable standard of price, however much its value may vary.

In the second place, a change in the value of gold does not interfere with its functions as a measure of value. The change affects all commodities simultaneously, and therefore, *coeteris paribus*, leaves their relative values *inter se*, unaltered, although those values are now expressed in higher or lower gold-prices.

Just as we can estimate the value of any commodity by a definite quantity of the use-value of some other commodity, so in estimating the value of the former in gold, we assume nothing more than that the production of a given quantity of gold costs, at a given period, a given amount of labor. As regards the fluctuations of prices generally, they are subject to the laws of elementary relative value investigated in a former chapter.

A general rise in the prices of commodities can result only from either a rise in their values—the value of money remaining constant—or from a fall in the value of money, the values of commodities remaining constant. On the other hand, a general fall in prices can result only from either a fall in the values of commodities—the value of money remaining constant—or from a rise in the value of money, the values of commodities remaining constant. It therefore by no means follows that a rise in the value of money necessarily implies a proportional fall in the prices of commodities, or that a fall in the value of money implies a proportional rise in prices. Such a change of price applies only in the case of commodities whose value remains constant. With those, for example whose value rises simultaneously with, and proportionally to, that of money, there is no alteration in price. And if their value rise either slower or faster than that of money, the fall or rise in their prices will be determined by the difference between the change in their value and that of money; and so on.

Let us now go back to the consideration of the price-form.

By degrees there arises a discrepancy between the current money names of the various weights of the precious metal figuring as money, and the actual weights which those names originally represented. This discrepancy is the result of historical causes, among which the chief are: (1) The importation of foreign money into an imperfectly developed community. This happened in Rome in its early days, where gold and silver coins circulated at first as foreign commodities. The names of these foreign coins never coincide with those of the indigenous weights. (2) As wealth increases, the less precious metal is cast out by the more precious from its place as a measure of value, copper by silver, silver by gold, however much this order of sequence may contradict poetical chronology.* The word pound, for instance, was the money-name given to an actual pound weight of silver. When gold replaced silver as a measure of value, the same name was applied according to the ratio between the values of silver and gold, to perhaps one-fifteenth of a pound of gold. The word pound, as a money-name, thus becomes differentiated from the same word as a weight-name. (3) The debasing of money was carried on for centuries by kings and princes to such an extent that, of the original weights of the coins, nothing in fact remained but the names.

These historical causes convert the separation of the money-name from the weight-name into an established habit within the community. Since the standard of money is on the one hand purely conventional, and must on the other hand find general acceptance, it is in the end regulated by law.

★ ★ ★

The prices, or quantities of gold, into which the values of commodities are ideally changed are therefore now expressed in the names of coins, or in the legally valid names of the subdivisions of the gold standard.

★ ★ ★

Price is the money-name of the labor realized in a commodity. Hence the expression of the equivalence of a commodity with the sum of money constituting its price is a tautology, just as in general the expression of the relative value of a commodity is a statement

---

*Moreover, it has no general historical validity.

of the equivalence of two commodities. But although price, being the exponent of the magnitude of a commodity's value, is the exponent of its exchange-ratio with money, it does not follow that the exponent of this exchange-ratio is necessarily the exponent of the magnitude of the commodity's value.

* * *

Magnitude of value expresses a relation of social production, it expresses the connection that necessarily exists between a certain article and the portion of the total labor-time of society required to produce it. As soon as magnitude of value is converted into price, this relation takes the shape of a more or less accidental exchange-ratio between a single commodity and another, the money-commodity. But this exchange-ratio may express either the real magnitude of that commodity's value or the quantity of gold deviating from that value for which, according to circumstances, it may be parted with. The possibility, therefore, of quantitative incongruity between price and magnitude of value, or the deviation of the former from the latter, is inherent in the price-form itself. This is no defect, but on the contrary, admirably adapts the price-form to a mode of production whose inherent laws impose themselves only as the mean of apparently lawless irregularities that compensate one another.

The price-form, however, is not only compatible with the possibility of a quantitative incongruity between magnitude of value and price, i.e., between the former and its expression in money, but it may also conceal a qualitative inconsistency, so much so that, although money is nothing but the value-form of commodities, price ceases altogether to express value. Objects that in themselves are no commodities, such as conscience, honour, etc., are capable of being offered for sale by their holders, and of thus acquiring, through their price, the form of commodities. Hence an object may have a price without having value. The price in that case is imaginary, like certain quantities in mathematics. On the other hand, the imaginary price-form may sometimes conceal either a direct or indirect real value-relation; for instance, the price of uncultivated land, which is without value, because no human labor has been incorporated in it.

Price, like relative value in general, expresses the value of a commodity (e.g., a ton of iron) by stating that a given quantity of the equivalent (e.g., an ounce of gold) is directly exchangeable for iron. But it by no means states the converse, that iron is directly exchangeable for gold. In order, therefore, that a commodity may in practice act effectively as exchange value, it must quit its bodily shape, must transform itself from mere imaginary into real gold, although to the commodity such transubstantiation may be more difficult than to the Hegelian "concept," the transition from "necessity" to "freedom," or to a lobster the casting of his shell, or to Saint Jerome the putting off of the old Adam. Though a commodity may, side by side with its actual form (iron, for instance), take in our imagination the form of gold, it cannot at one and the same time actually be both iron and gold. To fix its price, it suffices to equate it to gold in the imagination. But to enable it to render to its owner the service of a universal equivalent, it must be actually replaced by gold.

★ ★ ★

A price therefore implies both that a commodity is exchangeable for money, and also that it must be so exchanged. On the other hand, gold serves as an ideal measure of value only because it has already, in the process of exchange, established itself as the money-commodity. Under the ideal measure of values there lurks the hard cash.

SECTION 2—THE MEDIUM OF CIRCULATION

A. THE METAMORPHOSIS OF COMMODITIES

Insofar as exchange is a process by which commodities are transferred from hands in which they are non-use-values to hands in which they become use-values it is a social circulation of matter. The product of one form of useful labor replaces that of another.

★ ★ ★

The comprehension of this change of form is, as a rule, very imperfect. The cause of this imperfection is, apart from indistinct notions of value itself, that every change of form in a commodity results from the exchange of two commodities, an ordinary one and the money-commodity. If we keep in view the material fact alone that a commodity has been exchanged for gold, we overlook the very thing that we ought to observe—namely, what has happened to the form of the commodity. We overlook the facts that gold, when a mere commodity, is not money, and that when other commodities express their prices in gold, this gold is but the money-form of those commodities themselves.

Commodities, first of all, enter into the process of exchange just as they are. The process then differentiates them into commodities and money, and thus produces an external opposition corresponding to the internal opposition inherent in them, as being at once use-values and values. Commodities as use-values now stand opposed to money as exchange value. On the other hand, both opposing sides are commodities, unities of use-value and value. But this unity of differences manifests itself at two opposite poles, and at each pole in an opposite way. Being poles they are as necessarily opposite as they are connected. On the one side of the equation we have an ordinary commodity, which is in reality a use-value. Its value is expressed only ideally in its price, by which it is equated to its opponent, the gold, as to the real embodiment of its value. On the other hand the gold, in its metallic reality, ranks as the embodiment of value, as money. Gold, as gold, is exchange value itself. As to its use-value, that has only an ideal existence, represented by the series of expressions of relative value in which it stands face to face with all other commodities, the sum of whose uses makes up the sum of the various uses of gold. These antagonistic forms of commodities are the real forms in which the process of their exchange moves and takes place.

★ ★ ★

The exchange of commodities is accompanied by the following changes in their form:

Commodity—Money—Commodity.
C—M—C.

The result of the whole process, so far as concerns the objects themselves, C–C, is the exchange of one commodity for another, the circulation of materialized social labor. When this result is attained, the process is at an end.

C—M. First metamorphosis, or sale.

The leap taken by value from the body of the commodity into the body of the gold is the *salto mortale* of the commodity. If it falls short then, although the commodity itself is not harmed, its owner decidedly is. The social division of labor causes his labor to be as one-sided as his wants are many-sided. This is precisely the reason why the product of his labor serves him solely as exchange value. But it cannot acquire the properties of a socially recognized universal equivalent except by being converted into money. That money, however, is in someone else's pocket. In order to entice the money out of that pocket, our friend's commodity must, above all things, be a use-value to the owner of the money. For this, it is necessary that the labor expended upon it be of a kind that is socially useful, of a kind that constitutes a branch of the social division of labor. But division of labor is a system of production which has grown up spontaneously and continues to grow behind the backs of the producers. The commodity to be exchanged may possibly be the product of some new kind of labor that pretends to satisfy newly arisen requirements, or even to give rise itself to new requirements. A particular operation, though conducted yesterday, perhaps, forming one out of the many operations conducted by one producer in creating a given commodity, may today separate itself from this connection, may establish itself as an independent branch of labor and send its incomplete product to market as an independent commodity. The circumstances may or may not be ripe for such a separation. Today the product satisfies a social want. Tomorrow the article may, either altogether or partially, be superseded by some other appropriate product.

★ ★ ★

The division of labor converts the product of labor into a commodity, and thereby makes necessary its further conversion into money. At the same time it also makes the accomplishment of this trans-substantiation quite accidental. Here, however, we are only concerned with the phenomenon in its integrity, and we therefore assume its progress to be normal. Moreover, if the conversion takes place at all, that is, if the commodity is not absolutely unsaleable, its metamorphosis does take place, although the price realized may be abnormally above or below the value.

★ ★ ★

Up to this point we have considered men in only one economical capacity, that of owners of commodities, a capacity in which they appropriate the product of the labor of others by alienating that of their own labor. Hence, for one commodity owner to meet with another who has money, it is necessary either that the product of the labor of the latter person, the buyer, should be in itself money, should be gold, the material of which money consists, or that his product should already have changed its skin and have stripped off its original form of a useful object. In order that it may play the part of money, gold must of course enter the market at some point or

other. This point is to be found at the source of production of the
metal where gold is bartered, as the immediate product of labor, for
some other product of equal value. From that moment it always
represents the realized price of some commodity. Apart from its exchange for other commodities at the source of its production, gold,
in whoever's hands it may be, is the transformed shape of some
commodity alienated by its owner; it is the product of a sale or of
the first metamorphosis, C–M. Gold, as we saw, became ideal
money, or a measure of values, in consequence of all commodities
measuring their values by it, and thus contrasting it ideally with
their natural shape as useful objects and making it the shape of their
value. It became real money by the general alienation of commodities, by actually changing places with their natural forms as
useful objects, and thus becoming in reality the embodiment of
their values. When they assume this money-shape, commodities
strip off every trace of their natural use-value, and of the particular
kind of labor to which they owe their creation, in order to transform themselves into the uniform, socially recognized incarnation
of homogeneous human labor.

★ ★ ★

The first metamorphosis of one commodity, its transformation
from a commodity into money, is therefore also invariably the second metamorphosis of some other commodity, the retransforma-
tion of the latter from money into a commodity.[*]

M–C, or purchase. The second and concluding metamorphois of a commodity.

Because money is the metamorphosed shape of all other commodities, the result of their general alienation, it is alienable itself

---

[*]The actual producer of gold or silver forms an exception. He exchanges his product directly for another commodity, without having first sold it.

without restriction or condition. It reads all prices backwards and thus, so to say, depicts itself in the bodies of all other commodities which offer to it the material for the realization of its own use-value. At the same time the prices, wooing glances cast at money by commodities, define the limits of its convertibility by pointing to its quantity. Since every commodity, on becoming money, disappears as a commodity, it is impossible to tell from the money itself how it got into the hands of its possessor, or what article has been changed into it. *Non olet*, from whatever source it may come. Representing on the one hand a sold commodity, it represents on the other hand a commodity to be bought.

★ ★ ★

The concluding metamorphosis of a commodity thus constitutes an aggregation of metamorphoses of various other commodities.

If we now consider the completed metamorphosis of a commodity, it appears in the first place that it is made up of two opposite and complementary movements, C–M and M–C. Those two antithetical transmutations of a commodity are brought about by two antithetical social acts on the part of the owner, and these acts in their turn stamp the character of the economical parts played by him. As the person who makes a sale, he is a seller; as the person who makes a purchase, he is a buyer. But just as, upon every such transmutation of a commodity, its two forms, commodity-form and money-form, exist simultaneously but at opposite poles, so every seller has a buyer opposed to him, and every buyer a seller. While one particular commodity is going through its two transmutations in succession, from a commodity into money and from money into another commodity, the owner of the commodity changes in succession his part from that of seller to that of buyer. These characters of seller and buyer are therefore not permanent, but attach themselves in turns to the various persons engaged in the circulation of commodities.

The complete metamorphosis of a commodity, in its simplest form, implies four extremes and three *dramatis personae*. First, a commodity comes face to face with money; the latter is the form taken by the value of the former, and exists in all its hard reality, in the pocket of the buyer. A commodity-owner is thus brought into contact with a possessor of money. As soon as the commodity has been changed into money, the money becomes its transient equivalent-form, the use-value whose equivalent-form is to be found in the bodies of other commodities. Money, the final term of the first transmutation, is at the same time the starting point for the second. The person who is a seller in the first transaction thus becomes a buyer in the second, during which a third commodity-owner appears on the scene as a seller.

The two phases, each inverse to the other, that make up the metamorphosis of a commodity constitute together a circular movement, a circuit: commodity-form, stripping off of this form, and return to the commodity-form. No doubt, the commodity appears here under two different aspects. At the starting point it is not a use-value to its owner; at the finishing point it is. So, too, the money appears in the first phase as a solid crystal of value, a crystal into which the commodity eagerly solidifies, and in the second, dissolves into the mere transient equivalent-form destined to be replaced by a use-value.

The two metamorphoses constituting the circuit are at the same time two inverse partial metamorphoses of two other commodities.

★ ★ ★

The total of all the different circuits constitutes *the circulation of commodities*.

The circulation of commodities differs from the direct exchange of products (barter) not only in form, but in substance. The process of circulation does not, as the direct barter of products does, become extinguished upon the use values changing places and hands.

The money does not vanish on dropping out of the circuit of the metamorphosis of a given commodity. It is constantly being precipitated into new places in the arena of circulation vacated by other commodities.

B. THE CURRENCY OF MONEY.

The change of form C–M–C, by which the circulation of the material products of labor is brought about, requires that a given value in the shape of a commodity shall begin the process and shall, also in the shape of a commodity, end it. The movement of the commodity is therefore a circuit. On the other hand, the form of this movement precludes a circuit from being made by the money. The result is not the return of the money, but its continued removal further and further away from its starting-point. This course constitutes its currency (*cours de la monnaie*).

The currency of money is the constant and monotonous repetition of the same process. The commodity is always in the hands of the seller; the money, as a means of purchase, always in the hands of the buyer. And money serves as a means of purchase by realising the price of the commodity. This realization transfers the commodity from the seller to the buyer, and removes the money from the hands of the buyer into those of the seller, where it again goes through the same process with another commodity. That this one-sided character of the money's motion arises out of the two-sided character of the commodity's motion is a circumstance that is hidden. The very nature of the circulation of commodities begets the opposite appearance. The first metamorphosis of a commodity is visibly not only the money's movement, but also that of the commodity itself; in the second metamorphosis, on the contrary, the movement appears to us as the movement of the money alone. In the first phase of its circulation the commodity changes place with the money. Thereupon the commodity, under its aspect as a useful object, falls out of circulation into consumption.* In its stead we have its value-shape—the money. It then goes through the second phase of its circulation, not in its own natural shape, but in the shape of money. The continuity of the movement is therefore maintained by the money alone, and the same movement that, as regards the commodity, consists of two processes of an antithetical character is, when considered as the movement of the money, always one and the same process, a continued change of places with ever fresh commodities. Hence the result brought about by the circulation of commodities, namely, the replacing of one commodity by another, takes the appearance of having been effected not by means of the change of form of the commodities, but rather by the money acting as a medium of circulation, by an action that circulates commodities, to all appearance motionless in themselves, and transfers them from hands in which they are non-use-values to hands in which they are use-values; and that in a direction constantly opposed to the direction of the money. The latter is continually withdrawing commodities from circulation and stepping into their places, and in this way continually moving further and further from its starting-point. Hence, although the movement of the money is merely the expression of the circulation of commodities, the contrary appears to be the actual fact, and the circulation of commodities seems to be the result of the movement of the money.

Again, money functions as a means of circulation only because in it the values of commodities have independent reality. Hence its movement as the medium of circulation is, in fact, merely the movement of commodities while changing their forms. This fact must therefore make itself plainly visible in the currency of money.

*Even when the commodity is sold over and over again, a phenomenon that at present does not exist for us, it falls, when definitely sold for the last time, out of the sphere of circulation into that of consumption, where it serves either as means of subsistence or means of production.

The twofold change of form in a commodity is reflected in the twice repeated change of place of the same piece of money during the complete metamorphosis of a commodity and in its constantly repeated change of place, as metamorphosis follows metamorphosis, and each becomes interlaced with the others.

* * *

If only one phase of the metamorphosis is gone through, if there are only sales or only purchases, then a given piece of money changes its place only once. Its second change corresponds to and expresses the second metamorphosis of the commodity, its reconversion from money into another commodity intended for use. It is a matter of course that all this is applicable to the simple circulation of commodities alone, the only form that we are now considering.

Every commodity, when it first steps into circulation and undergoes its first change of form, does so only to fall out of circulation again and to be replaced by other commodities. Money on the contrary, as the medium of circulation, keeps continually within the sphere of circulation and moves about in it. The question therefore arises, how much money does this sphere constantly absorb?

In a given country there take place every day at the same time, but in different localities, numerous one-sided metamorphoses of commodities, or in other words, numerous sales and numerous purchases. The commodities are equated beforehand in the imagination, by their prices, to definite quantities of money. And since, in the form of circulation now under consideration, money and commodities always come bodily face to face, one at the positive pole of purchase, the other at the negative pole of sale, it is clear that the amount of the means of circulation required is determined beforehand by the sum of the prices of all these commodities. As a matter of fact, the money in reality represents the quantity or sum of gold ideally expressed beforehand by the sum of the prices of the commodities. The equality of these two sums is therefore self-evident. We know, however, that the values of commodities remaining constant, their prices vary with the value of gold (the material of money), rising in proportion as it falls and falling in proportion as it rises. Now if, in consequence of such a rise or fall in the value of gold, the sum of the prices of commodities fall or rise, the quantity of money in currency must fall or rise to the same extent. The change in the quantity of the circulating medium is, in this case, it is true, caused by money itself, yet not in virtue of its function as a medium of circulation, but of its function as a measure of value. First, the price of the commodities varies inversely as the value of the money, and then the quantity of the medium of circulation varies directly as the price of the commodities. Exactly the same thing would happen if, for instance, instead of the value of gold falling, gold were replaced by silver as the measure of value, or if, instead of the value of silver rising, gold were to cast silver out from being the measure of value. In the one case, more silver would be current than gold was before; in the other case, less gold would be current than silver was before. In each case the value of the material of money, i.e., the value of the commodity that serves as the measure of value, would have undergone a change and therefore, so too would the prices of commodities which express their values in money, and so too would the quantity of money current whose function it is to realise those prices. We have already seen that the sphere of circulation has an opening through which gold (or the material of money generally) enters into it as a commodity with a given value. Hence, when money enters on its functions as a measure of value, when it expresses prices, its value is already determined. If its value now falls, this fact is first evidenced by a change in the prices of those commodities that are directly bartered for the precious metals at the sources of their production. The greater part of all other commodities, especially in the imperfectly developed stages of civil society, will continue for a long time to be estimated by the former antiquated and illusory value of the measure of value. Nevertheless, one commodity infects another through their common value-relation, so that their prices, expressed in gold or in silver, gradually settle down into the proportions determined by their comparative values, until finally the values of all commodities are estimated in terms of the new value of the metal that constitutes money. This process is accompanied by the continued increase in the quantity of the precious metals, an increase caused by their streaming in to replace the articles directly bartered for them at their sources of production. Therefore, in proportion as commodities in general acquire their true prices, in proportion as their values become estimated according to the fallen value of the precious metal, in the same proportion the quantity of that metal necessary for realising those new prices is provided beforehand.

On this supposition then, the quantity of the medium of circulation is determined by the sum of the prices that have to be realized. If now we further suppose the price of each commodity to be given, the sum of the prices clearly depends on the mass of commodities in circulation.

★ ★ ★

If the mass of commodities remains constant, the quantity of circulating money varies with the fluctuations in the prices of those commodities. It increases and diminishes because the sum of the prices increases or diminishes according to the change of price. To produce this effect, it is by no means requisite that the prices of all commodities should rise or fall simultaneously. A rise or a fall in the prices of a number of leading articles is sufficient in the one case to increase, in the other to diminish, the sum of the prices of all commodities, and therefore to put more or less money in circulation. Whether the change in the price corresponds to an actual change of value in the commodities or whether it be the result of mere fluctuations in market prices, the effect on the quantity of the medium of circulation remains the same.

★ ★ ★

The total circulation of commodities in a given country during a given period is made up on the one hand of numerous isolated and simultaneous partial metamorphoses, sales which are at the same time purchases in which each coin changes its place only once, or makes only one move; on the other hand, of numerous distinct series of metamorphoses partly running side by side and partly coalescing with each other, in each series of which each coin makes a number of moves, the number being greater or less according to circumstances. The total number of moves made by all the circulating coins of one denomination being given, we can arrive at the average number of moves made by a single coin of that denomination, or at the average velocity of the currency of money. The quantity of money thrown into circulation at the beginning of each day is of course determined by the sum of the prices of all the commodities circulating simultaneously side by side. But once in circulation, coins are, so to say, made responsible for one another. If the one increases its velocity, the other either retards its own or altogether falls out of circulation; for the circulation can absorb only such a quantity of gold as when, multiplied by the mean number of moves made by one single coin or element, it is equal to the sum of the prices to be realized. Hence if the number of moves made by the separate pieces increase, the total number of those pieces in circulation diminishes. If the number of the moves diminish, the total number of pieces increases. Since the quantity of money capable of being absorbed by the circulation is established for a given mean velocity of currency, all that is necessary in order to derive a given number of sovereigns from the circulation is to throw the same number of one-pound notes into it, a trick well known to all bankers.

Just as the currency of money, generally considered, is but a reflection of the circulation of commodities, or of the antithetical metamorphoses they undergo, so, too, the velocity of that currency reflects the rapidity with which commodities change their forms, the continued interlacing of one series of metamorphoses with another, the hurried social interchange of matter, the rapid disappearance of commodities from the sphere of circulation, and the equally rapid substitution of fresh ones in their places. Hence, in the velocity of the currency we have the fluent unity of the antithetical and complementary phases, the unity of the conversion of the useful aspect of commodities into their value-aspect, and their re-conversion from the latter aspect to the former, or the unity of the two processes of sale and purchase. On the other hand; the retardation of the currency reflects the separation of these two processes into isolated antithetical phases, reflects the stagnation in the change of form, and therefore, in the social interchange of matter. The circulation itself, of course, gives no clue to the origin of this stagnation; it merely is evidence of the phenomenon itself. The general public, who simultaneously with the retardation of the currency, see money appear and disappear less frequently at the periphery of circulation, naturally attribute this retardation to a quantitive deficiency in the circulating medium.

The total quantity of money functioning during a given period as the circulating medium is determined, on the one hand, by the sum of the prices of the circulating commodities, and on the other hand, by the rapidity with which the antithetical phases of the metamorphoses follow one another. On this rapidity depends what proportion of the sum of the prices can, on average, be realized by each single coin. But the sum of the prices of the circulating commodities depends on the quantity, as well as on the prices, of the commodities. However, these three factors—state of prices, quantity of circulating commodities, and velocity of money-currency—are all variable. Hence, the sum of the prices to be realized, and consequently the quantity of the circulating medium depending on that sum, will vary with the numerous variations of these three factors in combination. Of these variations we shall consider those alone that have been the most important in the history of prices.

While prices remain constant, the quantity of the circulating medium may increase owing to the number of circulating commodities increasing, or to the velocity of currency decreasing, or to a combination of the two. On the other hand the quantity of the circulating medium may decrease with a decreasing number of commodities, or with an increasing rapidity of their circulation.

With a general rise in the prices of commodities, the quantity of the circulating medium will remain constant, provided the number of commodities in circulation decreases proportionally to the increase in their prices, or provided the velocity of currency increases at the same rate as prices rise, the number of commodities in circulation remaining constant. The quantity of the circulating medium may decrease owing to the number of commodities decreasing more rapidly, or to the velocity of currency increasing more rapidly, than prices rise.

With a general fall in the prices of commodities, the quantity of the circulating medium will remain constant, provided the number of commodities increases proportionately to their fall in price, or provided the velocity of currency decreases in the same proportion. The quantity of the circulating medium will increase, provided the number of commodities increases quicker, or the rapidity of circulation decreases quicker, than the prices fall.

The variations of the different factors may mutually compensate each other, so that notwithstanding their continued instability, the sum of the prices to be realized and the quantity of money in circulation remain constant; consequently, we find, especially if we take long periods into consideration, that the deviations from the average level of the quantity of money current in any country are much smaller than we should at first sight expect, apart of course from excessive perturbations periodically arising from industrial and commercial crises, or, less frequently, from fluctuations in the value of money.

The law that the quantity of the circulating medium is determined by the sum of the prices of the commodities circulating and the average velocity of currency may also be stated as follows: given the sum of the values of commodities, and the average rapidity of their metamorphoses, the quantity of precious metal current as money depends on the value of that precious metal.

c. COIN, AND SYMBOLS OF VALUE

That money takes the shape of coin springs from its function as the circulating medium. The weight of gold represented in the imagination by the prices or money-names of commodities must confront those commodities, within the circulation, in the shape of coins or pieces of gold of a given denomination. Coining, like the establishment of a standard of prices, is the business of the State. The different national uniforms worn at home by gold and silver as coins, and doffed again in the market of the world, indicate the separation between the internal or national spheres of the circulation of commodities, and their universal sphere.

The only difference, therefore, between coin and bullion is one of shape, and gold can at any time pass from one form to the other. But no sooner does coin leave the mint than it immediately finds itself on the high-road to the melting pot. During their currency, coins wear away, some more, others less. Name and substance, nominal weight and real weight, begin their process of separation. Coins of the same denomination become different in value because they are different in weight. The weight of gold, fixed upon as the standard of prices, deviates from the weight that serves as the circulating medium, and the latter thereby ceases any longer to be a real equivalent of the commodities whose prices it realizes. The natural tendency of circulation to convert coins into a mere semblance of what they profess to be, into a symbol of the weight of metal they are officially supposed to contain, is recognized by modern legislation, which fixes the loss of weight sufficient to demonetise a gold coin, or to make it no longer legal tender.

The fact that the currency of coins itself effects a separation between their nominal and their real weight, creating a distinction between them as mere pieces of metal on the one hand, and as coins with a definite function on the other—this fact implies the latent possibility of replacing metallic coins by tokens of some other material, by symbols serving the same purposes as coins. The practical difficulties in the way of coining extremely minute quantities of gold or silver, and the circumstance that at first the less precious metal is used as a measure of value instead of the more precious, copper instead of silver, silver instead of gold, and that the less precious circulates as money until dethroned by the more precious—all these facts explain the parts historically played by silver and copper tokens as substitutes for gold coins. Silver and copper tokens take the place of gold in those regions of circulation where coins pass from hand to hand most rapidly, and are subject to the maximum amount of wear and tear. This occurs where sales and purchases on a very small scale are continually happening. In order to prevent these satellites from establishing themselves permanently in the place of gold, positive enactments determine the extent to which they must be compulsorily received as payment instead of gold. The particular tracks pursued by the different species of coin in currency run naturally into each other. The tokens keep company with gold in order to pay fractional parts of the smallest gold coin; gold is, on the one hand, constantly pouring into retail circulation, and on the other hand is just as constantly being thrown out again by being changed into tokens.

The weight of metal in the silver and copper tokens is arbitrarily fixed by law. When in currency, they wear away even more rapidly than gold coins. Hence their functions are totally independent of their weight, and consequently of all value. The function of gold as coin becomes completely independent of the metallic value of that gold. Therefore things that are relatively without value, such as paper notes, can serve as coins in its place. This purely symbolic character is to a certain extent masked in metal tokens. In paper money it stands out plainly. In fact, *ce n'est que le premier pas qui coûte.*

We allude here only to inconvertible paper money issued by the State and having compulsory circulation. It has its immediate origin in the metallic currency. Money based upon credit implies on the other hand conditions which from our standpoint of the simple circulation of commodities, are as yet totally unknown to us. But we may affirm this much, that just as true paper money takes its rise in the function of money as the circulating medium, so money based upon credit takes root spontaneously in the function of money as the means of payment.

The State puts in circulation bits of paper on which their various denominations, say £1, £5, etc., are printed. Insofar as they actually take the place of gold to the same amount, their movement is subject to the laws that regulate the currency of money itself. A law peculiar to the circulation of paper money can spring up only from the proportion in which that paper money represents gold. Such a law exists; stated simply, it is as follows: the issue of paper money must not exceed in amount the gold (or silver as the case may be) which would actually circulate if not replaced by symbols. Now the quantity of gold which the circulation can absorb constantly fluctuates about a given level. Still, the mass of the circulating medium in a given country never sinks below a certain minimum easily ascertained by actual experience. The fact that this minimum mass continually undergoes changes in its constituent parts, or that the pieces of gold of which it consists are being constantly replaced by fresh ones, causes of course no change either in its amount or in the continuity of its circulation. It can therefore be replaced by paper symbols. If, on the other hand, all the conduits of circulation were today filled with paper money to the full extent of their capacity for absorbing money, they might tomorrow be overflowing in consequence of a fluctuation in the circulation of commodities. There would no longer be any standard. If the paper money exceed its proper limit, which is the amount of gold coins of the like denomination that can actually be current, it would, apart from the danger of falling into general disrepute, represent only that quantity of gold which, in accordance with the laws of the circulation of commodities, is required, and is alone capable of being represented by paper.

★ ★ ★

Paper-money is a token representing gold or money. The relation between it and the values of commodities is this, that the latter are ideally expressed in the same quantities of gold that are symbolically represented by the paper. Only insofar as paper-money represents gold, which like all other commodities has value, is it a symbol of value.

Finally, someone may ask why gold is capable of being replaced by tokens that have no value. But, as we have already seen, it is capable of being so replaced only insofar as it functions exclusively as coin, or as the circulating medium, and as nothing else. Now, money has other functions besides this one, and the isolated function of serving as the mere circulating medium is not necessarily the only one attached to gold coin, although this is the case with those abraded coins that continue to circulate. Each piece of money is a mere coin, or means of circulation, only so long as it actually circulates. But this is just the case with that minimum mass of gold, which is capable of being replaced by paper-money. That mass remains constantly within the sphere of circulation, continually functions as a circulating medium, and exists exclusively for that purpose. Its movement therefore represents nothing but the continued alternation of the inverse phases of the metamorphosis C–M–C, phases in which commodities confront their value-forms, only to disappear again immediately. The independent existence of the exchange value of a commodity is here a transient apparition by means of which the commodity is immediately replaced by another commodity. Hence, in this process which continually makes money pass from hand to hand, the mere symbolical existence of money suffices. Its functional existence absorbs, so to say, its material existence. Being a transient and objective reflex of the prices of commodities, it serves only as a symbol of itself, and is therefore capable of being replaced by a token. One thing is, however, requisite; this token must have an objective social validity of its own, and this the paper symbol acquires by its forced currency. This compulsory action of the State can take effect only within that inner sphere of circulation which is coterminous with the territories of the community, but it is also only within that sphere that money completely responds to its function of being the circulating medium, or becomes coin.

SECTION 3—MONEY

The commodity that functions as a measure of value and, either in its own person or by a representative, as the medium of circulation, is money. Gold (or silver) is therefore money. It functions as money, on the one hand, when it has to be present in its own golden person. It is then the money-commodity, neither merely ideal, as in its function of a measure of value, nor capable of being represented, as in its function of circulating medium. On the other hand, it also functions as money when by virtue of its function, whether that function be performed in person or by representative, it congeals into the sole form of value, the only adequate form of existence of exchange-value, in opposition to use-value, represented by all other commodities.

A. HOARDING

The continual movement in circuits of the two antithetical metamorphoses of commodities, or the never ceasing alternation of sale and purchase, is reflected in the restless currency of money, or in the function that money performs of a perpetuum mobile of circulation. But as soon as the series of metamorphoses is interrupted, as soon as sales are not supplemented by subsequent purchases, money ceases to be mobilised; it is tranformed from movable into immovable, from coin into money.

With the very earliest development of the circulation of commodities, there is also developed the necessity, and the passionate desire, to hold fast the product of the first metamorphosis. This product is the transformed shape of the commodity, or its gold-chrysalis. Commodities are thus sold not for the purpose of buying others, but in order to replace their commodity-form by their money-form. From being the mere means of effecting the circulation of commodities, this change of form becomes the goal. The changed form of the commodity is thus prevented from functioning as its unconditionally alienable form, or as its merely transient money-form. The money becomes petrified into a hoard, and the seller becomes a hoarder of money.

In the early stages of the circulation of commodities, it is the surplus use-values alone that are converted into money. Gold and silver thus become of themselves social expressions for superfluity of wealth.

★ ★ ★

As the production of commodities further develops, every producer of commodities is compelled to make sure of the *nexus rerum,* or the social pledge. His wants are constantly making themselves felt, and necessitate the continual purchase of other people's commodities, while the production and sale of his own goods require time and depend upon circumstances. In order then to be able to buy without selling, he must have sold previously without buying.

This operation, conducted on a general scale, appears to imply a contradiction. But the precious metals at the sources of their production are directly exchanged for other commodities. And here we have sales (by the owners of commodities) without purchases (by the owners of gold or silver). And subsequent sales by other producers, unfollowed by purchases, merely bring about the distribution of the newly produced precious metals among all the owners of commodities. In this way, all along the line of exchange, hoards of gold and silver of varied extent are accumulated. With the possibility of holding and storing up exchange value in the shape of a particular commodity, the greed for gold arises also. Along with the extension of circulation, the power of money increases. Since gold does not disclose what has been transformed into it, everything, commodity or not, is convertible into gold. Everything becomes saleable and buyable. The circulation becomes the great social retort into which everything is thrown, to come out again as a gold-crystal. Just as every qualitative difference between commodities is extinguished in money, so money, on its side, like the radical leveller that it is, does away with all distinctions. But money itself is a commodity, an external object, capable of becoming the private property of any individual. Thus social power becomes the private power of private persons.

★ ★ ★

A commodity, in its capacity as a use-value, satisfies a particular want, and is a particular element of material wealth. But the value of a commodity measures the degree of its attraction for all other elements of material wealth, and therefore measures the social wealth of its owner.

★ ★ ★

In order that gold may be held as money and made to form a hoard, it must be prevented from circulating, or from transforming itself into a means of enjoyment. The hoarder, therefore, makes a sacrifice of the lusts of the flesh to his gold fetish. On the other hand, he can withdraw from circulation no more than what he has thrown into it in the shape of commodities. The more he produces, the more he is able to sell.

★ ★ ★

By the side of the gross form of a hoard, we find also its aesthetic form in the possession of gold and silver articles. This grows with the wealth of civil society. In this way there is created, on the one hand, a constantly extending market for gold and silver, unconnected with their functions as money, and on the other hand, a latent source of supply, to which recourse is had principally in times of crisis and social disturbance.

Hoarding serves various purposes in the economy of the metallic circulation. Its first function arises out of the conditions to which the currency of gold and silver coins is subject. We have seen how, along with the continual fluctuations in the extent and rapidity of the circulation of commodities and in their prices, the quantity of money current unceasingly ebbs and flows. This mass must, therefore, be capable of expansion and contraction. At one time money must be attracted in order to act as circulating coin, at another, circulating coin must be repelled in order to act again as more or less stagnant money. In order that the mass of money actually current may constantly saturate the absorbing power of the circulation, it is necessary that the quantity of gold and silver in a country be greater than the quantity required to function as coin. This condition is fulfilled by money taking the form of hoards. These reserves serve as conduits for the supply or withdrawal of money to or from the circulation, which in this way never overflows its banks.

B. MEANS OF PAYMENT

In the simple form of the circulation of commodities hitherto considered, we found a given value always presented to us in a double shape, as a commodity at one pole, as money at the opposite pole. The owners of commodities came therefore into contact as the respective representatives of what were already equivalents. But with the development of circulation, conditions arise under which the alienation of commodities becomes separated, by an interval of time, from the realization of their prices. One sort of article requires a longer, another a shorter time for its production. Again, the production of different commodities depends on different seasons of the year. One sort of commodity may be born on its own market place, another has to make a long journey to market. Commodity-owner No. 1 may therefore be ready to sell before No. 2 is ready to buy. When the same transactions are continually repeated between the same persons, the conditions of sale are regulated in accordance with the conditions of production. On the other hand, the use of a given commodity, of a house, for instance, is sold (in common parlance, let) for a definite period. Here, it is only at the end of the term that the buyer has actually received the use-value of the commodity. He therefore buys it before he pays for it. The vendor sells an existing commodity, the purchaser buys as the mere representative of money, or rather of future money. The vendor becomes a creditor, the purchaser becomes a debtor. Since the metamorphosis of commodities, or the development of their value-form, appears here under a new aspect, money also acquires a fresh function; it becomes the means of payment.

The character of creditor or of debtor results here from the simple circulation. The change in the form of that circulation stamps buyer and seller with this new die. At first, therefore, these new parts are just as transient and alternating as those of seller and buyer, and are in turns played by the same actors. But the opposition is not nearly so pleasant, and is far more capable of crystallization. The same characters can, however, be assumed independently of the circulation of commodities. The class-struggles of the ancient world took the form chiefly of a contest between debtors and creditors, which in Rome ended in the ruin of the plebeian debtors. They were displaced by slaves. In the middle-ages the contest ended with the ruin of the feudal debtors, who lost their political power together with the economical basis on which it was established. Nevertheless, the money relation of debtor and creditor that existed at these two periods reflected only the deeper-lying antagonism between the general economical conditions of existence of the classes in question.

Let us return to the circulation of commodities. The appearance of the two equivalents, commodities and money, at the two poles of the process of sale has ceased to be simultaneous. The money functions now, first as a measure of value in the determination of the price of the commodity sold; the price fixed by the contract measures the obligation of the debtor, or the sum of money that he has to pay at a fixed date. Secondly, it serves as an ideal means of purchase. Although existing only in the promise of the buyer to pay, it causes the commodity to change hands. It is not before the day fixed for payment that the means of payment actually steps into circulation, leaving the hand of the buyer for that of the seller. The circulating medium was transformed into a hoard, because the process stopped short after the first phase, because the converted shape of the commodity, viz., the money, was withdrawn from circulation. The means of payment enters circulation, but only after the commodity has left it. The money is no longer the means that brings about the process. It only brings it to a close, by stepping in as the absolute form of existence of exchange value, or as the universal commodity. The seller turned his commodity into money in order thereby to satisfy some want; the hoarder did the same in order to keep his commodity in its money-shape, and the debtor in order to be able to pay; if he does not pay, his goods will be sold by the sheriff. The value-form of commodities, money, is therefore now the end and aim of a sale, and that owing to a social necessity springing out of the process of circulation itself.

The buyer converts money back into commodities before he has turned commodities into money: in other words, he achieves the second metamorphosis of commodities before the first. The seller's commodity circulates, and realizes its price, but only in the shape of a legal claim upon money. It is converted into a use-value before it has been converted into money. The completion of its first metamorphosis follows only at a later period.

The obligations falling due within a given period represent the sum of the prices of the commodities, the sale of which gave rise to those obligations. The quantity of gold necessary to realize this sum depends, in the first instance, on the rapidity of currency of the means of payment. That quantity is conditioned by two circumstances: first, the relations between debtors and creditors form a sort of chain in such a way that A, when he receives money from his debtor B, straightway hands it over to his creditor C, and so on; the second circumstance is the length of the intervals between the different due-days of the obligations. The continuous chain of payments, or retarded first metamorphoses, is essentially different from that interlacing of the series of metamorphoses which we considered on a previous page. By the currency of the circulating medium, the connection between buyers and sellers is not merely expressed. This connection is originated by, and exists in, the circulation alone. Contrariwise, the movement of the means of payment expresses a social relation that existed long before.

The fact that a number of sales take place simultaneously, and side by side, limits the extent to which coin can be replaced by the rapidity of currency. On the other hand, this fact is a new lever in economizing the means of payment. In proportion as payments are concentrated at one spot, special institutions and methods are developed for their liquidation. Such in the middle ages were the *virements* at Lyons. The debts due to A from B, to B from C, to C from A, and so on, have only to be confronted with each other in order to annul each other to a certain extent like positive and negative quantities. There thus remains only a single balance to pay. The greater the amount of the payments concentrated, the less is this balance relative to that amount, and the less is the mass of the means of payment in circulation.

The function of money as the means of payment implies a contradiction without a *terminus medius*. Insofar as the payments balance one another, money functions only ideally as money of account, as a measure of value. Insofar as actual payments have to be made, money does not serve as a circulating medium, as a mere transient agent in the interchange of products, but as the individual incarnation of social labor, as the independent form of existence of exchange value, as the universal commodity. This contradiction comes to a head in those phases of industrial and commercial crises which are known as monetary crises. Such crises occur only where the ever-lengthening chain of payments, and an artificial system of settling them, has been fully developed. Whenever there is a general and extensive disturbance of this mechanism, no matter what its cause, money becomes suddenly and immediately transformed from its merely ideal shape of money of account into hard cash. Profane commodities can no longer replace it. The use-value of commodities becomes valueless, and their value vanishes in the presence of its own independent form. On the eve of the crisis, the bourgeois, with the self-sufficiency that springs from intoxicating prosperity, declares money to be a vain imagination. Commodities alone are money. But now the cry is everywhere: money alone is a commodity! As a deer pants after fresh water, so pants his soul after money, the only wealth. In a crisis, the antithesis between commodities and their value-form—money—becomes heightened into an absolute contradiction. Hence, in such events, the form under which money appears is of no importance. The money famine continues, whether payments have to be made in gold or in credit money such as bank notes.

If we now consider the sum total of the money current during a given period, we shall find that, given the rapidity of currency of the circulating medium and of the means of payment, it is equal to the sum of the prices to be realized, plus the sum of the payments falling due, minus the payments that balance each other, minus finally the number of circuits in which the same piece of coin serves in turn as means of circulation and of payment. Hence, even when prices, rapidity of currency, and the extent of the economy in payments are given, the quantity of money current and the mass of commodities circulating during a given period, such as a day, no longer correspond. Money that represents commodities long withdrawn from circulation continues to be current. Commodities circulate whose equivalent in money will not appear on the scene till some future day. Moreover, the debts contracted each day, and the payments falling due on the same day, are quite incommensurable quantities.

Credit-money springs directly out of the function of money as a means of payment. Certificates of the debts owing for the purchased commodities circulate for the purpose of transferring those debts to others. On the other hand, to the same extent as the system of credit is extended, so is the function of money as a means of payment. In that character it takes various forms peculiar to itself under which it makes itself at home in the sphere of great commercial transactions. Gold and silver coin, on the other hand, are mostly relegated to the sphere of retail trade.

When the production of commodities has sufficiently extended itself, money begins to serve as the means of payment beyond the sphere of the circulation of commodities. It becomes the commodity that is the universal subject-matter of all contracts. Rents, taxes, and such like payments are transformed from payments in kind into money payments.

★ ★ ★

From the law of the rapidity of currency of the means of payment, it follows that the quantity of the means of payment required for all periodical payments, whatever their source, is in inverse proportion to the length of their periods.

The development of money into a medium of payment makes it necessary to accumulate money against the dates fixed for the payment of the sums owed. While hoarding, as a distinct mode of acquiring riches, vanishes with the progress of civil society, the formation of reserves of the means of payment grows with that progress.

c. Universal Money

When money leaves the home sphere of circulation, it strips off the local garbs which it there assumes of a standard of prices, of coin, of tokens, and of a symbol of value, and returns to its original form of bullion. In the trade between the markets of the world, the value of commodities is expressed so as to be universally recognized. Hence their independent value-form also, in these cases, confronts them in the shape of universal money. It is only in the markets of the world that money acquires to the full extent the character of the commodity whose bodily form is also the immediate social incarnation of human labor in the abstract. Its real mode of existence in this sphere adequately corresponds to its ideal concept.

Within the sphere of home circulation, there can be but one commodity which, by serving as a measure of value, becomes money. In the markets of the world a double measure of value holds sway—gold and silver.[*]

---

[*]Hence the absurdity of every law prescribing that the banks of a country shall form reserves of that precious metal alone which circulates at home.

Money of the world serves as the universal medium of payment, as the universal means of purchasing, and as the universally recognized embodiment of all wealth. Its function as a means of payment in the settling of international balances is its chief one. Hence the watchword of the mercantilists—balance of trade. Gold and silver serve as international means of purchasing chiefly and necessarily in those periods when the customary equilibrium in the interchange of products between different nations is suddenly disturbed. And lastly, it serves as the universally recognized embodiment of social wealth whenever the question is not of buying or paying, but of transferring wealth from one country to another, and whenever this transference in the form of commodities is rendered impossible, either by special conjunctures in the markets, or by the purpose itself that is intended.

Just as every country needs a reserve of money for its home circulation, so, too, it requires one for external circulation in the markets of the world. The functions of hoards, therefore, arise in part out of the function of money, as the medium of the home circulation and home payments, and in part out of its function of money of the world. For this latter function, the genuine money-commodity, actual gold and silver, is necessary.

★ ★ ★

The current of the stream of gold and silver is a double one. On the one hand, it spreads itself from its sources over all the markets of the world in order to become absorbed, to various extents, into the different national spheres of circulation, to fill the conduits of currency, to replace abraded gold and silver coins, to supply the material of articles of luxury, and to petrify into hoards. This first current is started by the countries that exchange their labor, realized in commodities, for the labor embodied in the precious metals by gold and silver-producing countries. On the other hand, there is a continual flowing backwards and forwards of gold and silver between the different national spheres of circulation, a current whose motion depends on the ceaseless fluctuations in the course of exchange.

Countries in which the bourgeois form of production is developed to a certain extent limit the hoards concentrated in the strong rooms of the banks to the minimum required for the proper performance of their peculiar functions. Whenever these hoards are strikingly above their average level, it is, with some exceptions, an indication of stagnation in the circulation of commodities, of an interruption in the even flow of their metamorphoses.

PART II

The Transformation of
Money into Capital

CHAPTER IV

THE GENERAL FORMULA
FOR CAPITAL

THE CIRCULATION of commodities is the starting point of capital. The production of commodities, their circulation, and that more developed form of their circulation called commerce—these form the historical groundwork from which it arises. The modern history of capital dates from the creation in the sixteenth century of a world-embracing commerce and a world-embracing market.

If we disregard the material substance of the circulation of commodities, that is, the exchange of the various use-values, and consider only the economic forms produced by this process of circulation, we find its final result to be money: this final product of the circulation of commodities is the first form in which capital appears.

As a matter of history, capital, as opposed to landed property, invariably takes the form at first of money; it appears as moneyed wealth, as the capital of the merchant and of the usurer. But we have no need to refer to the origin of capital in order to discover that the first form of appearance of capital is money. We can see it daily with our very eyes. All new capital, to commence with, comes on the stage, that is, on the market, whether of commodities, labor, or money, even in our days, in the shape of money that by a definite process has to be transformed into capital.

The first distinction we notice between money that is money only, and money that is capital, is nothing more than a difference in their form of circulation.

★ ★ ★

The final result of every separate circuit in which a purchase and consequent sale are completed forms of itself the starting point of a new circuit. The simple circulation of commodities—selling in order to buy—is a means of carrying out a purpose unconnected with circulation, namely, the appropriation of use-values, the satisfaction of wants. The circulation of money as capital is, on the contrary, an end in itself, for the expansion of value takes place only within this constantly renewed movement. The circulation of capital has therefore no limits. Thus the conscious representative of this movement, the possessor of money, becomes a capitalist. His person, or rather his pocket, is the point from which the money starts and to which it returns. The expansion of value becomes his subjective aim, and it is only insofar as the appropriation of ever more wealth in the abstract becomes the sole motive of his operations that he functions as a capitalist, that is, as capital personified and endowed with consciousness and a will. Use-values must therefore never be looked upon as the real aim of the capitalist; neither must the profit on any single transaction.

★ ★ ★

The independent form, i.e., the money-form, which the value of commodities assumes in the case of simple circulation, serves only one purpose, namely, their exchange, and vanishes in the final result of the movement. On the other hand, both the money and the commodity represent only different modes of existence of value itself, the money its general mode, and the commodity its particular or, so to say, disguised mode. It is constantly changing from one form to the other without thereby becoming lost, and thus assumes an automatically active character. If now we take in turn each of the two different forms which self-expanding value successively assumes in the course of its life, we then arrive at these two propositions: Capital is money; Capital is commodities. In truth, however, value is here the active factor in a process in which, while constantly assuming the form in turn of money and commodities, it at the same time changes in magnitude, differentiates itself by throwing off surplus-value from itself; the original value, in other words, expands spontaneously. Because the movement, in the course of which it adds surplus value, is its own movement, its expansion therefore is automatic expansion. Because it is value, it has acquired the occult quality of being able to add value to itself. It brings forth living offspring or, at the least, lays golden eggs.

Value, therefore, being the active factor in such a process, and assuming at one time the form of money, at another that of commodities, but through all these changes preserving itself and expanding, requires some independent form by means of which its identity may at any time be established. And this form it possesses only in the shape of money. It is under the form of money that value begins and ends and begins again, every act of its own spontaneous generation.

CHAPTER V

CONTRADICTIONS IN THE GENERAL FORMULA OF CAPITAL

THE FORM WHICH circulation takes when money becomes capital is opposed to all the laws we have hitherto investigated bearing on the nature of commodities, value and money, and even of circulation itself. What distinguishes this form from that of the simple circulation of commodities is the inverted order of succession of the two antithetical processes, sale and purchase. How can this purely formal distinction between these processes change their character as if by magic?

But that is not all. This inversion has no existence for two out of the three persons who transact business together. As capitalist, I buy commodities from A and sell them again to B, but as a simple owner of commodities, I sell them to B and then purchase fresh ones from A. A and B see no difference between the two sets of transactions. They are merely buyers or sellers. And I on each occasion meet them as a mere owner of either money or commodities, as a buyer or a seller, and what is more, in both sets of transactions I am opposed to A only as a buyer and to B only as a seller, to the one only as money, to the other only as commodities, and to neither of them as capital or a capitalist, or as representative of anything that is more than money or commodities, or that can produce any effect beyond what money and commodities can. For me the purchase from A and the sale to B are part of a series. But the connection between the two acts exists for me alone. A does not trouble himself about my transaction with B, nor does B about my business with A. And if I offered to explain to them the meritorious nature of my action in inverting the order of succession, they would probably point out to me that I was mistaken as to that order of succession, and that the whole transaction, instead of beginning with a purchase and ending with a sale, began, on the contrary, with a sale and was concluded with a purchase. In truth, my first act, the purchase, was from the standpoint of A, a sale, and my second act, the sale, was from the standpoint of B, a purchase. Not content with that, A and B would declare that the whole series was superfluous and nothing but hocus pocus; that for the future B would buy direct from A, and A sell direct to B. Thus the whole transaction would be reduced to a single act forming an isolated, non-complemented phase in the ordinary circulation of commodities, a mere sale from A's point of view, and from B's, a mere purchase. The inversion, therefore, of the order of succession, does not take us outside the sphere of the simple circulation of commodities, and we must rather look as to whether there is in this simple circulation anything permitting an expansion of the value that enters into circulation, and consequently, a creation of surplus-value.

Let us take the process of circulation in a form under which it presents itself as a simple and direct exchange of commodities. This is always the case when two owners of commodities buy from each other, and on the settling day the amounts mutually owed are equal and cancel each other. The money in this case is money of account and serves to express the value of the commodities by their prices, but is not itself, in the shape of hard cash, confronted with them. So far as regards use-values, it is clear that both parties may gain some advantage. Both part with goods that, as use-values, are of no service to them, and receive others that they can make use of. And there may also be a further gain. A, who sells wine and buys corn, possibly produces more wine, with given labor time, than farmer B could, and B, on the other hand, more corn than wine-grower A could. A, therefore, may get, for the same exchange value, more corn, and B more wine, than each would respectively get without any exchange by producing his own corn and wine. With reference, therefore, to use-value, there is good ground for saying that "exchange is a transaction by which both sides gain." It is otherwise with exchange value. "A man who has plenty of wine and no corn interacts with a man who has plenty of corn and no wine; an exchange takes place between them of corn to the value of 50, for wine of the same value. This act produces no increase of exchange value either for the one or the other; for each of them already possessed, before the exchange, a value equal to that which he acquired by means of that operation." The result is not altered by introducing money as a medium of circulation between the commodities, and making the sale and the purchase two distinct acts. The value of a commodity is expressed in its price before it goes into circulation, and is therefore a precedent condition of circulation, not its result.

Abstractedly considered, that is, apart from circumstances not immediately flowing from the laws of the simple circulation of commodities, there is in an exchange nothing (if we except the replacing of one use-value by another) but a metamorphosis, a mere change in the form of the commodity. The same exchange value, i.e., the same quantity of incorporated social labor, remains throughout in the hands of the owner of the commodity first in the shape of his own commodity, then in the form of the money for which he exchanged it, and lastly, in the shape of the commodity he buys with that money. This change of form does not imply a change in the magnitude of the value. But the change which the value of the commodity undergoes in this process is limited to a change in its money form. This form exists first as the price of the commodity offered for sale, then as an actual sum of money which, however, was already expressed in the price, and lastly, as the price of an equivalent commodity. This change of form no more implies, taken alone, a change in the quantity of value, than does the change of a £5 note into sovereigns, half sovereigns, and shillings. So far therefore as the circulation of commodities effects a change in the form alone of their values, and is free from disturbing influences, it must be the exchange of equivalents.

★ ★ ★

Behind all attempts to represent the circulation of commodities as a source of surplus-value, there lurks a *quid pro quo,* a mixing up of use-value and exchange-value.

★ ★ ★

If commodities, or commodities and money, of equal exchange-value, and consequently equivalents, are exchanged, it is plain that no one derives more value from circulation than he throws into it. There is no creation of surplus-value. And, in its normal form, the circulation of commodities demands the exchange of equivalents.

★ ★ ★

The creation of surplus-value, and therefore the conversion of money into capital, can be explained neither on the assumption that commodities are sold above their value, nor that they are bought below their value.

★ ★ ★

Circulation, or the exchange of commodities, begets no value.

★ ★ ★

The circuit M–C–M', buying in order to sell dearer, is the general formula of capital as it appears *prima facie* within the sphere of circulation. It is seen most clearly in genuine merchants' capital. But the movement takes place entirely within the sphere of circulation. Since, however, it is impossible by circulation alone to account for the conversion of money into capital, for the formation of surplus-value, it would appear that merchants' capital is an impossibility so long as equivalents are exchanged; that, therefore, it can only have its origin in the twofold advantage gained, over both the selling and the buying producers, by the merchant who parasitically shoves himself in between them. If the transformation of merchants' money into capital is to be explained otherwise than by the producers' being simply cheated, a long series of intermediate steps would be necessary which, at present, when the simple circulation of commodities forms our only assumption, are entirely wanting.

What we have said with reference to merchants' capital applies still more to money-lenders' capital. In merchants' capital, the two extremes, the money that is thrown upon the market and the augmented money that is withdrawn from the market, are at least connected by a purchase and a sale, in other words, by the movement of the circulation. In money-lenders' capital the form M–C–M' is reduced to the two extremes without a mean, M–M', money exchanged for more money, a form that is incompatible with the nature of money and therefore remains inexplicable from the standpoint of the circulation of commodities.

★ ★ ★

We have shown that surplus-value cannot be created by circulation, and therefore, that in its formation, something must take place in the background which is not apparent in the circulation itself. But can surplus-value possibly originate anywhere else than in circulation, which is the sum total of all mutual relations of commodity-owners, as far as they are determined by their commodities? Apart from circulation, the commodity-owner is in relation only with his own commodity. So far as regards value, that relation is limited to this, that the commodity contains a quantity of his labor, that quantity being measured by a definite social standard. This quantity is expressed by the value of the commodity, and since the value is reckoned in money of account, this quantity is also expressed by the price, which we will suppose to be £10. But his labor is not represented both by the value of the commodity and by a surplus over that value, not by a price of 10 that is also a price of 11, not by a value that is greater than itself. The commodity owner can, by his labor, create value, but not self-expanding value. He can increase the value of his commodity by adding fresh labor, and therefore more value to the value in hand, by making, for instance, leather into boots. The same material has now more value, because it contains a greater quantity of labor. The boots have therefore more value than the leather, but the value of the leather remains what it was; it has not expanded itself, has not, during the making of the boots, annexed surplus value. It is therefore impossible that outside the sphere of circulation a producer of commodities can, without coming into contact with other commodity owners, expand value, and consequently convert money or commodities into capital.

It is therefore impossible for capital to be produced by circulation, and it is equally impossible for it to originate apart from circulation. It must have its original both in circulation and yet not in circulation.

We have, therefore, got a double result.

The conversion of money into capital has to be explained on the basis of the laws that regulate the exchange of commodities in such a way that the starting point is the exchange of equivalents.

CHAPTER VI

THE BUYING AND SELLING
OF LABOR-POWER

The change of value that occurs in the case of money intended to be converted into capital cannot take place in the money itself, since in its function of means of purchase and of payment it does no more than realise the price of the commodity it buys or pays for; and, as hard cash, it is value petrified, never varying. Just as little can it originate in the second act of circulation, the re-sale of the commodity, which does no more than transform the article from its bodily form back again into its money-form. The change must, therefore, take place in the commodity bought by the first act, M–C, but not in its value, for equivalents are exchanged, and the commodity is paid for at its full value. We are, therefore, forced to the conclusion that the change originates in the use-value, as such, of the commodity, i.e., in its consumption. In order to be able to extract value from the consumption of a commodity, our friend, Moneybags, must be so lucky as to find, within the sphere of circulation, in the market, a commodity whose use-value possesses the peculiar property of being a source of value, whose actual consumption, therefore, is itself an embodiment of labor, and consequently, a creation of value. The possessor of money does find on the market such a special commodity in the capacity for labor or labor-power.

By labor-power or capacity for labor is to be understood the aggregate of those mental and physical capabilities existing in a human being which he exercises whenever he produces a use-value of any description.

But in order that our owner of money may be able to find labor-power offered for sale as a commodity, various conditions must first be fulfilled. The exchange of commodities in itself implies no other relations of dependence than those which result from its own nature. On this assumption, labor-power can appear upon the market as a commodity only if, and insofar as, its possessor, the individual whose labor-power it is, offers it for sale, or sells it, as a commodity. In order that he may be able to do this, he must have it at his disposal, must be the untrammelled owner of his capacity for labor, i.e., of his person. He and the owner of money meet in the market and deal with each other as on the basis of equal rights with this difference alone, that one is buyer, the other seller; both, therefore, equal in the eyes of the law. The continuance of this relation demands that the owner of the labor-power should sell it only for a definite period, for if he were to sell it rump and stump, once for all, he would be selling himself, converting himself from a free man into a slave, from an owner of a commodity into a commodity. He must constantly look upon his labor-power as his own property, his own commodity, and this he can only do by placing it at the disposal of the buyer temporarily, for a definite period of time. By this means alone can he avoid renouncing his rights of ownership over it.

The second essential condition to the owner of money finding labor-power in the market as a commodity is this—that the laborer instead of being in the position to sell commodities in which his labor is incorporated, must be obliged to offer for sale as a commodity that very labor-power which exists only in his living self.

In order that a man may be able to sell commodities other than labor-power, he must of course have the means of production, as raw material, implements, etc. He requires also the means of subsistence. Nobody can live upon future products, or upon use-values in an unfinished state; and ever since the first moment of his appearance on the world's stage, man always has been and must still be a consumer, both before and while he is producing. In a society where all products assume the form of commodities, these commodities must be sold after they have been produced; it is only after their sale that they can serve in satisfying the requirements of their producer. The time necessary for their sale is added to that necessary for their production.

For the conversion of his money into capital, therefore, the owner of money must meet in the market with the free laborer, free in the double sense, that as a free man he can dispose of his labor-power as his own commodity, and that on the other hand he has no other commodity for sale, is short of everything necessary for the realization of his labor-power.

★ ★ ★

Definite historical conditions are necessary that a product may become a commodity. It must not be produced as the immediate means of subsistence of the producer himself. Had we gone further, and inquired under what circumstances all or even the majority of products take the form of commodities, we should have found that this can only happen with production of a very specific kind, capitalist production. Production and circulation of commodities can take place, although the great mass of the objects produced are intended for the immediate requirements of their producers, are not turned into commodities, and consequently social production is not yet by a long way dominated in its length and breadth by exchange-value. The appearance of products as commodities presupposed such a development of the social division of labor, that the separation of use-value from exchange-value, a separation which first begins with barter, must already have been completed. But such a degree of development is common to many forms of society which in other respects present the most varying historical features. On the other hand, if we consider money, its existence implies a definite stage in the exchange of commodities. The particular functions of money which it performs, either as the mere equivalent of commodities, or as means of circulation, or means of payment, as hoard or as universal money, point, according to the extent and relative preponderance of the one function or the other, to very different stages in the process of social production. Yet we know by experience that a relatively primitive circulation of commodities suffices for the production of all these forms. Otherwise with capital. The historical conditions of its existence are by no means given with the mere circulation of money and commodities. It can spring into life only when the owner of the means of production and subsistence meets in the market with the free laborer selling his labor-power. And this one historical condition comprises a world's history. Capital therefore announces from its first appearance a new epoch in the process of social production.[*]

★ ★ ★

The value of labor-power is determined, as in the case of every other commodity, by the labor-time necessary for the production, and consequently also the reproduction, of this special article. So far as it has value, it represents no more than a definite quantity of the average labor of society incorporated in it. Labor-power exists only as a capacity, or power of the living individual. Its production consequently presupposes his existence. Given the individual, the production of labor-power consists in his reproduction of himself or

[*]The capitalist epoch is therefore characterized by this, that labor-power takes in the eyes of the laborer himself the form of a commodity which is his property; his labor consequently becomes wage labor. On the other hand, it is only from this moment that the product of labor universally becomes a commodity.

his maintenance. For his maintenance he requires a given quantity of the means of subsistence. Therefore the labor-time requisite for the production of labor-power reduces itself to that necessary for the production of those means of subsistence; in other words, the value of labor-power is the value of the means of subsistence necessary for the maintenance of the laborer. Labor-power, however, becomes a reality only by its exercise; it sets itself in action only by working. But thereby a definite quantity of human muscle, nerve, brain, etc., is wasted, and these must be restored. This increased expenditure demands a larger income. If the owner of labor-power works today, tomorrow he must again be able to repeat the same process in the same conditions as regards health and strength. His means of subsistence must therefore be sufficient to maintain him in his normal state as a laboring individual. His natural wants, such as food, clothing, fuel, and housing, vary according to the climatic and other physical conditions of his country. On the other hand, the number and extent of his so-called necessary wants, and also the modes of satisfying them, are themselves the product of historical development and depend therefore to a great extent on the degree of civilisation of a country, more particularly on the conditions under which, and consequently on the habits and degree of comfort in which, the class of free laborers has been formed. In contradistinction therefore to the case of other commodities, there enters into the determination of the value of labor-power a historical and moral element. Nevertheless, in a given country, at a given period, the average quantity of the means of subsistence necessary for the laborer is practically known.

★ ★ ★

The labor-power withdrawn from the market by wear and tear and death must be continually replaced by, at the very least, an equal amount of fresh labor-power. Hence the sum of the means of subsistence necessary for the production of labor-power must include the means necessary for the laborer's substitutes, i.e., his children, in order that this race of peculiar commodity-owners may perpetuate its appearance in the market.

In order to modify the human organism so that it may acquire skill and handiness in a given branch of industry and become labor-power of a special kind, a special education or training is requisite. The expenses of this education (excessively small in the case of ordinary labor-power) enter *pro tanto* into the total value spent in its production.

The value of labor-power resolves itself into the value of a definite quantity of the means of subsistence. It therefore varies with the value of these means or with the quantity of labor requisite for their production.

Some of the means of subsistence, such as food and fuel, are consumed daily, and a fresh supply must be provided daily. Others such as clothes and furniture last for longer periods and require to be replaced only at longer intervals. But in whatever way the sum total of these outlays may be spread over the year, they must be covered by the average income, taking one day with another.

★ ★ ★

The minimum limit of the value of labor-power is determined by the value of the commodities, without the daily supply of which the laborer cannot renew his vital energy, consequently by the value of those means of subsistence that are physically indispensable. If the price of labor-power falls to this minimum, it falls below its value, since under such circumstances it can be maintained and developed only in a crippled state. But the value of every commodity is determined by the labor-time requisite to turn it out so as to be of normal quality.

★ ★ ★

One consequence of the peculiar nature of labor-power as a commodity is that its use-value does not, on the conclusion of this contract between the buyer and seller, immediately pass into the hands of the former. Its value, like that of every other commodity, is already fixed before it goes into circulation, since a definite quantity of social labor has been spent upon it; but its use-value consists in the subsequent exercise of its force. The alienation of labor-power and its actual appropriation by the buyer, its employment as a use-value, are separated by an interval of time. But in those cases in which the formal alienation by sale of the use-value of a commodity is not simultaneous with its actual delivery to the buyer, the money of the latter usually functions as means of payment.

★ ★ ★

The price of the labor-power is fixed by the contract, although it is not realized till later, like the rent of a house. The labor-power is sold, although it is only paid for at a later period. It will, therefore, be useful for a clear comprehension of the relation of the parties to assume provisionally that the possessor of labor-power, on the occasion of each sale, immediately receives the price stipulated to be paid for it.

★ ★ ★

The consumption of labor-power is at one and the same time the production of commodities and of surplus value. The consumption of labor-power is completed, as in the case of every other commodity, outside the limits of the market or of the sphere of circulation.

PART III

The Production of Absolute Surplus-Value

CHAPTER VII

THE LABOR-PROCESS AND THE PROCESS OF PRODUCING SURPLUS-VALUE

SECTION 1—THE LABOR PROCESS OR THE PRODUCTION OF USE-VALUES

The capitalist buys labor-power in order to use it; and labor-power in use is labor itself. The purchaser of labor-power consumes it by setting the seller of it to work. By working, the latter becomes actually what before he only was potentially—labor-power in action, a laborer. In order that his labor may reappear in a commodity, he must, before all things, expend it on something useful, on something capable of satisfying a want of some sort. Hence, what the capitalist sets the laborer to produce is a particular use-value, a specified article. The fact that the production of use-values, or goods, is carried on under the control of a capitalist and on his behalf does not alter the general character of that production. We shall therefore, in the first place, have to consider the labor-process independently of the particular form it assumes under given social conditions.

Labor is, in the first place, a process in which both man and nature participate, and in which man of his own accord starts, regulates, and controls the material reactions between himself and nature. He opposes himself to nature as one of her own forces, setting in motion arms and legs, head and hands, the natural forces of his body, in order to appropriate nature's productions in a form adapted to his own wants. By thus acting on the external world and changing it, he at the same time changes his own nature. He develops his slumbering powers and compels them to act in obedience to his sway. We are not now dealing with those primitive instinctive forms of labor that remind us of the mere animal. An immeasurable interval of time separates the state of things in which a man brings his labor-power to market for sale as a commodity from that state in which human labor was still in its first instinctive stage.

★ ★ ★

The elementary factors of the labor-process are 1, the personal activity of man, i.e., work itself; 2, the subject of that work; and 3, its instruments.

The soil (and this, economically speaking, includes water) in the virgin state in which it supplies man with necessities or the means of subsistence ready to hand exists independently of him, and is the universal subject of human labor. All those things which labor merely separates from immediate connection with their environment are subjects of labor spontaneously provided by nature. Such are fish which we catch and take from their element, water, timber which we fell in the virgin forest, and ores which we extract from their veins. If, on the other hand, the subject of labor has, so to say, been filtered through previous labor, we call it raw material; such is ore already extracted and ready for washing. All raw material is the subject of labor, but not every subject of labor is raw material; it can only become so after it has undergone some alteration by means of labor.

An instrument of labor is a thing, or a complex of things, which the laborer interposes between himself and the subject of his labor, and which serves as the conducter of his activity. He makes use of the mechanical, physical, and chemical properties of some substances in order to make other substances subservient to his aims. Leaving out of consideration such ready-made means of subsistence as fruits, in gathering which a man's own limbs serve as the instruments of his labor, the first thing of which the laborer possesses himself is not the subject of labor but its instrument. Thus nature becomes one of the organs of his activity, one that he annexes to his own bodily organs, adding stature to himself in spite of the Bible. The earth itself is an instrument of labor, but when used as such in agriculture implies a whole series of other instruments and a comparitively high development of labor. No sooner does labor undergo the least development than it requires specially prepared instruments. Thus in the oldest caves we find stone implements and weapons. In the earliest period of human history domesticated animals, i.e., animals which have been bred for the purpose and have undergone modifications by means of labor, play the chief part as instruments of labor along with specially prepared stones, wood, bones, and shells. The use and fabrication of instruments of labor, although existing in the germ among certain species of animals, is specifically characteristic of the human labor-process. Instruments of labor not only supply a standard of the degree of development which human labor has attained, but they are also indicators of the social conditions under which that labor is carried on.

★ ★ ★

In a wider sense we may include among the instruments of labor, in addition to those things that are used for directly transferring labor to its subject, and which therefore in one way or another serve as conductors of activity, all such objects as are necessary for carrying on the labor-process.

★ ★ ★

In the labor-process, therefore, man's activity, with the help of the instruments of labor, effects an alteration, designed from the commencement, in the material worked upon. The process disappears in the product; the latter is a use-value, nature's material adapted by a change of form to the wants of man. Labor has incorporated itself with its subject: the former is materialized, the latter transformed. That which in the laborer appeared as movement, now appears in the product as a fixed quality without motion.

If we examine the whole process from the point of view of its result, the product, it is plain that both the instruments and the subject of labor are means of production and that the labor itself is productive labor.*

Though a use-value, in the form of a product, issues from the labor-process, other use-values, products of previous labor, enter into it as means of production. The same use-value is both the product of a previous process and a means of production in a later process. Products are therefore not only results, but also essential conditions of labor.

* * *

Whether a use-value is to be regarded as raw material, as instrument of labor, or as product, this is determined entirely by its function in the labor process, by the position it there occupies: as this varies, so does its character.

Whenever therefore a product enters as a means of production into a new labor-process, it thereby loses its character of product, and becomes a mere factor in the process. A spinner treats spindles only as implements for spinning, and flax only as the material that he spins.

A machine which does not serve the purposes of labor is useless. In addition, it falls a prey to the destructive influence of natural forces. Living labor must seize upon these things and rouse them from their death-sleep, change them from mere possible use-values into real and effective ones.

* * *

If, on the one hand, finished products are not only results but also necessary conditions of the labor-process, on the other hand, their

---

*This method of determining what is productive labor from the standpoint of the labor-process alone is by no means directly applicable to the case of the capitalist process of production.

assumption into that process, their contact with living labor, is the sole means by which they can be made to retain their character of use-values, and be utilised.

Labor uses up its material factors, its subject and its instruments, consumes them, and is therefore a process of consumption. Such productive consumption is distinguished from individual consumption by this, that the latter uses up products as means of subsistence for the living individual; the former, as means whereby alone labor, the labor-power of the living individual, is enabled to act. The product, therefore, of individual consumption is the consumer himself; the result of productive consumption is a product distinct from the consumer.

Insofar then as its instruments and subjects are themselves products, labor consumes products in order to create products, or in other words, consumes one set of products by turning them into means of production for another set. But, just as in the beginning, the only participators in the labor-process were man and the earth, the latter of which exists independently of man, so even now we still employ in the process many means of production provided directly by nature that do not represent any combination of natural substances with human labor.

★ ★ ★

The general character of the labor-process is not changed by the fact that the laborer works for the capitalist instead of for himself; moreover, the particular methods and operations employed in boot-making or spinning are not immediately changed by the intervention of the capitalist. He must begin by taking the labor-power as he finds it in the market, and consequently be satisfied with labor of such a kind as would be found in the period immediately preceding the rise of the capitalists. Changes in the methods of production by the subordination of labor to capital, can take place only at a later period.

The labor-process, turned into the process by which the capitalist consumes labor-power, exhibits two characteristic phenomena. First, the laborer works under the control of the capitalist to whom his labor belongs; the capitalist taking good care that the work is done in a proper manner, and that the means of production are used with intelligence so that there is no unnecessary waste of raw material, and no wear and tear of the implements beyond what is necessarily caused by the work.

Secondly, the product is the property of the capitalist and not that of the laborer, its immediate producer.

★ ★ ★

By the purchase of labor-power, the capitalist incorporates labor as a living ferment with the lifeless constituents of the product. From his point of view, the labor-process is nothing more than the consumption of the commodity purchased, i.e., of labor-power; but this consumption cannot be effected except by supplying the labor-power with the means of production. The labor-process is a process between things that the capitalist has purchased, things that have become his property. The product of this process also belongs, therefore, to him, just as much as does the wine which is the product of a process of fermentation completed in his cellar.

SECTION 2—THE PRODUCTION OF SURPLUS-VALUE

The product appropriated by the capitalist is a use-value, as yarn, for example, or boots. But, although boots are, in one sense, the basis of all social progress, and our capitalist is a decided "progressist," he does not manufacture boots for their own sake. Use-values are only produced by capitalists because and insofar as they are the material substratum, the depositaries of exchange-value. Our capitalist has two objects in view: in the first place, he wants to produce a use-value that has a value in exchange, that is to say, an article destined to be sold, a commodity; and secondly, he desires to produce a commodity whose value shall be greater than the sum of the values of the commodities used in its production, that is, of the means of production and the labor-power, that he purchased with his good money in the open market. His aim is to produce not only a use-value, but a commodity also; not only use-value, but value; not only value, but at the same time surplus-value.

★ ★ ★

Let us now examine production as a creation of value.

We know that the value of each commodity is determined by the quantity of labor expended on and materialized in it, by the working-time necessary, under given social conditions, for its production. This rule also holds good in the case of the product that accrued to our capitalist as the result of the labor-process carried on for him. Assuming this product to be 10 lbs. of yarn, our first step is to calculate the quantity of labor realized in it.

For spinning the yarn, raw material is required; suppose in this case 10 lbs. of cotton. We have no need at present to investigate the value of this cotton, for our capitalist has, we will assume, bought it at its full value, say of ten shillings. In this price the labor required for the production of the cotton is already expressed in terms of the average labor of society. We will further assume that the wear and tear of the spindle which, for our present purpose, may represent all other instruments of labor employed, amounts to the value of 2s. If, then, twenty-four hours' labor, or two working days, is required to produce the quantity of gold represented by twelve shillings, we have here, to begin with, two days' labor already incorporated in the yarn.

★ ★ ★

The labor required for the production of the cotton, the raw material of the yarn, is part of the labor necessary to produce the yarn, and is therefore contained in the yarn. The same applies to the labor embodied in the spindle, without whose wear and tear the cotton could not be spun.

Hence, in determining the value of the yarn or the labor-time required for its production, all the special processes carried on at various times and in different places which were necessary first to produce the cotton and the wasted portion of the spindle, and then with the cotton and spindle to spin the yarn, may together be looked on as different and successive phases of one and the same process. The whole of the labor in the yarn is past labor; and it is a matter of no importance that the operations necessary for the production of its constituent elements were carried on at times which, referred to the present, are more remote than the final operation of spinning. If a definite quantity of labor, say thirty days, is requisite to build a house, the total amount of labor incorporated in it is not altered by the fact that the work of the last day is done twenty-nine days later than that of the first. Therefore the labor contained in the raw material and the instruments of labor can be treated just as if it were labor expended in an earlier stage of the spinning process, before the labor of actual spinning commenced.

The values of the means of production, i.e., the cotton and the spindle, whose values are expressed in the price of twelve shillings, are therefore constituent parts of the value of the yarn, or, in other words, of the value of the product.

Two conditions must nevertheless be fulfilled. First, the cotton and spindle must concur in the production of a use-value; they must in the present case become yarn. Value is independent of the particular use-value by which it is borne, but it must be embodied in a use-value of some kind. Secondly, the time occupied in the labor of production must not exceed the time really necessary under the given social conditions of the case. Therefore, if no more than 1 lb. of cotton is requisite to spin 1 lb. of yarn, care must be taken that no more than this weight of cotton is consumed in the production of 1 lb. of yarn; and similarly with regard to the spindle. Though the capitalist may have a hobby, and use a gold instead of a steel spindle, the only labor that counts for anything in the value of the yarn is that which would be required to produce a steel spindle, because no more is necessary under the given social conditions.

We now know what portion of the value of the yarn is owing to the cotton and the spindle. It amounts to twelve shillings or the value of two days' work. The next point of our consideration is: what portion of the value of the yarn is added to the cotton by the labor of the spinner?

We have now to consider this labor under a very different aspect from that which it had during the labor-process; there, we viewed it solely as that particular kind of human activity which changes cotton into yarn; there, the more the labor was suited to the work, the better the yarn, other circumstances remaining the same. The labor of the spinner was then viewed as specifically different from other kinds of productive labor, different on the one hand in its special aim, viz., spinning, different on the other hand in the special character of its operations, in the special nature of its means of production and in the special use-value of its product. For the operation of spinning, cotton and spindles are a necessity, but for making rifled cannon they would be of no use whatever. Here, on the contrary, where we consider the labor of the spinner only so far as it is value-creating, i.e., a source of value, his labor differs in no respect from the labor of the man who bores cannon, or (what here more closely concerns us), from the labor of the cotton-planter and spindle-maker incorporated in the means of production. It is solely by reason of this identity that cotton planting, spindle making, and spinning, are capable of forming the component parts, differing only quantitatively from each other, of one whole, namely, the value of the yarn. Here, we have nothing more to do with the quality, the nature, and the specific character of the labor, but merely with its quantity. And this simply requires to be calculated. We proceed upon the assumption that spinning is simple, unskilled labor, the average labor of a given state of society. Hereafter we shall see that the contrary assumption would make no difference.

While the laborer is at work, his labor constantly undergoes a transformation: from being motion, it becames an object without motion; from being the laborer working, it becomes the thing produced. At the end of one hour's spinning, that act is represented by a definite quantity of yarn; in other words, a definite quantity of labor, namely that of one hour, has become embodied in the cotton. We say labor, i.e., the expenditure of his vital force by the spinner, and not spinning labor, because the special work of spinning counts here only so far as it is the expenditure of labor-power in general, and not insofar as it is the specific work of the spinner.

In the process we are now considering it is of extreme importance that no more time be consumed in the work of transforming the cotton into yarn than is necessary under the given social conditions. If under normal, i.e., average social conditions of production, a pounds of cotton ought to be made into b pounds of yarn by one hour's labor, then a day's labor does not count as 12 hours' labor unless 12 a pounds of cotton have been made into 12 b pounds of yarn; for in the creation of value, the time that is socially necessary alone counts.

Not only the labor, but also the raw material and the product now appear in quite a new light, very different from that in which we viewed them in the labor-process pure and simple. The raw material serves now merely as an absorbent of a definite quantity of labor. By this absorption it is in fact changed into yarn because it is spun, because labor-power in the form of spinning is added to it; but the product, the yarn, is now nothing more than a measure of the labor absorbed by the cotton. If in one hour $1^2/_3$ lbs. of cotton can be spun into $1^2/_3$ lbs. of yarn, then 10 lbs. of yarn indicate the absorption of 6 hours' labor. Definite quantities of product, these quantities being determined by experience, now represent nothing but definite quantities of labor, definite masses of crystallized labor-time. They are nothing more than the materialisation of so many hours or so many days of social labor.

We are here no more concerned about the facts that the labor is the specific work of spinning, that its subject is cotton and its product yarn, than we are about the fact that the subject itself is already a product and therefore raw material. If the spinner, instead of spinning, were working in a coal mine, the subject of his labor, the coal, would be supplied by nature; nevertheless, a definite quantity of extracted coal, a hundred weight, for example, would represent a definite quantity of absorbed labor.

We assumed, on the occasion of its sale, that the value of a day's labor-power is three shillings, and that six hours' labor are incorporated in that sum; and consequently that this amount of labor is requisite to produce the necessities of daily life required on average by the laborer. If now our spinner, by working for one hour, can convert $1^2/_3$ lbs. of cotton into $1^2/_3$ lbs. of yarn, it follows that in six hours he will convert 10 lbs. of cotton into 10 lbs. of yarn. Hence, during the spinning process, the cotton absorbs six hours' labor. The same quantity of labor is also embodied in a piece of gold of the value of three shillings. Consequently by the mere labor of spinning, a value of three shillings is added to the cotton.

Let us now consider the total value of the product, the 10 lbs. of yarn. Two and a half days' labor have been embodied in it, of which two days were contained in the cotton and in the substance of the spindle worn away, and half a day was absorbed during the process of spinning. This two and a half days' labor is also represented by a piece of gold of the value of fifteen shillings. Hence, fifteen shillings is an adequate price for the 10 lbs. of yarn, or the price of one pound is eighteen pence.

Our capitalist stares in astonishment. The value of the product is exactly equal to the value of the capital advanced. The value so advanced has not expanded, no surplus-value has been created, and consequently money has not been converted into capital. The price of the yarn is fifteen shillings, and fifteen shillings were spent in the open market upon the constituent elements of the product or, what amounts to the same thing, upon the factors of the labor-process; ten shillings were paid for the cotton, two shillings for the substance of the spindle worn away, and three shillings for the labor-power. The swollen value of the yarn is of no avail, for it is merely the sum of the values formerly existing in the cotton, the spindle, and the labor-power; out of such a simple addition of existing values, no surplus-value can possibly arise. These separate values are now all concentrated in one thing; but so they were also in the sum of fifteen shillings, before it was split up into three parts, by the purchase of the commodities.

There is in reality nothing very strange in this result. The value of one pound of yarn being eighteen pence, if our capitalist buys 10 lbs. of yarn in the market, he must pay fifteen shillings for them. It is clear that whether a man buys his house ready built or gets it built for him, in neither case will the mode of acquisition increase the amount of money laid out on the house.

★ ★ ★

Let us examine the matter more closely. The value of a day's labor-power amounts to 3 shillings, because on our assumption half a day's labor is embodied in that quantity of labor-power, i.e., because the means of subsistence that are daily required for the production of labor-power cost half a day's labor. But the past labor that is embodied in the labor-power, and the living labor that it can call into action; the daily cost of maintaining it, and its daily expenditure in work, are two totally different things. The former determines the exchange-value of the labor-power, the latter is its use-value. The fact that half a day's labor is necessary to keep the laborer alive during 24 hours does not in any way prevent him from working a whole day. Therefore, the value of labor-power and the value which that labor-power creates in the labor process are two entirely different magnitudes; and this difference of the two values was what the capitalist had in view when he was purchasing the labor-power. The useful qualities that labor-power possesses, and by virtue of which it makes yarn or boots, were to him nothing more than a *conditio sine qua non*; for in order to create value, labor must be expended in a useful manner. What really influenced him was the specific use-value which this commodity possesses of being *a source not only of value, but of more value than it has itself.* This is the special service that the capitalist expects from labor-power, and in this transaction he acts in accordance with the "eternal laws" of the exchange of commodities. The seller of labor-power, like the seller of any other commodity, realizes its exchange-value and parts with its use-value. He cannot take the one without giving the other. The use-value of labor-power, or in other words, labor, belongs just as little to its seller, as the use-value of oil after it has been sold belongs to the dealer who has sold it. The owner of the money has paid the value of a day's labor-power; his, therefore, is the use of it for a day; a day's labor belongs to him. The circumstance, that on the one hand the daily sustenance of labor-power costs only half a day's labor, while on the other hand the very same labor-power can work during a whole day, that consequently the value which its use during one day creates is double what he pays for that use, this circumstance is, without doubt, a piece of good luck for the buyer, but by no means an injury to the seller.

Our capitalist foresaw this state of things. The laborer therefore finds in the workshop the means of production necessary for working not only during six, but during twelve hours. Just as during the six hours' process our 10 lbs. of cotton absorbed six hours' labor and became 10 lbs. of yarn, so now, 20 lbs. of cotton will absorb 12 hours' labor and be changed into 20 lbs. of yarn. Let us now examine the product of this prolonged process. There is now materialized in this 20 lbs. of yarn the labor of five days, of which four days are due to the cotton and the lost steel of the spindle, the remaining day having been absorbed by the cotton during the spinning process. Expressed in gold, the labor of five days is thirty shillings. This is therefore the price of the 20 lbs. of yarn, giving, as before, eighteen pence as the price of a pound. But the sum of the values of the commodities that entered into the process amounts to 27 shillings. The value of the yarn is 30 shillings. Therefore the value of the product is $1/9$ greater than the value advanced for its production; 27 shillings have been transformed into 30 shillings; a surplus-value of 3 shillings has been created. The trick has at last succeeded; money has been converted into capital.

Every condition of the problem is satisfied, while the laws that regulate the exchange of commodities have been in no way violated. Equivalent has been exchanged for equivalent. For the capitalist as buyer paid for each commodity, for the cotton, the spindle, and the labor-power, its full value. He then did what is done by every purchaser of commodities; he consumed their use-value. The consumption of the labor-power, which was also the process of producing commodities, resulted in 20 lbs. of yarn, having a value of 30 shillings. The capitalist, formerly a buyer, now returns to market as a seller of commodities. He sells his yarn at eighteen pence a pound, which is its exact value. Yet for all that he withdraws 3 shillings more from circulation than he originally threw into it. This metamorphosis, this conversion of money into capital, takes place both within the sphere of circulation and also outside it; within the circulation, because it is conditioned by the purchase of the labor-power in the market; outside the circulation, because what is done within it is only a stepping-stone to the production of surplus-value, a process which is entirely confined to the sphere of production.

By turning his money into commodities that serve as the material elements of a new product and as factors in the labor-process, by incorporating living labor with their dead substance, the capitalist at the same time converts value, i.e., past, materialized, and dead labor into capital, into value big with value, a live monster that is fruitful and multiplies.

If we now compare the two processes of producing value and of creating surplus-value, we see that the latter is nothing but the continuation of the former beyond a definite point. If on the one hand the process is not carried beyond the point where the value paid by the capitalist for the labor-power is replaced by an exact equivalent, it is simply a process of producing value; if on the other hand it is continued beyond that point, it becomes a process of creating surplus-value.

If we proceed further and compare the process of producing value with the labor-process pure and simple, we find that the latter consists of the useful labor, the work, that produces use-values. Here we contemplate the labor as producing a particular article; we view it under its qualitative aspect alone with regard to its end and aim. But viewed as a value-creating process, the same labor-process presents itself under its quantitative aspect alone. Here it is a question merely of the time occupied by the laborer in doing the work; of the period during which the labor-power is usefully expended. Here, the commodities that take part in the process do not count any longer as necessary adjuncts of labor-power in the production of a definite, useful object. They count merely as depositaries of so much absorbed or materialized labor; that labor, whether previously embodied in the means of production or incorporated in them for the first time during the process by the action of labor-power, counts in either case only according to its duration; it amounts to so many hours or days as the case may be.

Moreover, only so much of the time spent in the production of any article is counted as, under the given social conditions, is necessary. The consequences of this are various. In the first place, it becomes necessary that the labor should be carried on under normal conditions. If a self-acting mule is the implement in general use for spinning, it would be absurd to supply the spinner with a staff and spinning wheel. The cotton too must not be such rubbish as to cause extra waste in being worked, but must be of suitable quality; otherwise the spinner would be found to spend more time in producing a pound of yarn than is socially necessary, in which case the excess time would create neither value nor money. But whether the material factors of the process are of normal quality or not depends not upon the laborer, but entirely upon the capitalist. Then again, the labor-power itself must be of average efficacy. In the trade in which it is being employed, it must possess the average skill, handiness, and quickness prevalent in that trade, and our capitalist took good care to buy labor-power of such normal goodness. This power must be applied with the average amount of exertion and with the usual degree of intensity; and the capitalist is as careful to see that this is done as that his workmen are not idle for a single moment. He has bought the use of the labor-power for a definite period, and he insists upon his rights. He has no intention of being robbed. Lastly, and for this purpose our friend has a penal code of his own, all wasteful consumption of raw material or instruments of labor is strictly forbidden, because what is so wasted represents labor superfluously expended, labor that does not count in the product or enter into its value.*

We now see that the difference between labor, considered on the one hand as producing utilities, and on the other hand as creating value, a difference which we discovered by our analysis of a commodity, resolves itself into a distinction between two aspects of the process of production.

The process of production, considered on the one hand as the unity of the labor-process and the process of creating value, is the

---

*This is one of the circumstances that makes production by slave labor such a costly process.

production of commodities; considered on the other hand as the unity of the labor-process and the process of producing surplus-value, it is the capitalist process of production, or capitalist production of commodities.

CHAPTER VIII

CONSTANT CAPITAL
AND VARIABLE CAPITAL

The various factors of the labor-process play different parts in forming the value of the product. The laborer adds fresh value to the subject of his labor by expending upon it a given amount of additional labor, no matter what the specific character and utility of that labor may be. On the other hand, the values of the means of production used up in the process are preserved, and present themselves afresh as constituent parts of the value of the product; the values of the cotton and the spindle, for instance, reappear again in the value of the yarn. The value of the means of production is therefore preserved by being transferred to the product. This transfer takes place during the conversion of those means into a product, or in other words, during the labor-process. It is brought about by labor; but how?

The laborer does not perform two operations at once, one in order to add value to the cotton, the other in order to preserve the value of the means of production or, in what amounts to the same thing, to transfer to the yarn, to the product, the value of the cotton on which he works, and part of the value of the spindle with which he works. But, by the very act of adding new value, he preserves their former values. Since, however, the addition of new value to the subject of his labor and the preservation of its former value are two entirely distinct results produced simultaneously by the laborer during one operation, it is plain that this twofold nature of the result can be explained only by the twofold nature of his labor; at one and the same time, it must in one character create value, and in another character preserve or transfer value.

Now, in what manner does every laborer add new labor and consequently new value? Evidently, only by laboring productively in a particular way; the spinner by spinning, the weaver by weaving, the smith by forging. But, while thus incorporating labor generally, this is value, it is by the particular form alone of the labor, by the spinning, the weaving, and the forging respectively, that the means of production, the cotton and spindle, the yarn and loom, and the iron and anvil become constituent elements of the product, of a new use-value. Each use-value disappears, but only to reappear under a new form in a new use-value. Now, we saw that if a use-value is effectively consumed in the production of a new use-value, the quantity of labor expended in the production of the consumed article forms a portion of the quantity of labor necessary to produce the new use-value; this portion is therefore labor transferred from the means of production to the new product. Hence, the laborer preserves the values of the consumed means of production, or transfers them as portions of its value to the product, not by virtue of his additional labor abstractedly considered, but by virtue of the particular useful character of that labor, by virtue of its special productive form. Insofar then as labor is such specific productive activity, insofar as it is spinning, weaving, or forging, it raises by mere contact the means of production from the dead, makes them living factors of the labor-process, and combines with them to form the new products.

★ ★ ★

The addition of new value takes place not by virtue of his labor being spinning in particular, or joinering in particular, but because it is labor in the abstract, a portion of the total labor of society; and we see next that the value added is of a given definite amount, not because his labor has a special utility, but because it is exerted for a definite time. On the one hand, then, it is by virtue of its general character, as being expenditure of human labor-power in the abstract, that spinning adds new value to the values of the cotton and the spindle; and on the other hand, it is by virtue of its special character, as being a concrete, useful process, that the same labor of spinning both transfers the values of the means of production to the product, and preserves them in the product. Hence at one and the same time there is produced a two-fold result.

By the simple addition of a certain quantity of labor, new value is added, and by the quality of this added labor, the original values of the means of production are preserved in the product.

★ ★ ★

Value exists only in articles of utility, in objects: we leave out of consideration its purely symbolical representation by tokens. (Man himself, viewed as the impersonation of labor-power, is a natural object, a thing, although a living conscious thing, and labor is the manifestation of this power residing in him.) If therefore an article loses its utility, it also loses its value.

★ ★ ★

In the labor-process the means of production transfer their value to the product only so far as along with their use-value they lose also their exchange value. They give up to the product that value alone which they themselves lose as means of production. But in this respect the material factors of the labor-process do not all behave alike.

★ ★ ★

Means of production never transfer more value to the product than they themselves lose during the labor-process by the destruction of their own use-value. If such an instrument has no value to lose, if, in other words, it is not the product of human labor, it transfers no value to the product. It helps to create use-value without contributing to the formation of exchange value. In this class are included all means of production supplied by nature without human assistance, such as land, wind, water, metals *in situ*, and timber in virgin forests.

Yet another interesting phenomenon here presents itself. Suppose a machine to be worth £1000, and to wear out in 1000 days. Then one thousandth part of the value of the machine is daily transferred to the day's product. At the same time, though with diminishing vitality, the machine as a whole continues to take part in the labor-process. Thus it appears that one factor of the labor-process, a means of production, continually enters as a whole into that process, while it enters into the process of the formation of value by fractions only. The difference between the two processes is here reflected in their material factors by the same instrument of production taking part as a whole in the labor-process, while at the same time as an element in the formation of value, it enters only by fractions.

On the other hand, a means of production may take part as a whole in the formation of value, while into the labor-process it enters only bit by bit.

★ ★ ★

The means of production can never add more value to the product than they themselves possess independently of the process in which they assist. However useful a given kind of raw material, or a machine, or other means of production may be, though it may cost £150, or say, 500 days' labor, it cannot, under any circumstances, add to the value of the product more than £150. Its value is determined not by the labor-process into which it enters as a means of production, but by that out of which it has issued as a product. In the labor-process it only serves as a mere use-value, a thing with useful properties, and could not, therefore, transfer any value to the product unless it possessed such value previously.

While productive labor is changing the means of production into constituent elements of a new product, their value undergoes a metempsychosis. It deserts the consumed body to occupy the newly created one. But this transmigration takes place, as it were, behind the back of the laborer. He is unable to add new labor, to create new value, without at the same time preserving old values, and this because the labor he adds must be of a specific useful kind; and he cannot do work of a useful kind without employing products as the means of production of a new product, and thereby transferring their value to the new product. The property which labor-power in action, living labor, possesses of preserving value at the same time that it adds it, is therefore a gift of nature which costs the laborer nothing, but which is very advantageous to the capitalist inasmuch as it preserves the existing value of his capital. So long as trade is good, the capitalist is too much absorbed in money-grubbing to take notice of this gratuitous gift of labor. A violent interruption of the labor-process by a crisis makes him sensitively aware of it.

As regards the means of production, what is really consumed is their use-value, and the consumption of this use-value by labor results in the product. There is no consumption of their value, and it would therefore be inaccurate to say that it is reproduced. It is rather preserved; not by reason of any operation it undergoes itself in the process, but because the article in which it originally exists vanishes into some other article. Hence, in the value of the product, there is a reappearance of the value of the means of production, but there is, strictly speaking, no reproduction of that value. That which is produced is a new use-value in which the old exchange-value reappears.

It is otherwise with the subjective factor of the labor-process, with labor-power in action. While the laborer, by virtue of his labor being of a specialized kind that has a special object, preserves and transfers to the product the value of the means of production, he at the same time, by the mere act of working, creates each instant an additional or new value. Suppose the process of production is stopped just when the workman has produced an equivalent for the value of his own labor-power when, for example, by six hours' labor, he has added a value of three shillings. This value is the surplus of the total value of the product over the portion of its value that is due to the means of production. It is the only original bit of value formed during this process, the only portion of the value of the product created by this process. Of course, we do not forget that this new value only replaces the money advanced by the capitalist in the purchase of the labor-power and spent by the laborer on the necessities of life. With regard to the money spent, the new value is merely a reproduction; nevertheless, it is an actual, and not, as in the case of the value of the means of production, only an apparent, reproduction. The substitution of one value for another, is here effected by the creation of new value.

The labor-process may continue beyond the time necessary to reproduce and incorporate in the product a mere equivalent for the value of the labor-power. Instead of the six hours that are sufficient for the latter purpose, the process may continue for twelve hours. The action of labor-power, therefore, not only reproduces its own value, but produces value over and above it. This surplus-value is the difference between the value of the product and the value of the elements consumed in the formation of that product, in other words, of the means of production and the labor-power.

★ ★ ★

The surplus of the total value of the product, over the sum of the values of its constituent factors, is the surplus of the expanded capital over the capital originally advanced. The means of production on the one hand, labor-power on the other, are merely the different modes of existence which the value of the original capital assumed when from being money it was transformed into the various factors of the labor-process. That part of capital then, which is represented by the means of production, by the raw material, auxiliary material, and the instruments of labor, does not, in the process of production, undergo any quantitative alteration of value. I therefore call it the constant part of capital, or more shortly, *constant capital*.

On the other hand, that part of capital represented by labor-power does, in the process of production, undergo an alteration of value. It both reproduces the equivalent of its own value and also produces an excess, a surplus-value, which may itself vary more or less according to circumstances. This part of capital is continually being transformed from a constant into a variable magnitude. I therefore call it the variable part of capital, or shortly, *variable capital*. The same elements of capital which, from the point of view of the labor-process, present themselves respectively as the objective and subjective factors, as means of production and labor-power, present themselves, from the point of view of the process of creating surplus-value, as constant and variable capital.

CHAPTER IX

THE RATE OF
SURPLUS-VALUE

SECTION 1—THE DEGREE OF EXPLOITATION
OF LABOR-POWER

The surplus-value generated in the process of production by C, the capital advanced, or in other words, the self-expansion of the value of the capital C, presents itself for our consideration, in the first place, as a surplus, as the amount by which the value of the product exceeds the value of its constituent element.

The capital C is made up of two components; one, the sum of money c laid out upon the means of production, and the other, the sum of money v expended upon the labor-power; c represents the portion that has become constant capital, and v the portion that has become variable capital. At first then, C=c + v: for example, if £500 is the capital advanced, its components may be such that the £500=410 const. + £90 var. When the process of production is finished, we get a commodity whose value=(c + v) + s, where s is the surplus-value; or taking our former figures, the value of this commodity may be (£410 const. + £90 var.) + £90 surpl. The original capital has now changed from C to C', from £500 to £590. The difference is s or a surplus value of £90. Since the value of the constituent elements of the product is equal to the value of the advanced capital, it is mere tautology to say that the excess of the value of the product over the value of its constituent elements is equal to the expansion of the capital advanced or to the surplus-value produced.

* * *

We have seen that the laborer, during one portion of the labor-process, produces only the value of his labor-power, that is, the value of his means of subsistence. Now since his work forms part of a system based on the social division of labor, he does not directly produce the actual necessities which he himself consumes; he produces instead a particular commodity, yarn for example, whose value is equal to the value of those necessities or of the money with which they can be bought. The portion of his day's labor devoted to this purpose will be greater or less in proportion to the value of the necessities that he daily requires on average or, what amounts to the same thing, in proportion to the labor-time required on average to produce them. If the value of those necessities represents on average the expenditure of six hours' labor, the workman must on average work for six hours to produce that value. If instead of working for the capitalist, he worked independently on his own account, he would, other things being equal, still be obliged to labor for the same number of hours in order to produce the value of his labor-power, and thereby to gain the means of subsistence necessary for his conservation or continued reproduction. But as we have seen, during that portion of his day's labor in which he produces the value of his labor-power, say three shillings, he produces only an equivalent for the value of his labor-power already advanced by the capitalist; the new value created only replaces the variable capital advanced. It is owing to this fact that the production of the new value of three shillings resembles a mere reproduction. That portion of the working day, then, during which this reproduction takes place, I call "*necessary*" labor-time, and the labor expended during that time I call "*necessary*" labor.* Necessary as regards the laborer, because it is independent of the particular social form of his labor; necessary as regards capital and the world of capitalists, because their existence also depends on the continued existence of the laborer.

During the second period of the labor-process, that in which his labor is no longer necessary labor, the workman, it is true, labors, expends labor-power; but since his labor is no longer necessary labor, he creates no value for himself. He creates surplus-value which, for the capitalist, has all the charms of a creation out of nothing. This portion of the working day I name surplus labor-time, and to the labor expended during that time I give the name of surplus-labor. It is every bit as important for a correct understanding of surplus-value to conceive it as a mere congelation of surplus-labor-time, as nothing but materialized surplus-labor, as it is, for a proper comprehension of value, to conceive it as a mere congelation of so many hours of labor, as nothing but materialized labor. The essential difference between the various economic forms of society, between, for instance, a society based on slave labor and one based on wage labor, lies only in the mode in which this surplus-labor is in each case extracted from the actual producer, the laborer.

Since, on the one hand, the values of the variable capital and of the labor-power purchased by that capital are equal, and the value of this labor-power determines the necessary portion of the working day, and since, on the other hand, the surplus-value is determined by the surplus portion of the working day, it follows that surplus-value bears the same ratio to variable capital that surplus-

---

*In this work, we have, up to now, employed the term "necessary labor-time" to designate the time necessary under given social conditions for the production of any commodity. Henceforward we use it to designate also the time necessary for the production of the particular commodity, labor-power.

labor does to necessary labor, or in other words, the rate of surplus-value

$$\frac{s}{v} = \frac{surplus\ labor}{necessary\ labor}$$

Both ratios, $\frac{s}{v}$ and $\frac{surplus\ labor}{necessary\ labor}$ express the same thing in different ways; in the one case by reference to materialized, incorporated labor, in the other by reference to living, fluent labor.

The rate of surplus-value is therefore an exact expression for the degree of exploitation of labor-power by capital, or of the laborer by the capitalist.[*]

★ ★ ★

The method of calculating the rate of surplus-value is shortly, as follows. We take the total value of the product and put the constant capital which merely reappears in it, equal to zero. What remains is the only value that has, in the process of producing the commodity, actually been created. If the amount of surplus-value is given, we have only to deduct it from this remainder to find the variable capital. And *vice versa*, if the latter is given, and we require to find the surplus-value. If both are given, we have only to perform the concluding operation, viz., to calculate $\frac{s}{v}$,

the ratio of the surplus-value to the variable capital.

---

[*]Although the rate of surplus-value is an exact expression for the degree of exploitation of labor-power, it is, in no sense, an expression for the absolute amount of exploitation. For example, if the necessary labor=5 hours and the surplus-labor=5 hours, the degree of exploitation is 100%. The amount of exploitation is here measured by 5 hours. If, on the other hand, the necessary labor=6 hours, and the surplus-labor=6 hours, the degree of exploitation remains, as before, 100%, while the actual amount of exploitation has increased 20%, namely from five hours to six.

SECTION 4—SURPLUS PRODUCE

The portion of the product that represents the surplus-value, we call "surplus-produce." Just as the rate of surplus-value is determined by its relation, not to the sum total of the capital, but to its variable part; in like manner, the relative quantity of surplus-produce is determined by the ratio that this produce bears, not to the remaining part of the total product, but to that part of it in which is incorporated the necessary labor. Since the production of surplus-value is the chief end and aim of capitalist production, it is clear that the greatness of a man's or a nation's wealth should be measured not by the absolute quantity produced, but by the relative magnitude of the surplus-produce.

The sum of the necessary labor and the surplus-labor, i.e., of the periods of time during which the workman replaces the value of his labor-power and produces the surplus-value, this sum constitutes the actual time during which he works, i.e., the working day.

CHAPTER X

THE WORKING DAY

SECTION 1—THE LIMITS OF THE WORKING DAY

We started with the supposition that labor-power is bought and sold at its value. Its value, like that of all other commodities, is determined by the working time necessary to its production. If the production of the average daily means of subsistence of the laborer takes up 6 hours, he must work, on average, 6 hours every day to produce his daily labor-power, or to reproduce the value received as the result of its sale. The necessary part of his working day amounts to 6 hours, and is, therefore, *coeteris paribus*, a given quantity. But with this, the extent of the working day itself is not yet given.

★ ★ ★

The working day is not a constant, but a variable quantity. One of its parts, certainly, is determined by the working time required for the reproduction of the labor-power of the laborer himself. But its total amount varies with the duration of the surplus-labor. The working day is, therefore, determinable, but is, *per se*, indeterminate.

Although the working day is not a fixed, but a fluent quantity, it can, on the other hand, only vary within certain limits. The minimum limit is, however, not determinable; of course, if we make the extension line BC or the surplus-labor=0, we have a minimum limit, i.e., the part of the day which the laborer must necessarily work for his own maintenance. On the basis of capitalist production, however, this necessary labor can form a part only of the working day; the working day itself can never be reduced to this minimum. On the other hand, the working day has a maximum limit. It cannot be prolonged beyond a certain point. This maximum limit is conditioned by two things. First, by the physical bounds of labor-power. Within the 24 hours of the natural day a man can expend only a definite quantity of his vital force. A horse, in like manner, can only work from day to day, 8 hours. During part of the day this force must rest, sleep; during another part the man has to satisfy other physical needs, to feed, wash, and clothe himself. Besides these purely physical limitations, the extension of the working day encounters moral ones. The laborer needs time for satisfying his intellectual and social wants, the extent and number of which are conditioned by the general state of social advancement. The variation of the working day fluctuates, therefore, within physical and social bounds. But both these limiting conditions are of a very elastic nature and allow the greatest latitude. So we find working days of 8, 10, 12, 14, 16, 18 hours, i.e., of the most different lengths.

The capitalist has bought the labor-power at its day-rate. To him its use-value belongs during one working day. He has thus acquired the right to make the laborer work for him during one day. But what is a working day?

In any event, less than a natural day. By how much? The capitalist has his own views of this *ultima Thule*, the necessary limit of the working day. As capitalist, he is only capital personified. But capital has one single life impulse, the tendency to create value and surplus-value, to make its constant factor, the means of production, absorb the greatest possible amount of surplus-labor .

The time during which the laborer works is the time during which the capitalist consumes the labor-power he has purchased of him.

If the laborer consumes his disposable time for himself, he robs the capitalist.

★ ★ ★

On the other hand, the peculiar nature of the commodity sold implies a limit to its consumption by the purchaser, and the laborer maintains his right as seller when he wishes to reduce the working day to one of definite normal duration. There is here, therefore, an antinomy, right against right, both equally bearing the seal of the law of exchanges. Between equal rights force decides. Hence it is that in the history of capitalist production, the determination of what is a working day presents itself as the result of a struggle, a struggle between collective capital, i.e., the class of capitalists, and collective labor, i.e., the working class.

SECTION 2—THE GREED FOR SURPLUS LABOR MANUFACTURER AND BOYARD

Capital has not invented surplus-labor. Wherever a part of society possesses the monopoly of the means of production, the laborer, free or not free, must add to the working time necessary for his own maintenance an extra working time in order to produce the means of subsistence for the owners of the means of production, whether this proprietor be the Etruscan theocrat, *civis Romanus*, Norman baron, American slave owner, Wallachian Boyard, modern landlord, or capitalist. It is, however, clear that in any given economic formation of society where not the exchange-value but the use-value of the product predominates, surplus-labor will be limited by a given set of wants which may be greater or less, and that here no boundless thirst for surplus-labor arises from the nature of the production itself. Hence in antiquity overwork becomes horrible only when the object is to obtain exchange-value in its specific independent money-form: in the production of gold and silver. Compulsory working to death is here the recognized form of overwork. But as soon as people, whose production still moves within the lower forms of slave-labor, corveé-labor, etc., are drawn into the whirlpool of an international market dominated by the capitalistic mode of production, the sale of their products for export becoming their principal interest, the civilized horrors of over-work are grafted on the barbaric horrors of slavery, serfdom, etc. Hence the negro labor in the Southern States of the American Union preserved something of a patriarchal character, so long as production was chiefly directed to immediate local consumption. But in proportion, as the export of cotton became of vital interest to these states, the over-working of the negro and sometimes the using up of his life in 7 years' of labor became a factor in a calculated and calculating system. It was no longer a question of obtaining from him a certain quantity of useful products. It was now a question of production of surplus-labor itself. So was it also with the corvée, e.g., in the Danubian Principalities (now Roumania).

★ ★ ★

If the Réglement organique of the Danubian provinces was a positive expression of the greed for surplus-labor which every paragraph legalized, the English Factory Acts are the negative expression of the same greed. These acts curb the passion of capital for a limitless draining of labor-power by forcibly limiting the working day by state regulations, made by a state that is ruled by capitalist and landlord. Apart from the working-class movement that daily grew more threatening, the limiting of factory labor was dictated by the same necessity which spread guano over the English fields. The same blind eagerness for plunder that in the one case exhausted the soil had, in the other, torn up by the roots the living force of the nation. Periodic epidemics speak on this point as clearly as the diminishing military standard in Germany and France.

★ ★ ★

The worker is here nothing more than personified labor-time.

SECTION 4—DAY AND NIGHT WORK. THE RELAY SYSTEM

Constant capital, the means of production, considered from the standpoint of the creation of surplus-value, only exist to absorb labor, and with every drop of labor a proportional quantity of surplus-labor. While they fail to do this, their mere existence causes a relative loss to the capitalist, for they represent during the time they lie fallow a useless advance of capital. And this loss becomes positive and absolute as soon as the intermission of their employment necessitates additional outlay at the recommencement of work. The prolongation of the working day beyond the limits of the natural day, into the night, only acts as a palliative. It quenches only in a slight degree the vampire thirst for the living blood of labor. To appropriate labor during all the 24 hours of the day is, therefore, the inherent tendency of capitalist production. But as it is physically impossible to exploit the same individual labor-power constantly during the night as well as the day, to overcome this physical hindrance an alternation becomes necessary between the work-people whose powers are exhausted by day, and those who are used up by night. This alternation may be effected in various ways; e.g., it may be so arranged that part of the workers are one week employed on day work, the next week on night work. It is well-known that this relay system, this alternation of two sets of workers, held full sway in the full-blooded youth-time of the

English cotton manufacture, and that at the present time it still flourishes, among others, in the cotton spinning of the Moscow district.

SECTION 5—THE STRUGGLE FOR
A NORMAL WORKING DAY

"What is a working day? What is the length of time during which capital may consume the labor-power whose daily value it buys? How far may the working day be extended beyond the working time necessary for the reproduction of labor-power itself?" To these questions capital replies: the working day contains the full 24 hours, with the deduction of the few hours of repose without which labor-power absolutely refuses its services again. Hence it is self-evident that the laborer is nothing else, his whole life through, than labor-power, that therefore all his disposable time is by nature and law labor-time, to be devoted to the self-expansion of capital. Time for education, for intellectual development, for the fulfilling of social functions and for social intercourse, for the free-play of his bodily and mental activity, even the rest time of Sunday—moonshine! But in its blind unrestrainable passion, its werewolf hunger for surplus-labor, capital oversteps not only the moral, but even the merely physical maximum bounds of the working day. It usurps the time for growth, development, and healthy maintenance of the body. It steals the time required for the consumption of fresh air and sunlight. It haggles over a meal-time, incorporating it where possible with the process of production itself, so that food is given to the laborer as to a mere means of production, as coal is supplied to the boiler, grease and oil to the machinery. It reduces the sound sleep needed for the restoration, reparation, refreshment of the bodily powers to just so many hours of torpor as the revival of an organism, absolutely exhausted, renders essential. It is not the normal maintenance of the labor-power which is to determine the limits of the working day; it is the greatest possible daily expenditure of labor-power, no matter how diseased, compulsory, and painful it may be, which is to determine the limits of the laborers' period of repose. Capital cares nothing for the length of life of labor-power. All that concerns it is simply and solely the maximum of labor-power that can be rendered fluent in a working day. It attains this end by shortening the extent of the laborer's life, as a greedy farmer snatches increased produce from the soil by robbing it of its fertility.

The capitalistic mode of production (essentially the production of surplus-value, the absorption of surplus-labor) produces thus, with the extension of the working day, not only the deterioration of human labor-power by robbing it of its typical moral and physical conditions of development and function. It produces also the premature exhaustion and death of this labor-power itself. It extends the laborer's time of production during a given period by shortening his actual life-time.

★ ★ ★

Free competition brings out the inherent laws of capitalist production in the shape of external coercive laws having power over every individual capitalist.

The establishment of a normal working day is the result of centuries of struggle between capitalist and laborer.

★ ★ ★

After capital had taken centuries in extending the working day to its normal maximum limit, and then beyond this to the limit of the natural day of 12 hours, there followed on the birth of machinism and modern industry in the last third of the eighteenth century, a violent encroachment like that of an avalanche in its intensity and extent. All bounds of morals and nature, age and sex, day and night, were broken down. Even the ideas of day and night, of rustic simplicity in the old statutes, became so confused that an English judge, as late as 1860, needed a quite Talmudic sagacity to explain "judicially" what was day and what was night.

As soon as the working class, stunned at first by the noise and turmoil of the new system of production, recovered, in some measure, its senses, its resistance began, and first in the native land of machinism, in England. For 30 years, however, the concessions conquered by the workpeople were purely nominal. Parliament passed 5 Labor Laws between 1802 and 1833, but was shrewd enough not to vote a penny for their carrying out, for the requisite officials, etc.

They remained a dead letter.

A normal working day for modern industry only dates from the Factory Act of 1833.

CHAPTER XI

RATE AND MASS OF SURPLUS-VALUE

The variable capital of a capitalist is the expression in money of the total value of all the labor-powers that he employs simultaneously. Its value is, therefore, equal to the average value of one labor-power, multiplied by the number of labor-powers employed. With a given value of labor-power, therefore, the magnitude of the variable capital varies directly as the number of laborers employed simultaneously. If the daily value of one labor-power=3s., then a capital of 300s must be advanced in order to exploit daily 100 labor-powers, of n times 3s., in order to exploit daily n labor-powers.

In the same way, if a variable capital of 3s., being the daily value of one labor-power, produces a daily surplus-value of 3s., a variable capital of 300s. will produce a daily surplus-value of 300s., and one of n times 3s. a daily surplus-value of nx3s. The mass of the surplus-value produced is therefore equal to the surplus-value which the working-day of one laborer supplies multiplied by the number of laborers employed. But as further the mass of surplus-value which a single laborer produces (the value of labor-power being given) is determined by the rate of the surplus-value, this law follows: the mass of the surplus-value produced is equal to the amount of the variable capital advanced, multiplied by the rate of surplus-value; in other words: it is determined by the compound ratio between the number of labor-powers exploited simultaneously by the same capitalist and the degree of exploitation of each individual labor-power.

Let the mass of the surplus-value be S, the surplus-value supplied by the individual laborer in the average day s, the variable capital daily advanced in the purchase of one individual labor-power v, the sum total of the variable capital V, the value of an average labor-power P, its degree of exploitation

$$\frac{á\ (surplus\text{-}labor)}{a\ (necessary\text{-}labor)}$$

and the number of laborers employed n; we have:

$$S = \left[\begin{array}{c} \dfrac{s}{v} \ \text{x V} \\[2em] P \ \text{x} \ \dfrac{á}{a} \ \text{x n} \end{array}\right.$$

It is always supposed not only that the value of an average labor-power is constant, but that the laborers employed by a capitalist are reduced to average laborers. There are exceptional cases in which the surplus-value produced does not increase in proportion to the number of laborers exploited, but then the value of the labor-power does not remain constant.

In the production of a definite mass of surplus-value, therefore, the decrease of one factor may be compensated by the increase of the other. If the variable capital diminishes, and at the same time the rate of surplus-value increases in the same ratio, the mass of surplus-value produced remains unaltered. If on our earlier assumption the capitalist must advance 300s in order to exploit 100 laborers a day, and if the rate of surplus-value amounts to 50%, this variable capital of 300s. yields a surplus-value of 150s. or of l00 x 3 working hours. If the rate of surplus-value doubles, or the working day, instead of being extended from 6 to 9, is extended from 6 to 12 hours and at the same time variable capital is lessened by half and reduced to 150s., it yields also a surplus-value of 150s. or 50 x 6 working hours. Diminution of the variable capital may therefore be compensated by a proportionate rise in the degree of exploitation of labor-power, or the decrease in the number of the laborers employed by a proportionate extension of the working-day. Within certain limits therefore the supply of labor exploitable by capital is independent of the supply of laborers. On the contrary, a fall in the rate of surplus-value leaves unaltered the mass of the surplus-value produced, if the amount of the variable capital, or number of the laborers employed, increases in the same proportion.

Nevertheless, the compensation of a decrease in the number of laborers employed, or of the amount of variable capital advanced, by a rise in the rate of surplus-value, or by the lengthening of the working-day, has impassable limits. Whatever the value of labor-power may be, whether the working time necessary for the maintenance of the laborer is 2 or 10 hours, the total value that a laborer can produce, day in, day out, is always less than the value in which 24 hours of labor are embodied, less than 12s., if 12s. is the money expression for 24 hours of realized labor.

★ ★ ★

The absolute limit of the average working-day—this being by nature always less than 24 hours—sets an absolute limit to the compensation of a reduction of variable capital by a higher rate of surplus-value, or of the decrease of the number of laborers exploited by a higher degree of exploitation of labor-power. This palpable law is of importance for the clearing up of many phenomena arising from a tendency (to be worked out later on) of capital to reduce as much as possible the number of laborers employed by it, or its variable constituent transformed into labor-power, in contradiction to its other tendency to produce the greatest sensible mass of surplus-value. On the other hand, if the mass of labor-power employed, or the amount of variable capital, increases, but not in proportion to the fall in the rate of surplus-value, the mass of the surplus-value produced falls.

A third law results from the determination of the mass of the surplus-value produced by two factors: rate of surplus-value and amount of variable capital advanced. The rate of surplus-value, or the degree of exploitation of labor-power, and the value of labor-power, or the amount of necessary working time being given—it is self-evident that the greater the variable capital, the greater would be the mass of the value produced and of the surplus-value. If the limit of the working-day is given, and also the limit of its necessary constituent, the mass of value and surplus-value that an individual capitalist produces is clearly exclusively dependent on the mass of labor that he sets in motion. But this, under the conditions supposed above, depends on the mass of labor-power, or the number of laborers whom he exploits, and this number in its turn is determined by the amount of the variable capital advanced. With a given rate of surplus-value, and a given value of labor-power, therefore, the masses of surplus-value produced vary directly as the amounts of the variable capitals advanced. Now we know that the capitalist divides his capital into two parts. One part he lays out in means of production. This is the constant part of his capital. The other part he lays out in living labor-power. This part forms his variable capital. On the basis of the same mode of social production, the division of capital into constant and variable differs in different branches of production, and within the same branch of production, too, this relation changes with changes in the technical conditions and in the social combinations of the processes of production. But in whatever proportion a given capital breaks up into a constant and a variable part, whether the latter is to the former as 1:2 or 1:10 or 1:x, the law just laid down is not affected by this. For, according to our previous analysis, the value of the constant capital reappears in the value of the product, but does not enter into the newly produced value, the newly created value-product. To employ 1,000 spinners, more raw material, spindles, etc., are, of course, required, than to employ 100. The value of these additional means of production however may rise or fall, remain unaltered, be large or small; it has no influence on the process of creation of surplus-value by means of the labor-powers that put them in motion. The law demonstrated above now, therefore, takes this form: the masses of value and of surplus-value produced by different capitals—the value of labor-power being given and its degree of exploitation being equal—vary directly as the amounts of the variable constituents of these capitals, i.e., as their constituents transformed into living labor-power.

★ ★ ★

The labor which is set in motion by the total capital of a society, day in, day out, may be regarded as a single collective working-day. If, e.g., the number of laborers is a million, and the average working-day of a laborer is 10 hours, the social working-day consists of ten million hours. With a given length of this working-day, whether its limits are fixed physically or socially, the mass of surplus-value can only be increased by increasing the number of laborers, i.e., of the laboring population. The growth of population here forms the mathematical limit to the production of surplus-value by the total social capital. On the contrary, with a given amount of population, this limit is formed by the possible lengthening of the working-day.

From the treatment of the production of surplus-value, so far, it follows that not every sum of money, or of value, is at pleasure transformable into capital. To effect this transformation, in fact, a certain minimum of money or of exchange-value must be presupposed in the hands of the individual possessor of money or commodities. The minimum of variable capital is the cost price of a single labor-power, employed the whole year through, day in, day out, for the production of surplus-value. If this laborer were in possession of his own means of production, and were satisfied to live as a laborer, he need not work beyond the time necessary for the re-production of his means of subsistence, say 8 hours a day. He would, besides, only require the means of production sufficient for 8 working hours. The capitalist, on the other hand, who makes him do, besides these 8 hours, say 4 hours' surplus-labor, requires an additional sum of money for furnishing the additional means of production. On our supposition, however, he would have to employ two laborers in order to live, on the surplus-value appropriated daily, as well as, and no better than a laborer, i.e., to be able to satisfy his necessary wants. In this case the mere maintenance of life would be the end of his production, not the increase of wealth; but this latter is implied in capitalist production. That he may live only twice as well as an ordinary laborer, and besides turn half of the surplus-value produced into capital, he would have to raise, with the number of laborers, the minimum of the capital advanced 8 times. Of course he can, like his laborer, take to work himself, participate directly in the process of production, but he is then only a hybrid between capitalist and laborer, a "small master." A certain stage of capitalist production necessitates that the capitalist be able to devote the whole of the time during which he functions as a capitalist, i.e., as personified capital, to the appropriation and therefore control of the labor of others, and to the selling of the products of this labor. The possessor of money or commodities actually turns into a capitalist in such cases only where the minimum sum advanced for production greatly exceeds the maximum of the middle ages.

★ ★ ★

The minimum of the sum of value that the individual possessor of money or commodities must command, in order to metamorphose himself into a capitalist, changes with the different stages of development of capitalist production, and is at given stages different in different spheres of production, according to their special and technical conditions. Certain spheres of production demand, even at the very outset of capitalist production, a minimum of capital that is not as yet found in the hands of single individuals. This gives rise partly to state subsidies to private persons, as in France in the time of Colbert, and as in many German states up to our own epoch; partly to the formation of societies with legal monopoly for the exploitation of certain branches of industry and commerce, the forerunners of our own modern joint-stock companies.

Within the process of production, as we have seen, capital acquired the command over labor, i.e., over functioning laboring-power or the laborer himself. Personified capital, the capitalist takes care that the laborer does his work regularly and with the proper degree of intensity.

Capital further developed into a coercive relation which compels the working class to do more work than the narrow round of its own life-wants prescribes. As a producer of the activity of others, as a pumper-out of surplus-labor and exploiter of labor-power, it surpasses in energy, recklessness, and efficiency all earlier systems of production based on directly compulsory labor.

At first, capital subordinates labor on the basis of the technical conditions in which it historically finds it. It does not, therefore, change immediately the mode of production. The production of surplus-value—in the form hitherto considered by us—by means of simple extension of the working-day, proved, therefore, to be independent of any change in the mode of production itself. It was not less active in the old-fashioned bakeries than in the modern cotton factories.

If we consider the process of production from the point of view of the simple labor-process, the laborer stands in relation to the means of production not in their quality as capital, but as the mere means and material of his own intelligent productive activity. In tanning, e.g., he deals with the skins as his simple object of labor. It is not the capitalist whose skin he tans. But it is different as soon as we deal with the process of production from the point of view of the process of creation of surplus-value. The means of production are at once changed into means for the absorption of the labor of others. It is now no longer the laborer that employs the means of production, but the means of production that employ the laborer. Instead of being consumed by him as material elements of his productive activity, they consume him as the ferment necessary to their own life-process, and the life-process of capital consists only in its movement as value constantly expanding, constantly multiplying itself. Furnaces and workshops that stand idle by night, and absorb no living labor, are "a mere loss" to the capitalist. Hence, furnaces and workshops constitute lawful claims upon the night-labor of the workpeople. The simple transformation of money into the material factors of the process of production, into means of production, transforms the latter into a title and a right to the labor and surplus-labor of others.

PART IV

Production of
Relative Surplus-Value

CHAPTER XII

THE CONCEPT OF RELATIVE SURPLUS-VALUE

That portion of the working-day which merely produces an equivalent for the value paid by the capitalist for his labor-power has, up to this point, been treated by us as a constant magnitude; and such in fact it is, under given conditions of production and at a given stage in the economical development of society. Beyond this, his necessary labor-time, the laborer, we saw, could continue to work for 2, 3, 4, 6, etc., hours. The rate of surplus-value and the length of the working day depended on the magnitude of this prolongation. Though the necessary labor-time was constant, we saw, on the other hand, that the total working-day was variable. Now suppose we have a working-day whose length, and whose apportionment between necessary labor and surplus-labor, are given. Let the whole line a c, a————b—c, represent, for example, a working-day of 12 hours; the portion of a b 10 hours of necessary labor, and the portion b c 2 hours of surplus-labor. How now can the production of surplus-value be increased, i.e., how can the surplus-labor be prolonged, without, or independently of, any prolongation of a c?

Although the length of a c is given, b c appears to be capable of prolongation, if not by extension beyond its end c, which is also the end of the working day a c, yet, at all events, by pushing back its starting point b in the direction of a. Assume that b´—b in the line, a b´ b c is equal to half of b c

a———————b´—b—c

or to one hour's labor-time. If now, in a c, the working day of 12 hours, we move the point b to b´, b c becomes b´ c; the surplus-labor increases by one-half, from 2 hours to 3 hours, although the working day remains as before at 12 hours. This extension of the surplus labor-time from b c to b´ c, from 2 hours to 3 hours, is, however, evidently impossible without a simultaneous contraction of the necessary labor-time from a b into a b´, from 10 hours to 9 hours. The prolongation of the surplus-labor would correspond to a shortening of the necessary labor; or a portion of the labor-time previously consumed, in reality, for the laborer's own benefit, would be converted into labor-time for the benefit of the capitalist. There would be an alteration, not in the length of the working day, but in its division into necessary labor-time and surplus labor-time.

On the other hand, it is evident that the duration of the surplus-labor is given when the length of the working day and the value of labor-power are given. The value of labor-power, i.e., the labor-time requisite to produce labor-power, determines the labor-time necessary for the reproduction of that value. If one working hour is embodied in six pence, and the value of a day's labor-power is five shillings, the laborer must work 10 hours a day in order to replace the value paid by capital for his labor-power, or to produce an equivalent for the value of his daily necessary means of subsistence. Given the value of these means of subsistence, the value of his labor-power is given; and given the value of his labor-power, the duration of his necessary labor-time is given. The duration of the surplus-labor, however, is arrived at by subtracting the necessary labor-time from the total working day. Ten hours subtracted from twelve leave two, and it is not easy to see how, under the given conditions, the surplus-labor can possibly be prolonged beyond two hours. No doubt, the capitalist can, instead of five shillings, pay the laborer four shillings and six pence or even less. For the reproduction of this value of four shillings and six pence, nine hours labor-time would suffice; and consequently three hours of surplus-labor, instead of two, would accrue to the capitalist, and the surplus-value would rise from one shilling to eighteen pence. This result, however, would be obtained only by lowering the wages of the laborer below the value of his labor-power. With the four shillings and six pence which he produces in nine hours, he commands one-tenth less of the necessities of life than before, and consequently the proper reproduction of his labor-power is crippled. The surplus-labor would in this case be prolonged only by an overstepping of its normal limits; its domain would be extended only by a usurpation of part of the domain of necessary labor-time. Despite the important part which this method plays in actual practice, we are excluded from considering it in this place by our assumption that all commodities, including labor-power, are bought and sold at their full value. Granted this, it follows that the labor-time necessary for the production of labor-power, or for the reproduction of its value, cannot be lessened by a fall in the laborer's wages below the value of his labor-power, but only by a fall in this value itself. Given the length of the working day, the prolongation of the surplus-labor must of necessity originate in the curtailment of the necessary labor-time; the latter cannot arise from the former. In the example we have taken, it is necessary that the value of labor-power should actually fall by one-tenth in order that the necessary labor-time may be diminished by one-tenth, i.e., from ten hours to nine, and in order that the surplus-labor may consequently be prolonged from two hours to three.

Such a fall in the value of labor-power implies, however, that the same necessities of life which were formerly produced in ten hours can now be produced in nine hours. But this is impossible without an increase in the productiveness of labor. For example, suppose a shoemaker, with given tools, makes in one working day of twelve hours, one pair of boots. If he must make two pairs in the same time, the productiveness of his labor must be doubled; and this cannot be done except by an alteration in his tools or in his mode of working, or in both. Hence, the conditions of production, i.e., his mode of production, and the labor-process itself, must be revolutionized. By increase in the productiveness of labor, we mean, generally, an alteration in the labor-process of such a kind as to shorten the labor-time socially necessary for the production of a commodity, and to endow a given quantity of labor with the power of producing a greater quantity of use-value. Hitherto in treating surplus-value arising from a simple prolongation of the working day, we have assumed the mode of production to be given and invariable. But when surplus-value has to be produced by the conversion of necessary labor into surplus-labor, it by no means suffices for capital to take over the labor-process in the form under which it has been historically handed down, and then simply to prolong the duration of that process. The technical and social conditions of the process, and consequently the very mode of production, must be revolutionized before the productiveness of labor can be increased. By that means alone can the value of labor-power be made to sink, and the portion of the working day necessary for the reproduction of that value, be shortened.

The surplus-value produced by prolongation of the working day, I call *absolute surplus-value*. On the other hand, the surplus-value arising from the curtailment of the necessary labor-time, and from the corresponding alteration in the respective lengths of the two components of the working day, I call *relative surplus-value*.

In order to effect a fall in the value of labor-power, the increase in the productiveness of labor must seize upon those branches of industry whose products determine the value of labor-power, and consequently either belong to the class of customary means of subsistence or are capable of supplying the place of those means. But the value of a commodity is determined not only by the quantity of labor which the laborer directly bestows upon that commodity, but also by the labor contained in the means of production. For instance, the value of a pair of boots depends not only on the cobbler's labor, but also on the value of the leather, wax, thread, etc. Hence, a fall in the value of labor-power is also brought about by an increase in the productiveness of labor, and by a corresponding cheapening of commodities in those industries which supply the instruments of labor and the raw material that form the material elements of the constant capital required for producing the necessities of life. But an increase in the productiveness of labor in those branches of industry which supply neither the necessities of life, nor the means of production for such necessities, leaves the value of labor-power undisturbed.

The cheapened commodity, of course, causes only a *pro tanto* fall in the value of labor-power, a fall proportional to the extent of that commodity's employment in the reproduction of labor-power. Shirts, for instance, are a necessary means of subsistence, but are only one out of many. The totality of the necessities of life consists, however, of various commodities, each the product of a distinct industry; and the value of each of those commodities enters as a component part into the value of labor-power. This latter value decreases with the decrease of the labor-time necessary for its reproduction, the total decrease being the sum of all the different curtailments of labor-time effected in those various and distinct industries. This general result is treated here as if it were the immediate result directly aimed at in each individual case. Whenever an individual capitalist cheapens shirts, for instance, by increasing the productiveness of labor, he by no means necessarily aims at reducing the value of labor-power and shortening, *pro tanto*, the necessary labor-time. But it is only insofar as he ultimately contributes to this result that he assists in raising the general rate of surplus-value. The general and necessary tendencies of capital must be distinguished from their forms of manifestation.

It is not our intention to consider here the way in which the laws innate in capitalist production manifest themselves in the movements of individual masses of capital where they assert themselves as coercive laws of competition and are brought home to the mind and consciousness of the individual capitalist as the directing motives of his operations. But this much is clear; a scientific analysis of competition is not possible before we have a conception of the inner nature of capital.

★ ★ ★

The value of commodities is in inverse ratio to the productiveness of labor. And so, too, is the value of labor-power, because it depends on the values of commodities. Relative surplus-value is, on the contrary, directly proportional to that productiveness. It rises with rising and falls with falling productiveness. The value of money being assumed to be constant, an average social working day of 12 hours always produces the same new value, six shillings, no matter how this sum may be apportioned between surplus-value and wages. But if, in consequence of increased productiveness, the value of the necessities of life fall, and the value of a day's labor-power be thereby reduced from five shillings to three, the surplus-value increases from one shilling to three. Ten hours were necessary for the reproduction of the value of the labor-power; now only six are required. Four hours have been set free, and can be annexed to the domain of surplus-labor. Hence there is innate in capital an inclination and constant tendency to heighten the productiveness of labor in order to cheapen commodities, and by such cheapening to cheapen the laborer himself.

The value of a commodity is, in itself, of no interest to the capitalist. What alone interests him is the surplus-value that dwells in it, and is realisable by sale. Realization of the surplus-value necessarily carries with it the refunding of the value that was advanced. Now, since relative surplus-value increases in direct proportion to the development of the productiveness of labor while, on the other hand, the value of commodities diminishes in the same proportion; since one and the same process cheapens commodities, and augments the surplus-value contained in them; we have here the solution of the riddle: why does the capitalist, whose sole concern is the production of exchange-value, continually strive to depress the exchange-value of commodities?

★ ★ ★

The shortening of the working day is, therefore, by no means what is aimed at, in capitalist production, when labor is economized by increasing its productiveness. It is only the shortening of the labor-time necessary for the production of a definite quantity of that is aimed at.

CHAPTER XIII

COOPERATION

CAPITALIST PRODUCTION only then really begins when each individual capital employs simultaneously a comparatively large number of laborers; when consequently the labor-process is carried out on an extensive scale and yields relatively large quantities of products. A greater number of laborers working together, at the same time, in one place (or, if you will, in the same field of labor), in order to produce the same sort of commodity under the mastership of one capitalist, constitutes both historically and logically the starting point of capitalist production. With regard to the mode of production itself, manufacture, in its strict meaning, is hardly to be distinguished in its earliest stages from the handicraft trades of the guilds otherwise than by the greater number of workmen simultaneously employed by one and the same individual capital. The workshop of the mediaeval master handicraftsman is simply enlarged.

At first, therefore, the difference is purely quantitative. We have shown that the surplus-value produced by a given capital is equal to the surplus-value produced by each workman multiplied by the number of workmen simultaneously employed. The number of workmen in itself does not affect, either the rate of surplus-value or the degree of exploitation of labor-power. If a working day of 12 hours be embodied in six shillings, 1200 such days will be embodied in 1200 times 6 shillings. In one case 12 x 1200 working hours, and in the other 12 such hours are incorporated in the product. In the production of value a number of workmen rank merely as so many individual workmen; and it therefore makes no difference in the value produced whether the 1200 men work separately or united under the control of one capitalist.

Nevertheless, within certain limits, a modification takes place. The labor realized in value is labor of an average social quality; is consequently the expenditure of average labor-power. Any average magnitude, however, is merely the average of a number of separate magnitudes all of one kind, but differing as to quantity. In every industry, each individual laborer, be he Peter or Paul, differs from the average laborer. These individual differences, or "errors" as they are called in mathematics, compensate one another and vanish whenever a certain minimum number of workmen are employed together.

★ ★ ★

Even without an alteration in the system of working, the simultaneous employment of a large number of laborers effects a revolution in the material conditions of the labor-process. The buildings in which they work, the store-houses for the raw material, the implements and utensils used simultaneously or in turns by the workmen; in short, a portion of the means of production, are now consumed in common. On the one hand, the exchange-value of these means of production is not increased; for the exchange-value of a commodity is not raised by its use-value being consumed more thoroughly and to greater advantage. On the other hand, they are used in common, and therefore on a larger scale than before. A room where twenty weavers work at twenty looms must be larger than the room of a single weaver with two assistants. But it costs less labor to build one workshop for twenty persons than to build ten to accommodate two weavers each; thus the value of the means of production that are concentrated for use in common on a large scale does not increase in direct proportion to the expansion and to the increased useful effect of those means. When consumed in common, they give up a smaller part of their value to each single product; partly because the total value they part with is spread over a greater quantity of products, and partly because their value, though absolutely greater, is, having regard to their sphere of action in the process, relatively less than the value of isolated means of production. Owing to this, the value of a part of the constant capital falls, and in proportion to the magnitude of the fall, the total value of the commodity also falls. The effect is the same as if the means of production had cost less. The economy in their application is entirely owing to their being consumed in common by a large number of workmen. Moreover, this character of being necessary conditions of social labor, a character that distinguishes them from the dispersed and relatively more costly means of production of isolated, independent laborers, of small masters, is acquired even when the numerous workmen assembled together do not assist one another, but merely work side by side. A portion of the instruments of labor acquires this social character before the labor-process itself does so.

Economy in the use of the means of production has to be considered under two aspects. First, as cheapening commodities, and thereby bringing about a fall in the value of labor-power. Secondly, as altering the ratio of the surplus-value to the total capital advanced, i.e., to the sum of the values of the constant and variable capital. The latter aspect will not be considered until we come to the third volume to which, with the object of treating them in their proper connection, we also relegate many other points that relate to the present question. The march of our analysis compels this splitting up of the subject matter, a splitting up that is quite in keeping with the spirit of capitalist production. For since, in this mode of production, the workman finds the instruments of labor existing independently of him as another man's property, economy in their use appears, with regard to him, to be a distinct operation, one that does not concern him and which, therefore, has no connection with the methods by which his own personal productiveness is increased.

When numerous laborers work together side by side, whether in one and the same process, or in different but connected processes, they are said to cooperate, or to work in cooperation.

★ ★ ★

The sum total of the mechanical forces exerted by isolated workmen differs from the social force that is developed when many hands take part simultaneously in one and the same undivided operation, such as raising a heavy weight, turning a winch, or removing an obstacle. In such cases the effect of the combined labor could either not be produced at all by isolated individual labor, or it could only be produced by a great expenditure of time, or on a very dwarfed scale. Not only have we here an increase in the productive power of the individual by means of cooperation, but the creation of a new power, namely, the collective power of masses.

★ ★ ★

Cooperation allows the work to be carried on over an extended space; it is consequently imperatively called for in certain undertakings, such as draining, constructing dykes, irrigation works, and the making of canals, roads and railways. On the other hand, while extending the scale of production, it renders possible a relative contraction of the arena. This contraction of arena simultaneous with, and arising from, extension of scale, whereby a number of useless expenses are cut down, is owing to the conglomeration of laborers, to the aggregation of various processes, and to the concentration of the means of production.

The combined working day produces, relatively to an equal sum of isolated working-days, a greater quantity of use-values, and consequently, diminishes the labor-time necessary for the production of a given useful effect. Whether the combined working-day, in a given case, acquires this increased productive power because it heightens the mechanical force of labor, or extends its sphere of action over a greater space, or contracts the field of production relatively to the scale of production, or at the critical moment sets large masses of labor to work, or excites emulation between individuals and raises their animal spirits, or impresses on the similar operations carried on by a number of men the stamp of continuity and many-sidedness, or performs simultaneously different operations, or economizes the means of production by use in common, or lends to individual labor the character of average social labor—whichever of these be the cause of the increase, the special productive power of the combined working day is, under all circumstances, the social productive power of labor, or the productive power of social labor. This power is due to cooperation itself. When the laborer cooperates systematically with others, he strips off the fetters of his individuality and develops the capabilities of his species.

As a general rule, laborers cannot cooperate without being brought together: their assemblage in one place is a necessary condition of their cooperation. Hence wage laborers cannot cooperate unless they are employed simultaneously by the same capital, the same capitalist, and unless therefore their labor-powers are bought simultaneously by him. The total value of these labor-powers, or the amount of the wages of these laborers for a day, or a week, as the case may be, must be ready in the pocket of the capitalist before the workmen are assembled for the process of production. The payment of 300 workmen at once, though only for one day, requires a greater outlay of capital than does the payment of a smaller number of men, week by week, during a whole year. Hence the number of the laborers that cooperate, or the scale of cooperation, depends, in the first instance, on the amount of capital that the individual capitalist can spare for the purchase of labor-power; in other words, on the extent to which a single capitalist has command over the means of subsistence of a number of laborers.

And as with the variable, so it is with the constant capital. For example, the outlay on raw material is 30 times as great for the capitalist who employs 300 men as it is for each of the 30 capitalists who employ 10 men. The value and quantity of the instruments of labor used in common do not, it is true, increase at the same rate as the number of workmen, but they do increase very considerably. Hence, concentration of large masses of the means of production in the hands of individual capitalists is a material condition for the cooperation of wage-laborers, and the extent of the cooperation or the scale of production depends on the extent of this concentration.

★ ★ ★

All combined labor on a large scale requires, more or less, a directing authority in order to secure the harmonious working of the individual activities, and to perform the general functions that have their origin in the action of the combined organism, as distinguished from the action of its separate organs. The work of directing, superintending, and adjusting becomes one of the functions of capital from the moment that the labor under the control of capital becomes cooperative. Once a function of capital, it acquires special characteristics.

The directing motive, the end and aim of capitalist production, is to extract the greatest possible amount of surplus-value, and consequently to exploit labor-power to the greatest possible extent. As the number of the cooperating laborers increases, so too does their resistance to the domination of capital, and with it, the necessity for capital to overcome this resistance by counter-pressure. The control exercised by the capitalist is not only a special function, due to the nature of the social labor-process, and peculiar to that process, but it is, at the same time, a function of the exploitation of a social labor-process, and is consequently rooted in the unavoidable antagonism between the expoiter and the living and laboring raw material he exploits.

Again, in proportion to the increasing mass of the means of production, now no longer the property of the laborer, but of the capitalist, the necessity increases for some effective control over the proper application of those means. Moreover, the cooperation of wage laborers is entirely brought about by the capital that employs them. Their union into one single productive body and the establishment of a connection between their individual functions are matters foreign and external to them, are not their own act, but the act of the capital that brings and keeps them together. Hence the connection existing between their various labors appears to them, ideally, in the shape of a preconceived plan of the capitalist, and practically in the shape of the authority of the same capitalist, in the shape of the powerful will of another, who subjects their activity to his aims. If, then, the control of the capitalist is in substance twofold by reason of the twofold nature of the process of production itself—which, on the one hand, is a social process for producing use-values, on the other, a process for creating surplus-value—in form that control is despotic. As cooperation extends its scale, this despotism takes forms peculiar to itself. Just as at first the capitalist is relieved from actual labor as soon as his capital has reached that minimum amount with which capitalist production as such begins, so now he hands over the work of direct and constant supervision of the individual workmen and groups of workmen to a special kind of wage laborer. An industrial army of workmen, under the command of a capitalist, requires, like a real army, officers (managers) and sergeants (foremen, overlookers) who, while the work is being done, command in the name of the capitalist. The work of supervision becomes their established and exclusive function. When comparing the mode of production of isolated peasants and artisans with production by slave labor, the political economist counts this labor of superintendence among the *faux frais* of production. But, when considering the capitalist mode of production, he on the contrary treats the work of control made necessary by the cooperative character of the labor process as identical with the different work of control, necessitated by the capitalist character of that process and the antagonism of interests between capitalist and laborer. It is not because he is a capitalist that a man is a leader of industry; on the contrary, he is a leader of industry because he is a capitalist. The leadership of industry is an attribute of capital, just as in feudal times the functions of general and judge were attributes of landed property.

The laborer is the owner of his labor-power until he has done bargaining for its sale with the capitalist; and he can sell no more than what he has—i.e., his individual, isolated labor-power. This state of things is in no way altered by the fact that the capitalist, instead of buying the labor-power of one man, buys that of 100, and enters into separate contracts with 100 unconnected men instead of with one. He is at liberty to set the 100 men to work without letting them cooperate. He pays them the value of 100 independent labor-powers, but he does not pay for the combined labor-power of the hundred. Being independent of each other, the laborers are isolated persons who enter into relations with the capitalist, but not with one another. This cooperation begins only with the labor process, but they have then ceased to belong to themselves. On entering that process, they become incorporated with capital. As cooperators, as members of a working organism, they are but special modes of existence of capital. Hence, the productive power developed by the laborer when working in cooperation is the productive power of capital. This power is developed gratuitously whenever the workmen are placed under given conditions, and it is capital that places them under such conditions.

★ ★ ★

Just as the social productive power of labor that is developed by cooperation appears to be the productive power of capital, so cooperation itself, contrasted with the process of production carried on by isolated independent laborers or even by small employers, appears to be a specific form of the capitalist process of production. It is the first change experienced by the actual labor-process when subjected to capital. This change takes place spontaneously. The simultaneous employment of a large number of wage-laborers in one and the same process, which is a necessary condition of this change, also forms the starting point of capitalist production. This point coincides with the birth of capital itself. If then, on the one hand, the capitalist mode of production presents itself to us historically as a necessary condition to the transformation of the labor-process into a social process, so, on the other hand, this social form of the labor-process presents itself as a method employed by capital for the more profitable exploitation of labor by increasing that labor's productiveness.

In the elementary form, under which we have hitherto viewed it, cooperation is a necessary concomitant of all production on a large scale, but it does not, in itself, represent a fixed form characteristic of a particular epoch in the development of the capitalist mode of production. At the most it appears to do so, and that only approximately, in the handicraft-like beginnings of manufacture, and in that kind of agriculture on a large scale which corresponds to the epoch of manufacture, and is distinguished from peasant agriculture mainly by the number of the laborers simultaneously employed, and by the mass of the means of production concentrated for their use. Simple cooperation is always the prevailing form in those branches of production in which capital operates on a large scale, and division of labor and machinery play but a subordinate part.

Cooperation ever constitutes the fundamental form of the capitalist mode of production; nevertheless, the elementary form of cooperation continues to subsist as a particular form of capitalist production side by side with the more developed form of that mode of production.

CHAPTER XIV

DIVISION OF LABOR
AND MANUFACTURE

SECTION 1—TWOFOLD ORIGIN OF MANUFACTURE

That cooperation which is based on division of labor assumes its typical form in manufacturing, and is the prevalent characteristic form of the capitalist process of production throughout the manufacturing period properly so called. That period, roughly speaking, extends from the middle of the sixteenth to the last third of the eighteenth century.

★ ★ ★

Manufacture either introduces division of labor into a process of production or further develops that division; on the other hand, it unites together handicrafts that were formerly separate. But whatever may have been its particular starting point, its final form is invariably the same—a productive mechanism whose parts are human beings.

For a proper understanding of the division of labor in manufacture, it is essential that the following points be firmly grasped. First, the decomposition of a process of production into its various successive steps coincides here strictly with the resolution of a handicraft into its successive manual operations. Whether complex or simple, each operation has to be done by hand, retains the character of a handicraft, and is therefore dependent on the strength, skill, quickness, and sureness of the individual workman in handling his tools. The handicraft continues to be the basis. This narrow technical basis excludes a really scientific analysis of any definite process of industrial production, since it is still a condition that each detail process gone through by the product must be capable of being done by hand and of forming, in its way, a separate handicraft. It is just because handicraft skill continues, in this way, to be the foundation of the process of production that each workman becomes exclusively assigned to a partial function, and that for the rest of his life, his labor-power is turned into the organ of this detail function.

Secondly, this division of labor is a particular sort of cooperation, and many of its disadvantages spring from the general character of cooperation, and not from this particular form of it.

SECTION 2–THE DETAIL LABORER
AND HIS IMPLEMENTS

The productiveness of labor depends not only on the proficiency of the workman, but on the perfection of his tools. Tools of the same kind, such as knives, drills, gimlets, hammers, etc. may be employed in different processes; and the same tool may serve various purposes in a single process. But as soon as the different operations of a labor-process are disconnected from each other, and each fractional operation acquires in the hands of the detail laborer a suitable and peculiar form, alterations become necessary in the implements that previously served more than one purpose. The direction taken by this change is determined by the difficulties experienced in consequence of the unchanged form of the implement. Manufacture is characterized by the differentiation of the instruments of labor—a differentiation whereby implements of a given sort acquire fixed shapes, adapted to each particular application, and by the specialization of those instruments, giving to each special instrument its full play only in the hands of a specific detail laborer. The manufacturing period simplifies, improves, and multiplies the implements of labor by adapting them to the exclusively special functions of each detail laborer. It thus creates at the same time one of the material conditions for the existence of machinery, which consists of a combination of simple instruments.

The detail laborer and his implements are the simplest dements of manufacture.

SECTION 4–DIVISION OF LABOR IN MANUFAC-TURE, AND DIVISION OF LABOR IN SOCIETY

Since the production and the circulation of commodities are the general prerequisites of the capitalist mode of production, division of labor in manufacture demands that division of labor in society at large should previously have attained a certain degree of development. Inversely, the former division reacts upon and develops and multiplies the latter. Simultaneously, with the differentiation of the instruments of labor, the industries that produce these instruments become more and more differentiated. If the manufacturing system seizes upon an industry which previously was carried on in connection with others, either as a chief or as a subordinate industry and by one producer, these industries immediately separate their connection and become independent. If it seizes upon a particular stage in the production of a commodity, the other stages of its production become converted into so many independent industries. In order to carry out more perfectly the division of labor in manufacture, a single branch of production is according to the varieties of its raw material, or the various forms that one and the same raw material may assume, split up into numerous, and to some extent, entirely new manufactures.

★ ★ ★

In spite of the numerous analogies and links connecting them, division of labor in the interior of a society and that in the interior of a workshop differ not only in degree, but also in kind. The analogy appears most indisputable where there is an invisible bond uniting the various branches of trade. For instance the cattle breeder produces hides, the tanner makes the hides into leather, and the shoemaker, the leather into boots. Here the thing produced by each of them is but a step towards the final form, which is the product of all their labors combined. There are, besides, all the various industries that supply the cattle-breeder, the tanner, and the shoemaker with the means of production. Now it is quite possible to imagine, with Adam Smith, that the difference between the above social division of labor and the division in manufacture is merely subjective, exists merely for the observer who, in a manufacture, can see with one glance all the numerous operations being performed on one spot, while in the instance given above, the spreading out of the work over great areas and the great number of people employed in each branch of labor obscure the connection. But what is it that forms the bond between the independent labors of the cattle-breeder, the tanner, and the shoemaker? It is the fact that their respective products are commodities. What, on the other hand, characterizes division of labor in manufactures? The fact that the detail laborer produces no commodities. It is only the common product of all the detail laborers that becomes a commodity. Division of labor in a society is brought about by the purchase and sale of the products of different branches of industry, while the connection between the detail operations in a workshop is due to the sale of the labor-power of several workmen to one capitalist, who applies it as combined labor-power. The division of labor in the workshop implies concentration of the means of production in the hands of one capitalist; the division of labor in society implies their dispersion among many independent producers of commodities. While within the workshop, the iron law of proportionality subjects definite numbers of workmen to definite functions, in the society outside the workshop, chance and caprice have full play in distributing the producers and their means of production among the various branches of industry. The different spheres of production, it is true, constantly tend to an equilibrium: for, on the one hand, while each producer of a commodity is bound to produce a use-value to satisfy a particular social want, and while the extent of these wants differs quantitatively, still there exists an inner relation which settles their proportions into a regular system, and that system is one of spontaneous growth; and, on the other hand, the law of the value of commodities ultimately determines how much of its disposable working-time society can expend on each particular class of commodities. But this constant tendency to equilibrium of the various spheres of production is exercised only in the shape of a reaction against the constant upsetting of this equilibrium. The *a priori* system on which the division of labor within the workshop is regularly carried out becomes in the division of labor within the society, an *a posteriori,* nature-imposed necessity controlling the lawless caprice of the producers, and perceptible in the barometrical fluctuations of the market prices. Division of labor within the workshop implies the undisputed authority of the capitalist over men who are but parts of a mechanism that belongs to him. The division of labor within the society brings into contact independent commodity-producers, who acknowledge no other authority but that of competition, of the coercion exerted by the pressure of their mutual interests; just as in the animal kingdom, the *bellum omnium contra omnes* more or less preserves the conditions of existence of every species. The same bourgeois mind which praises division of labor in the workshop, lifelong annexation of the laborer to a partial operation, and his complete subjection to capital, as being an organization of labor that increases its productiveness—that same bourgeois mind denounces with equal vigor every conscious attempt to socially control and regulate the process of production as an inroad upon such sacred things as the rights of property, freedom, and unrestricted play for the bent of the individual capitalist. It is very characteristic that the enthusiastic apologists of the factory system have nothing more damning to urge against a general organization of the labor of society than that would turn all society into one immense factory.

If, in a society with capitalist production, anarchy in the social division of labor and despotism in that of the workshop are mutual conditions the one of the other, we find, on the contrary, in those earlier forms of society in which the separation of trades has been spontaneously developed, then crystallized, and finally made permanent by law, on the one hand, a specimen of the organization of the labor of society, in accordance with an approved and authoritative plan, and on the other, the entire exclusion of division of labor in the workshop, or in all events a mere dwarflike or sporadic and accidental development of the same.

★ ★ ★

While division of labor in society at large, whether such division be brought about or not by exchange of commodities, is common to economical formations of society the most diverse, division of labor in the workshop, as practiced by manufacture, is a special creation of the capitalist mode of production alone.

SECTION 5–THE CAPITALISTIC CHARACTER OF MANUFACTURE

An increased number of laborers under the control of one capitalist is the natural starting-point of cooperation generally, as well as of manufacture in particular. But the division of labor in manufacture makes this increase in the number of workmen a technical necessity. The minimum number that any given capitalist is bound to employ is here prescribed by the previously established division of labor. On the other hand, the advantages of further division are obtainable only by adding to the number of workmen, and this can be done only by adding multiples of the various detail groups. But an increase in the variable component of the capital employed necessitates an increase in its constant component, too, in the workshops, implements, etc., and, in particular, in the raw material, the call for which grows quicker than the number of workmen. The quantity of it consumed in a given time, by a given amount of labor, increases in the same ratio as does the productive power of that labor in consequence of its division. Hence, it is a law, based on the very nature of manufacture, that the minimum amount of capital, which is bound to be in the hands of each capitalist, must keep increasing; in other words, that the transformation into capital of the social means of production and subsistence must keep extending.

In manufacture, as well as in simple cooperation, the collective working organism is a form of existence of capital. The mechanism that is made up of numerous individual detail laborers belongs to the capitalist. Hence, the productive power resulting from a combination of laborers appears to be the productive power of capital. Manufacture proper not only subjects the previously independent workman to the discipline and command of capital, but in addition, creates a hierarchic gradation of the workmen themselves. While simple cooperation leaves the mode of working by the individual for the most part unchanged, manufacture thoroughly revolutionizes it, and seizes labor-power by its very roots. It converts the laborer into a crippled monstrosity by forcing his detail dexterity at the expense of a world of productive capabilities and instincts. Not only is the detail work distributed to different individuals, but the individual himself is made the automatic motor of a fractional operation. If, at first, the workman sells his labor-power to capital because the material means of producing a commodity fail him, now his very labor-power refuses its services unless it has been sold to capital. Its functions can be exercised only in an environment that exists in the workshop of the capitalist after the sale. By nature unfitted to make anything independently, the manufacturing laborer develops productive activity as a mere appendage of the capitalist's workshop.

The knowledge, the judgment, and the will which, though in ever so small a degree, are practiced by the independent peasant or handicraftsman in the same way as the savage makes the whole art of war consist in the exercise of his personal cunning—these faculties are now required only for the workshop as a whole. Intelligence in production expands in one direction, because it vanishes in many others. What is lost by the detail laborers is concentrated in the capital that employs them. It is a result of the division of labor in manufactures that the laborer is brought face to face with the intellectual potencies of the material process of production, as the property of another, and as a ruling power. This separation begins in simple cooperation, where the capitalist represents to the single workman the oneness and the will of the associated labor. It is developed in manufacture which cuts down the laborer into a detail laborer. It is completed in modern industry, which makes science a productive force distinct from labor and presses it into the service of capital.

In manufacture, in order to make the collective laborer, and through him capital, rich in social productive power, each laborer must be made poor in individual productive powers.

★ ★ ★

By decomposition of handicrafts, by specialization of the instruments of labor, by the formation of detail laborers, and by grouping and combining the latter into a single mechanism, division of labor in manufacture creates a qualitative gradation and a quantitative proportion in the social process of production; it consequently creates a definite organization of the labor of society, and thereby develops at the same time new productive forces in the society. In its specific capitalist form—and under the given conditions, it could take no other form than a capitalistic one—manufacture is but a particular method of begetting relative surplus-value, or of augmenting at the expense of the laborer the self-expansion of capital—usually called social wealth, "Wealth of Nations," etc. It increases the social productive power of labor not only for the benefit of the capitalist instead of for that of the laborer, but it does this by crippling the individual laborers. It creates new conditions for the lordship of capital over labor. If, therefore, on the one hand it presents itself historically as progress and as a necessary phase in the economic development of society, on the other hand it is a refined and civilized method of exploitation.

Political economy, which as an independent science first sprang into being during the period of manufacture, views the social division of labor only from the standpoint of manufacture, and sees in it only the means of producing more commodities with a given quantity of labor and, consequently, of cheapening commodities and hurrying on the accumulation of capital. In most striking contrast with this accentuation of quantity and exchange-value, stands the attitude of the writers of classical antiquity, who hold exclusively by quality and use-value. In consequence of the separation of the social branches of production, commodities are better made, the various bents and talents of men select a suitable field, and without some restraint no important results can be obtained anywhere. Hence both product and producer are improved by division of labor. If the growth of the quantity produced is occasionally mentioned, this is only done with reference to the greater abundance of use-values.

★ ★ ★

During the manufacturing period proper, i.e., the period during which manufacture is the predominant form taken by capitalist production, many obstacles are opposed to the full development of the peculiar tendencies of manufacture. Although manufacture creates, as we have already seen, a simple separation of the laborers into skilled and unskilled simultaneously with their hierarchic arrangement in classes, the number of the unskilled laborers, owing to the preponderating influence of the skilled, remains very limited. Although it adapts the detail operations to the various degrees of maturity, strength, and development of the living instruments of labor,

thus conducive to exploitation of women and children, yet this tendency as a whole is wrecked on the habits and the resistance of the
male laborers. Although the splitting up of handicrafts lowers the
cost of forming the workman and thereby lowers his value, for the
more difficult detail work, a longer apprenticeship is necessary and,
even where it would be superfluous, is jealously insisted upon by
the workmen. In England, for instance, we find the laws of apprenticeship, with the seven years' probation, in full force down to
the end of the manufacturing period; and they are not thrown on
one side till the advent of Modern Industry. Since handicraft skill is
the foundation of manufacture, and since the mechanism of manufacture as a whole possesses no framework apart from the laborers
themselves, capital is constantly compelled to wrestle with the in-
subordination of the workmen.

CHAPTER XV

MACHINERY AND MODERN INDUSTRY

John Stuart Mill says in his *Principles of Political Economy*: "It is questionable if all the mechanical inventions yet made have lightened the day's toil of any human being." That is, however, by no means the aim of the capitalistic application of machinery. Like every other increase in the productiveness of labor, machinery is intended to cheapen commodities and, by shortening that portion of the working-day in which the laborer works for himself, to lengthen the other portion that he gives, without an equivalent, to the capitalist. In short, it is a means for producing surplus-value.

In manufacture, the revolution in the mode of production begins with the labor-power; in modern industry it begins with the instruments of labor.

SECTION 2–THE VALUE TRANSFERRED BY MACHINERY TO THE PRODUCT

Just as a man requires lungs to breathe, so he requires something that is work of man's hand, in order to consume physical forces productively. A water-wheel is necessary to exploit the force of water, and a steam engine to exploit the elasticity of steam. Once discovered, the law of the deviation of the magnetic needle in the field of an electric current, or the law of magnetisation of iron around which an electric current circulates, never cost a penny. But the exploitation of these laws for the purposes of telegraphy, etc., necessitates a costly and expensive apparatus. The tool, as we have seen, is not exterminated by the machine. From being a dwarf implement of the human organism, it expands and multiplies into the implement of mechanism created by man. Capital now sets the laborer to work not with a manual tool, but with a machine which itself handles the tools. Although, therefore, it is clear at first glance that, by incorporating both stupendous physical forces and the natural sciences with the process of production, Modern Industry raises the productiveness of labor to an extraordinary degree, it is by no means equally clear that this increased productive force is not, on the other hand, purchased by an increased expenditure of labor. Machinery, like every other component of constant capital, creates no new value, but yields up its own value to the product that it serves to beget. Insofar as the machine has value and, in consequence, parts with value to the product, it forms an element in the value of that product. Instead of being cheapened, the product is made dearer in proportion to the value of the machine. And it is clear that machines and systems of machinery, the characteristic instruments of labor of Modern Industry, are incomparably more loaded with value than the implements used in handicrafts and manufactures.

In the first place, it must be observed that the machinery, while always entering as a whole into the labor-process, enters into the value-begetting process only by bits. It never adds more value than it loses, on average, by wear and tear. Hence there is a great difference between the value of a machine and the value transferred in a given time by that machine to the product. The longer the life of the machine in the labor-process, the greater is that difference. It is true, no doubt, as we have already seen, that every instrument of labor enters as a whole into the labor-process, and only piecemeal, proportionally to its average daily loss by wear and tear into the value-begetting process. But this difference between the instrument as a whole and its daily wear and tear is much greater in a machine than in a tool because the machine, being made from more durable material, has a longer life; because its employment, being regulated by strictly scientific laws, allows of greater economy in the wear and tear of its parts and in the materials it consumes; and lastly, because its field of production is incomparably larger than that of a tool. The greater the productive power of the machinery compared with that of the tool, the greater is the extent of its gratuitous service compared with that of the tool. In Modern Industry man succeeded for the first time in making the product of his past labor work on a large scale gratuitously, like the forces of nature.

★ ★ ★

An analysis and comparison of the prices of commodities produced by handicrafts or manufacturers, and of the prices of the same commodities produced by machinery, shows generally that in the product of machinery, the value due to the instruments of labor increases relatively, but decreases absolutely. In other words, its absolute amount decreases, but its amount, relative to the total value of the product, of a pound of yarn, for instance, increases.[*]

It is evident that whenever it costs as much labor to produce a machine as is saved by the employment of that machine, there is nothing but a transposition of labor; consequently the total labor required to produce a commodity is not lessened or the productiveness of labor is not increased. It is clear, however, that there is a difference between the labor a machine costs, and the labor it saves,

---

[*]This portion of value which is added by the machinery decreases both absolutely and relatively when the machinery does away with horses and other animals that are employed as mere moving forces, and not as machines for changing the form of matter.

in other words, that the degree of its productiveness does not depend on the difference between its own value and the value of the implement it replaces. As long as the labor spent on a machine, and consequently the portion of its value added to the product, remains smaller than the value added by the workman to the product with his tool, there is always a difference of labor saved in favour of the machine. The productiveness of a machine is therefore measured by the human labor-power it replaces.

★ ★ ★

The use of machinery for the exclusive purpose of cheapening the product is limited in this way, that less labor must be expended in producing the machinery than is displaced by the employment of that machinery. For the capitalist, however, this use is still more limited. Instead of paying for the labor, he only pays the value of the labor-power employed; therefore, the limit to his using a machine is fixed by the difference between the value of the machine and the value of the labor-power replaced by it. Since the division of the day's work into necessary and surplus-labor differs in different countries, and even in the same country at different periods, or in different branches of industry; and further, since the actual wage of the laborer at one time sinks below the value of his labor-power, and at another rises above it, it is possible for the difference between the price of the machinery to vary very much, although the difference between the quantity of labor requisite to produce the machine and the total quantity replaced by it remain constant. But it is the former difference alone that determines the cost to the capitalist of producing a commodity and, through the pressure of competition, influences his action. Hence the invention these days of machines in England that are employed only in North America; just as in the sixteenth and seventeenth centuries, machines were invented in Germany to be used only in Holland, and just as many a

French invention of the eighteenth century was exploited in England alone.

SECTION 3–THE APPROXIMATE EFFECTS OF MACHINERY ON THE WORKMAN

The starting point of Modern Industry is the revolution in the instruments of labor, and this revolution attains its most highly developed form in the organized system of machinery in a factory. Let us consider some general effects of this revolution on the laborer himself.

★ ★ ★

Insofar as machinery dispenses with muscular power, it becomes a means of employing laborers of slight muscular strength, and those whose bodily development is incomplete but whose limbs are all the more supple. The labor of women and children was, therefore, the first thing sought for by capitalists who used machinery. That mighty substitute for labor and laborers forthwith changed into a means for increasing the number of wage-laborers by enrolling, under the direct sway of capital, every member of the workman's family, without distinction of age or sex. Compulsory work for the capitalist usurped the place not only of the children's play, but also of free labor at home within moderate limits for the support of the family.

The value of labor-power was determined not only by the labor-time necessary to maintain the individual adult laborer, but also by that necessary to maintain his family. Machinery, by throwing every member of that family onto the labor market, spreads the value of the man's labor-power over his whole family. It thus depreciates his labor-power. Thus we see that machinery, while augmenting the human material that forms the principal object of capital's exploiting power, at the same time raises the degree of exploitation.

Machinery also revolutionizes out and out the contract between the laborer and the capitalist which formally fixes their mutual relations. Taking the exchange of commodities as our basis, our first assumption was that capitalist and laborer met as free persons, as independent owners of commodities; the one possessing money and means of production, the other labor-power. But now the capitalist buys children and young persons under age. Previously, the workman sold his own labor power, which he disposed of nominally as a free agent. Now he sells wife and child. He has become a slave dealer.

★ ★ ★

If machinery be the most powerful means for increasing the productiveness of labor—i.e., for shortening the working time required in the production of a commodity, it becomes in the hands of capital the most powerful means, in those industries first invaded by it, for lengthening the working day beyond all bounds set by human nature. It creates, on the one hand, new conditions by which capital is enabled to give free scope to this, its constant tendency, and on the other hand, new motives with which to whet capital's appetite for the labor of others.

In the first place, in the form of machinery, the implements of labor become automatic, things moving and working independent of the work, man. They are thenceforth an industrial *perpetuum mobile* that would go on producing forever, had it not met with certain natural obstructions in the weak bodies and the strong wills of its human attendants.

★ ★ ★

Given the length of the working day, all other circumstances remaining the same, the exploitation of double the number of workmen demands not only a doubling of that part of constant capital which is invested in machinery and buildings, but also of that part which is laid out in raw material and auxiliary substances. The lengthening of the working day, on the other hand, allows production on an extended scale without any alteration in the amount of capital laid out on machinery and buildings. Not only is there, therefore, an increase of surplus-value, but the outlay necessary to obtain it diminishes. It is true that this takes place, more or less, with every lengthening of the working day; but in the case under consideration, the change is more marked, because the capital converted into the instruments of labor preponderates to a greater degree. The development of the factory system fixes a constantly increasing portion of the capital in a form in which, on the one hand, its value is capable of continual self-expansion, and in which, on the other hand, it loses both use-value and exchange-value whenever it loses contact with living labor.

★ ★ ★

Machinery produces relative surplus-value; not only by directly depreciating the value of labor-power, and by indirectly cheapening the same through cheapening the commodities that enter into its reproduction, but also, when it is first introduced sporadically into an industry, by converting the labor employed by the owner of that machinery into labor of a higher degree and greater efficacy, by raising the social value of the article produced above its individual value, and thus enabling the capitalist to replace the value of a day's labor-power by a smaller portion of the value of the day's product. During this transition period when the use of machinery is a sort of monopoly, the profits are therefore exceptional, and the capitalist endeavours to exploit thoroughly "the sunny time of this his first love" by prolonging the working-day as much as possible. The magnitude of the profit whets his appetite for more profit.

As the use of machinery becomes more general in a particular industry, the social value of the product sinks down to its individual value, and the law asserts itself that surplus-value does not arise from the labor-power that has been replaced by the machinery, but from the labor-power actually employed in working with the machinery. Surplus-values arises from the variable capital alone, and we saw that the-amount of surplus-value depends on two factors, *viz.*, the rate

of surplus-value and the number of the workmen simultaneously
employed. Given the length of the working day, the rate of surplus-
value is determined by the relative duration of the necessary labor
and of the surplus-labor in a day. The number of the laborers simultaneously employed depends, for its part, on the ratio of the
variable to the constant capital. Now, however much the use of
machinery may increase the surplus-labor at the expense of the necessary labor by heightening the productiveness of labor, it is clear
that it attains this result only by diminishing the number of workmen employed by a given amount of capital. It converts what was
formerly variable capital invested in labor-power into machinery
which, being constant capital, does not produce surplus-value.

★ ★ ★

If, then, the capitalistic employment of machinery on the one
hand supplies new and powerful motives to an excessive lengthening of the working day, and radically changes the methods of labor
and also the character of the social working organism in such a manner as to break down all opposition to this tendency, on the other
hand it produces, partly by opening out to the capitalist new strata
of the working class previously inaccessible to him, partly by setting
free the laborers it supplants, a surplus working population which is
compelled to submit to the dictation of capital.

★ ★ ★

The immoderate lengthening of the working day produced by
machinery in the hands of capital leads to a reaction on the part of
society, the very sources of whose life are menaced; and, thence, to
a normal working day whose length is fixed by law. Thenceforth
the intensification of labor develops into great importance.

★ ★ ★

It is self-evident that in proportion as the use of machinery
spreads, and the experience of a special class of workmen habitu-

ated to machinery accumulates, the rapidity and intensity of labor increase as a natural consequence. Apart from the increased yield of relative surplus-value through the heightened productiveness of labor, the same mass of value is now produced for the capitalist, say, by $3\frac{1}{3}$ hours of surplus labor, and $6\frac{2}{3}$ hours of necessary labor, as was previously produced by four hours of surplus labor and eight hours of necessary labor.

★ ★ ★

We now come to the question: How is the labor intensified? This is effected in two ways: by increasing the speed of the machinery, and by giving the workman more machinery to tend. Improved construction of the machinery is necessary, partly because without it greater pressure cannot be put on the workman, and partly because the shortened hours of labor force the capitalist to exercise the strictest watch over the cost of production. The improvements in the steam-engine have increased the piston speed, and at the same time have made it possible, by means of a greater economy of power, to drive with the same or even a smaller consumption of coal more machinery with the same engine. The improvements in the transmitting mechanism have lessened friction and, what so strikingly distinguishes modern from the older machinery, have reduced the diameter and weight of the shafting to a constantly decreasing minimum. Finally, the improvements in the operative machines have, while reducing their size, increased their speed and efficiency, as in the modern power-loom; or, while increasing the size of their frame-work, have also increased the extent and number of their working parts, as in spinning mules, or have added to the speed of these working parts by imperceptible alterations of detail, such as those which ten years ago increased the speed of the spindles in self-acting mules by one-fifth.

SECTION 4–THE FACTORY

Along with the tool, the skill of the workman in handling it passes over to the machine. The capabilities of the tool are emancipated from the restraints that are inseparable from human labor-power. Thereby the technical foundation on which is based the division of labor in manufacture is swept away. Hence, in the place of the hierarchy of specialized workmen that characterizes manufacture, there arises in the automatic factory a tendency to equalize and reduce to one and the same level every kind of work that has to be done by the minders of the machines; in the place of the artificially produced differentiations of the detail workmen, arises the natural differences of age and sex.

So far as division of labor reappears in the factory, it is primarily a distribution of the workmen among the specialized machines; and of masses of workmen, not however organized into groups, among the various departments of the factory, in each of which they work at a number of similar machines placed together; their cooperation, therefore, is only simple. The organized group, peculiar to manufacture, is replaced by the connection between the head workman and his few assistants. The essential division is into workmen who are actually employed on the machines (among whom are included a few who look after the engine), and into mere attendants (almost exclusively children) of these workmen. Among the attendants are reckoned more or less all "Feeders" who supply the machines with the material to be worked. In addition to these two principal classes, there is a numerically unimportant class of persons whose occupation it is to look after the whole of the machinery and repair it from time to time—such as engineers, mechanics, joiners, etc. This is a superior class of workmen, some of them scientifically educated, others brought up to a trade; it is distinct from the factory operative class, and merely aggregated to it. This division of labor is purely technical.

To work at a machine, the workman should be taught from childhood, in order that he may learn to adapt his own movements to the uniform and unceasing motion of an automaton. When the machinery, as a whole, forms a system of manifold machines working simultaneously and in concert, the cooperation based upon it requires the distribution of various groups of workmen among the different kinds of machines. But the employment of machinery does away with the necessity of crystallizing this distribution after the manner of Manufacture by the constant annexation of a particular man to a particular function. Since the motion of the whole system does not proceed from the workman, but from the machinery, a change of persons can take place at any time without an interruption of the work. At the same time that factory work exhausts the nervous system to the uttermost, it does away with the many-sided play of the muscles, and confiscates every atom of freedom, both in bodily and intellectual activity. Every kind of capitalist production insofar as it is not only a labor-process, but also a process of creating surplus-value, has this in common, that it is not the workman that employs the instruments of labor, but the instruments of labor that employ the workman. But it is only in the factory system that this inversion for the first time acquires technical and palpable reality. By means of its conversion into an automaton, the instrument of labor confronts the laborer during the labor-process in the shape of capital, of dead labor, that dominates and pumps dry living labor-power. The separation of the intellectual powers of production from the manual labor, and the conversion of those powers into the might of capital over labor, is, as we have already shown, finally completed by modern industry erected on the foundation of machinery. The special skill of each individual insignificant factory operative vanishes as an infinitesimal quantity before the science, the gigantic physical forces, and the mass of labor that are embodied in the factory mechanism and, together with that mechanism, constitute the power of the "master." The technical subordination of the workman to the uniform motion of the instruments of labor, and the peculiar composition of the body of workpeople, consisting as it does of individuals of both sexes and of all ages, give rise to a barrack discipline which is elaborated into a complete system in the factory, and which fully develops the before mentioned labor of overlooking, thereby dividing the workpeople into operatives and overlookers, into private soldiers and sergeants of an industrial army. The factory code in which capital formulates, like a private legislator, and at his own good will, his autocracy over his workpeople, unaccompanied by that division of responsibility in other matters so much approved of by the bourgeoisie, and unaccompanied by the still more approved representative system, this code is but the capitalistic caricature of that social regulation of the labor-process which becomes requisite in cooperation on a great scale, and in the employment in common of instruments of labor and especially of machinery. The place of the slave driver's lash is taken by the overlooker's book of penalties. All punishments naturally resolve themselves into fines and deductions from wages so that a violation of his laws is, if possible, more profitable to him than the keeping of them.

★ ★ ★

Is Fourier wrong when he calls factories "tempered bagnos?"

SECTION 6–THE THEORY OF COMPENSATION AS REGARDS THE WORKPEOPLE DISPLACED BY MACHINERY

James Mill, MacCulloch, Torrens, Senior, John Stuart Mill, and a whole series of bourgeois political economists insist that all machinery that displaces workmen simultaneously and necessarily sets free an amount of capital adequate to employ the same identical workmen.

★ ★ ★

The real facts, which are travestied by the optimism of economists, are as follows: The laborers, when driven out of the workshop by the machinery, are thrown upon the labor market, and there add to the number of workmen at the disposal of the capitalists. The laborers that are thrown out of work in any branch of industry can no doubt seek employment in some other branch. If they find it, and thus renew the bond between them and the means of subsistence, this takes place only by the intermediary of a new and additional capital that is seeking investment; not at all by the intermediary of the capital that formerly employed them and was afterwards converted into machinery. And even should they find employment, what a poor look-out is theirs! Crippled as they are by division of labor, these poor devils are worth so little outside their old trade that they cannot find admission into any industries except a few of inferior kind that are over-supplied with underpaid workmen. Further, every branch of industry attracts each year a new stream of men who furnish a contingent from which to fill up vacancies, and to draw a supply for expansion. As soon as machinery sets free a part of the workmen employed in a given branch of industry, the reserve men are also diverted into new channels of employment and become absorbed in other branches; meanwhile the original victims, during the period of transition, for the most part starve and perish.

★ ★ ★

Although machinery necessarily throws men out of work in those industries into which it is introduced, yet it may, notwithstanding this, bring about an increase of employment in other industries. This effect, however, has nothing in common with the so-called theory of compensation. Since every article produced by a machine is cheaper than a similar article produced by hand, we deduce the following infallible law: If the total quantity of the article produced by machinery is equal to the total quantity of the article previously produced by a handicraft or by manufacture and now made by machinery, then the total labor expended is diminished. The new labor spent on the instruments of labor, on the machinery, on the coal, and so on, must necessarily be less than the labor displaced by the use of the machinery; otherwise the product of the machine would be as dear, or dearer, than the product of the manual labor. But, as a matter of fact, the total quantity of the article produced by machinery with a diminished number of workmen, instead of remaining equal to, by far exceeds the total quantity of the hand-made article that has been displaced.

★ ★ ★

Hence, as the use of machinery extends in a given industry, the immediate effect is to increase production in the other industries that furnish the first with means of production. How far employment is thereby found for an increased number of men depends, given the length of the working-day and the intensity of labor, on the composition of the capital employed, i.e., on the ratio of its constant to its variable component. This ratio, in its turn, varies considerably with the extent to which machinery has already seized on, or is then seizing on, those trades.

SECTION 10–MODERN INDUSTRY
AND AGRICULTURE

If the use of machinery in agriculture is for the most part free from the injurious physical effect it has on the factory operative, its action in superseding the laborers is more intense, and finds less resistance.

★ ★ ★

In the sphere of agriculture, modern industry has a more revolutionary effect than elsewhere for this reason—that it annihilates the peasant, that bulwark of the old society, and replaces him by the wage laborer. Thus the desire for social changes and the class antagonisms are brought to the same level in the country as in the towns. The irrational, old-fashioned methods of agriculture are replaced by scientific ones. Capitalist production completely tears asunder the old bond of union which held together agriculture and manufacture in their infancy. But at the same time it creates the material conditions for a higher synthesis in the future, viz., the union of agriculture and industry on the basis of the more perfected forms they have each acquired during their temporary separation. Capitalist production, by collecting the population in great centers and causing an ever increasing preponderance of the town population, on the one hand concentrates the historical motive-power of society; on the other hand, it disturbs the circulation of matter between man and the soil, i.e., prevents the return to the soil of its elements consumed by man in the form of food and clothing; it therefore violates the conditions necessary to lasting fertility of the soil. By this action it destroys at the same time the health of the town laborer and the intellectual life of the rural laborer. But while upsetting the naturally grown conditions for the maintenance of that circulation of matter, it imperiously calls for its restoration as a system, as a regulating law of social production, and under a form appropriate to the full development of the human race. In agriculture as in manufacture, the transformation of production under the sway of capital means, at the same time, the martyrdom of the producer; the instrument of labor becomes the means of enslaving, exploiting, and impoverishing the laborer; the social combination and organization of labor-processes is turned into an organized mode of crushing the workman's individual vitality, freedom, and independence. The dispersion of the rural laborers over larger areas breaks their power of resistence while concentration increases that of the town operatives. In modern agriculture, as in the urban industries, the increased productiveness and quantity of the labor set in motion are bought at the cost of laying waste and consuming by disease labor-power itself. Moreover, all progress in capitalistic agriculture is a progress in the art not only of robbing the laborer, but of robbing the soil; all progress in increasing the fertility of the soil for a given time is progress towards ruining the lasting sources of that fertility. The more a country starts its development on the foundation of modern industry, like the United States, for example, the more rapid is this process of destruction. Capitalist production, therefore, develops technology and combines together various processes into a social whole only by sapping the original sources of all wealth—the soil and the laborer.

PART VI

Wages

CHAPTER XIX

THE TRANSFORMATION OF THE VALUE (AND RESPECTIVELY THE PRICE) OF LABOR-POWER INTO WAGES

O N THE SURFACE of bourgeois society the wage of the laborer appears as the price of labor, a certain quantity of money that is paid for a certain quantity of labor. Thus people speak of the value of labor and call its expression in money its necessary or natural price. On the other hand they speak of the market prices of labor, i.e., prices oscillating above or below its natural price.

But what is the value of a commodity? The objective form of the social labor expended in its production. And how do we measure the quantity of this value? By the quantity of the labor contained in it. How then is the value, e.g., of a 12 hours' working day, to be determined? By the 12 working hours contained in a working day, of 12 hours, which is an absurd tautology.

In order to be sold as a commodity in the market, labor must in all events exist before it is sold. But could the laborer give it an independent objective existence, he would sell a commodity and not labor.

Apart from these contradictions, a direct exchange of money, i.e., of realized labor, with living labor would either do away with the law of value which only begins to develop itself freely on the basis of capitalist production, or do away with capitalist production itself, which rests directly on wage-labor. The working day of 12 hours embodies itself, e.g., in a money value of 6s. Either equivalents are exchanged, and then the laborer receives 6s. for 12 hours' labor; the price of his labor would be equal to the price of his product. In this case he produces no surplus-value for the buyer of his labor; the 6s. are not transformed into capital, and the basis of capitalist production vanishes. But it is on this very basis that he sells his labor and that his labor is wage-labor. Or else he receives for 12 hours' labor less than 6s., i.e., less than 12 hours' labor. Twelve hours' labor are exchanged against 10, 6, etc., hours' labor. This equalization of unequal quantities does not merely eliminate the determination of value; such a self-destructive contradiction cannot even be enunciated or formulated as a law.

It is of no avail to deduce the exchange of more labor against less from their difference of form, the one being realized, the other living. This is the more absurd as the value of a commodity is determined not by the quantity of labor actually realized in it, but by the quantity of living labor necessary for its production. A commodity represents, say 6 working hours. If an invention is made by which it can be produced in 3 hours, the value, even of the commodity already produced, falls by half. It represents now 3 hours of social labor instead of the 6 formerly necessary. It is the quantity of labor required for its production, not the realized form of that labor, by which the amount of the value of a commodity is determined.

That which comes directly face to face with the possessor of money on the market is in fact not labor, but the laborer. What the latter sells is his labor-power. As soon as his labor actually begins, it has already ceased to belong to him; it can therefore no longer be sold by him. Labor is the substance, and the immanent measure of value, but *has itself no value.*

In the expression "value of labor," the idea of value is not only completely obliterated, but actually reversed. It is an expression as imaginary as the value of the earth. These imaginary expressions arise, however, from the relations of production themselves. They are categories for the phenomenal forms of essential relations. That in their appearance things often represent themselves in inverted form is pretty well known in every science except political economy.

Classical political economy borrowed from everyday life the category "price of labor" without further criticism, and then simply asked the question, "How is this price determined?" It soon recognized that in the change in the relations of demand and supply explained in regard to the price of labor, as in all other commodities, nothing except its price changes, i.e., the oscillations of the market price above or below a certain mean. If demand and supply balance, the oscillation of prices ceases, all other conditions remaining the same. But then demand and supply also cease to explain anything. The price of labor at the moment when demand and supply are in equilibrium is its natural price, determined independently of the relation of demand and supply. And how this price is determined is just the question. Or a larger period of oscillations in the market-price is taken, e.g., a year, and they are found to cancel each other, leaving a mean average quantity, a relatively constant magnitude. This had naturally to be determined other than by its own compensating variations. This price which always finally predominates over the accidental market-prices of labor and regulates them, this "necessary price" (physiocrats) or "natural price" of labor (Adam Smith) can, as with all other commodities, be nothing else than its value expressed in money. In this way political economy expected to penetrate athwart the accidental prices of labor to the value of labor. As with other commodities, this value was determined by the cost of production. But what is the cost of production—of the laborer, i.e., the cost of producing or reproducing the laborer himself? This question unconsciously substituted itself in political economy for the original one; for the search after the cost of production of labor as such turned in a circle and never left the spot.

What economists therefore call value of labor is in fact the value of labor-power as it exists in the personality of the laborer, which is as different from its function, labor, as a machine if from the work it performs. Occupied with the difference between the market-price of labor and its so-called value, with the relation of this value to the rate of profit, and to the values of the commodities produced by means of labor, etc., they never discovered that the course of the analysis had led not only from the market prices of labor to its presumed value, but had led to the resolution of this value of labor itself into the value of labor-power. Classical economy never arrived at a consciousness of the results of its own analysis; it accepted uncritically the categories "value of labor," "natural price of labor," etc., as final and as adequate expressions for the value-relation under consideration, and was thus led, as will be seen later, into inextricable confusion and contradiction, while it offered to the vulgar economists a secure basis of operations for their shallowness, which on principle worships appearances only.

Let us next see how value (and price) of labor-power present themselves in this transformed condition as wages.

We know that the daily value of labor-power is calculated upon a certain length of the laborer's life to which, again, corresponds a certain length of working-day. Assume the habitual working-day as 12 hours, the daily value of labor-power as 3s., the expression in money of a value that embodies 6 hours of labor. If the laborer receives 3s., then he receives the value of his labor-power functioning through 12 hours. If, now, this value of a day's labor-power is expressed as the value of a day's labor itself, we have the formula: Twelve hours' labor has a value of 3s. The value of labor-power thus determines the value of labor or, expressed in money, its necessary price. If, on the other hand, the price of labor-power differs from its value, in like manner the price of labor differs from its so-called value.

As the value of labor is only an irrational expression for the value of labor-power, it follows, of course, that the value of labor must always be less than the value it produces, for the capitalist always makes labor-power work longer than is necessary for the reproduction of its own value. In the above example, the value of the labor-power that functions through 12 hours is 3s., a value for the reproduction of which 6 hours are required. The value which the labor-power produces is, on the other hand, 6s., because it, in fact, functions during 12 hours, and the value it produces depends not on its own value, but on the length of time it is in action. Thus, we have a result absurd at first sight—that labor which creates a value of 6s. possesses a value of 3s.

We see, further: The value of 3s. by which a part only of the working day—i.e., 6 hours' labor—is paid for, appears as the value or price of the whole working-day of 12 hours, which thus includes 6 hours unpaid for. The wage-form thus extinguishes every trace of the division of the working-day into necessary labor and surplus-labor, into paid and unpaid labor. All labor appears as paid labor. In the corvée, the labor of the worker for himself and his compulsory labor for his lord differ in space and time in the clearest possible way. In slave-labor, even that part of the working-day in which the slave is only replacing the value of his own means of existence, in which, therefore, in fact, he works for himself alone, appears as labor for his master. All the slave's labor appears as unpaid labor. In wage-labor, on the contrary, even surplus-labor, or unpaid labor, appears as paid. There the property-relation conceals the labor of the slave for himself; here the money-relation conceals the unrequited labor of the wage-laborer.

Hence, we may understand the decisive importance of the transformation of value and price of labor-power into the form of wages, or into the value and price of labor itself. This phenomenal form, which makes the actual relation invisible and, indeed, shows the direct opposite of that relation, forms the basis of all the juridicial notions of both laborer and capitalist, of all the mystifications of the capitalistic mode of production, of all its illusions as to liberty, of all the apologetic shifts of the vulgar economists.

If history took a long time to get to the bottom of the mystery of wages, nothing, on the other hand, is more easy to understand than the necessity, the *raison d'être*, of this phenomenon.

The exchange between capital and labor at first presents itself to the mind in the same guise as the buying and selling of all other commodities. The buyer gives a certain sum of money, the seller an article of a nature different from money.

Further, exchange-value and use-value, being intrinsically incommensurable magnitudes, the expressions "value of labor," "price of labor," do not seem more irrational than the expressions "value of cotton," "price of cotton." Moreover, the laborer is paid after he has given his labor. In its function of means of payment, money realizes subsequently the value or price of the article supplied—i.e., in this particular case, the value or price of the labor supplied. Finally, the use-value supplied by the laborer to the capitalist is not, in fact, his labor-power, but its function, some definite useful labor, the work of tailoring, shoemaking, spinning, etc. That this same labor is, on the other hand, the universal value-creating element, and thus possesses a property by which it differs from all other commodities, is beyond the cognizance of the ordinary mind.

Let us put ourselves in the place of the laborer who receives for 12 hours' labor, say the value produced by 6 hours' labor, say 3s. For him, in fact, his 12 hours' labor is the means of buying the 3s. The value of his labor-power may vary with the value of his usual means of subsistence, from 3 to 4 shillings, or from 3 to 2 shillings; or, if the value of his labor-power remains constant, its price may, in consequence of changing relations of demand and supply, rise to 4s. or fall to 2s. But he always gives 12 hours of labor. Every change in the amount of the equivalent that he receives appears to him, therefore, necessarily as a change in the value or price of his 12 hours' work. This circumstance misled Adam Smith, who treated the working-day as a constant quantity, to the assertion that the value of labor is constant, although the value of the means of subsistence may vary, and the same working-day, therefore, may represent itself in more or less money for the laborer.

Let us consider, on the other hand, the capitalist. He wishes to receive as much labor as possible for as little money as possible. Practically, therefore, the only thing that interests him is the difference between the price of labor-power and the value which its function creates. But, then, he tries to buy all commodities as cheaply as possible, and always accounts for his profit by simple cheating, by buying under and selling over the value. Hence, he never comes to see that, if such a thing as the value of labor really existed and were really paid this value, no capital would exist, his money would not be turned into capital.

Moreover, the actual movement of wages presents phenomena which seem to prove that it's not the value of labor-power that is paid, but the value of its function, of labor itself. We may reduce these phenomena to two great classes: (1) Change of wages with the changing length of the working-day. One might as well conclude that it's not the value of a machine that is paid, but that of its working, because it costs more to hire a machine for a week than for a day. (2) The individual difference in the wages of different laborers who do the same kind of work. We find this individual difference, but are not deceived by it, in the system of slavery where, frankly and openly, without any circumlocution, labor-power itself is sold. But in the slave system, the advantage of a labor-power above the average, and the disadvantage of a labor-power below the average, affects the slave-owner; in the wage-labor system it affects the laborer himself, because his labor-power is, in the one case, sold by himself, in the other, by a third person.

For the rest, in respect to the phenomenal form "value and price of labor," or "wages," as contrasted with the essential relation manifested therein, viz., the value and price of labor-power, the same difference holds that holds in respect to all phenomena and their hidden substratum. The former appear directly and spontaneously as current modes of thought; the latter must first be discovered by science. Classical political economy nearly touches the true relation of things without, however, consciously formulating it. This it cannot so long as it sticks in its bourgeois skin.

CHAPTER XX

TIME-WAGES

Wages themselves again take many forms, a fact not recognizable in the ordinary economical treatises which, exclusively interested in the material side of the question, neglect every difference of form. An exposition of all these forms, however, belongs to the special study of wage-labor, not therefore to this work. Still the two fundamental forms must be briefly worked out here.

The sale of labor-power, as will be remembered, takes place for a definite period of time. The converted form under which the daily, weekly, etc., value of labor-power presents itself is hence that of time-wages, and therefore day-wages, etc.

Next it is to be noted that the laws set forth in the seventeenth chapter on the changes in the relative magnitudes of price of labor-power and surplus-value pass, by a simple transformation of form, into laws of wages. Similarly the distinction between the exchange-value of labor-power and the sum of the necessities of life into which this value is converted now reappears as the distinction between nominal and real wages. It would be useless to repeat here, with regard to the phenomenal form, what has been already worked out in the substantial form. We limit ourselves therefore to a few points characteristic of time-wages.

The sum of money which the laborer receives for his daily or weekly labor forms the amount of his nominal wages, or of his wages estimated in value. But it is clear that according to the length of the working-day, that is, according to the amount of actual labor daily supplied, the same daily or weekly wage may represent very different prices of labor, i.e., very different sums of money for the same quantity of labor. We must, therefore, in considering time-wages, again distinguish between the sum total of the daily or weekly wages, etc., and the price of labor. How then to find this price, i.e., the money-value of a given quantity of labor? The average price of labor is found when the average daily value of the labor-power is divided by the average number of hours in the working-day. If, e.g., the daily value of labor-power is 3 shillings, the value of the product of 6 working hours, and if the working-day is 12 hours, the price of 1 working hour is 3/12 shillings=3d. The price of the working hour thus found serves as the unit measure for the price of labor.

It follows therefore that the daily and weekly wages, etc., may remain the same, although the price of labor falls constantly. If, e.g., the habitual working-day is 10 hours and the daily value of the labor-power 3s., the price of the working hour is $3 \frac{3}{5}$ d. It falls to 3d. as soon as the working-day rises to 12 hours, to $2 \frac{2}{5}$ d. as soon as it rises to 15 hours. Daily or weekly wages remain, despite all this, unchanged. On the contrary, the daily or weekly wages may rise, although the price of labor remains constant or even falls. If, e.g., the working day is 10 hours, and the daily value of labor-power 3 shillings, the price of one working hour is $3 \frac{3}{5}$ d. If the laborer in consequence of increasing trade works 12 hours, the price of labor remaining the same, his daily wage now rises to 3 shillings $7 \frac{1}{5}$ d. without any variation in the price of labor. The same result might follow if, instead of the extensive amount of labor, its intensive amount increased. The rise of the nominal daily or weekly wages may therefore be accompanied by a price of labor that remains stationary or falls. The same holds as to the income of the laborer's family, as soon as the quantity of labor expended by the head of the family is increased by the labor of the members of his family. There are, therefore, methods of lowering the price of labor independent of the reduction of the nominal daily or weekly wages.

As a general law it follows that, given the amount of daily, weekly labor, etc., the daily or weekly wages depend on the price of labor, which itself varies either with the value of labor-power or with the difference between its price and its value. Given, on the other hand, the price of labor, the daily or weekly wages depend on the quantity of the daily or weekly labor.

The unit measure for time-wages, the price of the working-hour, is the quotient of the value of a day's labor-power, divided by the number of hours of the average working-day. Let the latter be 12 hours, and the daily value of labor-power 3 shillings, the value of the product of 6 hours of labor. Under these circumstances the price of a working-hour is 3d., and the value produced in it is 6d. If the laborer is now employed less than 12 hours (or less than 6 days in the week), e.g., only 6 or 8 hours, he receives, with this price of labor, only 2s. or 1s, 6d. a day. As our hypothesis stipulates he must work on average 6 hours daily in order to produce a day's wage corresponding merely to the value of his labor-power, and as according to the same hypothesis he works only half of every hour for himself and half for the capitalist, it is clear that he cannot obtain for himself the value of the product of 6 hours if he is employed less than 12 hours. In previous chapters we saw the destructive consequences of over-work; here we find the sources of the sufferings that result to the laborer from his insufficient employment.

If the hour's wage is fixed so that the capitalist does not bind himself to pay a day's or a week's wage, but only to pay wages for the hours during which he chooses to employ the laborer, he can employ him for a shorter time than that which is originally the basis of the calculation of the hour-wage, of the unit-measure of the price of labor. Since this unit is determined by the ratio

$$\frac{daily\ value\ of\ labor\text{-}power}{\text{working-day of a given number of hours}}$$

it, of course, loses all the meaning as soon as the working day ceases to contain a definite number of hours. The connection between the paid and the unpaid labor is destroyed. The capitalist can now wring from the laborer a certain quantity of surplus-labor without allowing him the labor-time necessary for his own subsistence. He can annihilate all regularity of employment, and according to his own convenience, caprice, and the interest of the moment, make the most enormous over-work alternate with relative or absolute cessation of work. He can, under the pretence of paying "the normal price of labor," abnormally lengthen the working-day without any corresponding compensation to the laborer. Hence the perfectly rational revolt in 1860 of the London laborers, employed in the building trades, against the attempt of the capitalists to impose on them this sort of wage by the hour. The legal limitation of the working-day puts an end to such mischief, although not, of course, to the diminution of employment caused by the competition of machinery, by changes in the quality of the laborers employed, and by crisis partial or general.

With an increasing daily or weekly wage the price of labor may remain nominally constant, and yet may fall below its normal level. This occurs every time that, the price of labor (reckoned per working hour) remaining constant, the working-day is prolonged beyond its customary length. If in the fraction:

$$\frac{daily\ value\ of\ labor\text{-}power}{\text{working day}}$$

the denominator increases, the numerator increases yet more rapidly. The value of labor-power, as dependent on its wear and tear, increases with the duration of its functioning, and in more rapid proportion than the increase of that duration. In many branches of industry where time-wage is the general rule without legal limits to the working-time, the habit has, therefore, spontaneously developed of regarding the working-day as normal only up to a certain point, e.g., up to the expiration of the tenth hour ("normal working-day," "the day's work," "the regular hours of work"). Beyond this limit the working-time is over-time and is, taking the hour as unit-measure, paid better ("extra pay"), although often in a proportion ridiculously small. The normal working-day exists here as a fraction of the actual working-day, and the latter, often during the whole year, lasts longer than the former. The increase in the price of labor with the extension of the working-day beyond a certain normal limit takes such a shape in various British industries that the low price of labor during the so-called normal time compels the laborer to work during the better paid overtime if he wishes to obtain a sufficient wage at all. Legal limitation of the working-day puts an end to these amenities.

It is a fact generally known that, the longer the working-days in any branch of industry, the lower are the wages. A. Redgrave, factory-inspector, illustrates this by a comparative review of the 20 years from 1839–1859, according to which wages rose in the factories under the 10 hours' law, whilst they fell in the factories in which the work lasted 14 to 15 hours daily.

From the law: "the price of labor being given, the daily or weekly wage depends on the quantity of labor expended," it follows, first of all, that the lower the price of labor, the greater must be the quantity of labor, or the longer must be the working-day for the laborer to secure even a miserable average-wage. The lowness of the price of labor acts here as a stimulus to the extension of the labor-time.

On the other hand, the extension of the working-time produces, in its turn, a fall in the price of labor, and with this a fall in the day's or week's wages.

The determination of the price of labor by:

$$\frac{\textit{daily value of labor-power}}{\text{working-day of a given number of hours}}$$

shows that a mere prolongation of the working-day lowers the price of labor, if no compensation steps in. But the same circumstances which allow the capitalist in the long run to prolong the working-day also allow him first, and compel him finally, to nominally lower the price of labor until the total price of the increased number of hours is lowered and, therefore, the daily or weekly wage. Reference to two circumstances is sufficient here. If one man does the work of 1 $^1/_2$ or 2 men, the supply of labor increases, although the supply of labor-power on the market remains constant. The competition thus created between the laborers allows the capitalist to beat down the price of labor, whilst the falling price of labor arrows him, on the other hand, to screw up still further the working-time. Soon, however, this command over abnormal quantities of unpaid labor, i.e., quantities in excess of the average social amount, becomes a source of competition among the capitalists themselves. A part of the price of the commodity consists of the price of labor. The unpaid part of the labor-price need not be reckoned in the price of the commodity. It may be presented to the buyer. This is the first step to which competition leads. The second step to which it drives is to exclude also from the selling-price of the commodity at least a part of the abnormal surplus-value created by the extension of the working-day. In this way an abnormally low selling-price of the commodity arises, at first sporadically, and becomes fixed by degrees; a lower selling price which henceforward becomes the constant basis of a miserable wage for an excessive working-time, as originally it was the product of these very circumstances.

CHAPTER XXI

PIECE-WAGES

WAGES BY THE piece are nothing else than a converted form of wages by time, just as wages by time are a converted form of the value or price of labor-power.

★ ★ ★

Piece-wages do not, in fact, distinctly express any relation of value. It is not, therefore, a question of measuring the value of the piece by the working-time incorporated in it, but on the contrary of measuring the working-time the laborer has expended by the number of pieces he has produced. In time-wages the labor is measured by its immediate duration, in piece-wages by the quantity of products in which the labor has embodied itself during a given time. The price of labor-time itself is finally determined by the equation; value of a day's labor=daily value of labor-power. Piecewage is, therefore, only a modified form of time-wage.

★ ★ ★

In time-wages, with few exceptions, the same wage holds for the same kind of work, whilst in piece-wages, though the price of the working-time is measured by a certain quantity of product, the day's or week's wage will vary with the individual differences of the laborers, of whom one supplies in a given time the minimum of product only, another the average, a third more than the average.

With regard to actual receipts, there is therefore great variety according to the different skill, strength, energy, staying-power, etc., of the individual laborers. Of course this does not alter the general relations between capital and wage-labor.

★ ★ ★

Piece-wage is the form of wages most in harmony with the capitalist mode of production. Although by no means new—it figures side by side with time-wages officially in the French and English labor statutes of the fourteenth century—it only conquers a larger field for action during the period of Manufacture, properly so-called.

★ ★ ★

In the workshops under the Factory Acts, piece-wage becomes the general rule, because capital there can only increase the efficacy of the working-day by intensifying labor.

With the changing productiveness of labor the same quantum of product represents a varying working-time. Therefore, piece-wage also varies, for it is the money expression of a determined working time. In other words, piece-wage is lowered in the same proportion as the number of the pieces produce in the same time rises, and therefore as the working time spent on the same piece falls. This change in piece-wage, so far purely nominal, leads to constant battles between capitalist and laborer, either because (1): the capitalist uses it as a pretext for actually lowering the price of labor, or because increased productive power of labor is accompanied by an increased intensity of the same; or because (2): the laborer takes seriously the appearance of piece-wages, viz., that his product is paid for, and not his labor-power, and therefore revolts against a lowering of wages unaccompanied by a lowering in the selling price of the commodity.

The capitalist rightly knocks on the head such pretensions as gross errors as to the nature of wage-labor. He cries out against this usurping attempt to lay taxes on the advance of industry, and declares roundly that the productiveness of labor does not concern the laborer at all.

CHAPTER XXII

NATIONAL DIFFERENCES
OF WAGES

The simple translation of the value or of the price of labor-power into the exoteric form of wages transforms all these laws into laws of the fluctuations of wages. That which appears in these fluctuations of wages within a single country as a series of varying combinations, may appear in different countries as contemporaneous difference of national wages. In the comparison of the wages in different nations, we must therefore take into account all the factors that determine changes in the amount of the value of labor-power; the price and the extent of the prime necessities of life as naturally and historically developed, the cost of training the laborers, the part played by the labor of women and children, the productiveness of labor, its extensive and intensive magnitude. Even the most superficial comparison requires the reduction first of the average day-wage for the same trades, in different countries, to a uniform working-day. After this reduction to the same terms of the day-wages, time-wage must again be translated into piece-wage, as the latter only can be a measure both of the productivity and the intensity of labor.

In every country there is a certain average intensity of labor, below which the labor for the production of a commodity requires more than the socially necessary time, and therefore does not reckon as labor of normal quality. Only a degree of intensity above the national average affects, in a given country, the measure of value of the mere duration of the working time. This is not the case on the universal market, whose integral parts are the individual countries. The average intensity of labor changes from country to country; here it is greater, there less. These national averages form a scale whose unit of measure is the average unit of universal labor. The more intense national labor, therefore, as compared with the less intense, produces in the same time more value, which expresses itself in more money.

But the law of value in its international application is yet more modified by this, that on the world-market the more productive national labor reckons also as the more intense, so long as the more productive nation is not compelled by competition to lower the selling price of its commodities to the level of their value.

In proportion as capitalist production is developed in a country, in the same proportion do the national intensity and productivity of labor there rise above the international level. The different quantities of commodities of the same kind, produced in different countries in the same working time, have therefore unequal international values which are expressed in different prices, i.e., in sums of money varying according to international values. The relative value of money will, therefore, be less in the nation with a more developed capitalist mode of production than in the nation with less developed. It follows, then, that the nominal wages, the equivalent of labor-power expressed in money, will also be higher in the first nation than in the second; which does not at all prove that this holds also for the real wages, i.e., for the means of subsistence placed at the disposal of the laborer.

But even apart from these relative differences of the value of money in different countries, it will be found frequently that the daily or weekly, etc., wage in the first nation is higher than in the second, whilst the relative price of labor, i.e., the price of labor as compared both with surplus-value and with the value of the product, stands higher in the second than in the first.

PART VII

The Accumulation of Capital

The conversion of a sum of money into means of production and labor-power is the first step taken by the quantum of value that is going to function as capital. This conversion takes place in the market within the sphere of circulation. The second step, the process of production, is complete as soon as the means of production have been converted into commodities whose value exceeds that of their component parts and, therefore, contains the capital originally advanced, plus a surplus-value. These commodities must then be thrown into circulation. They must be sold, their value realized in money, this money afresh converted into capital, and so over and over again. This circular movement, in which the same phases are continually gone through in succession, forms the circulation of capital.

The first condition of accumulation is that the capitalist must have contrived to sell his commodities, and to reconvert into capital the greater part of the money so received. In the following pages we shall assume that capital circulates in its normal way.

The capitalist who produces surplus-value—i.e., who extracts unpaid labor directly from the laborers and fixes it in commodities, is indeed the first appropriator, but by no means the ultimate owner, of this surplus-value. He has to share it with capitalists, with

landowners, etc., who fulfill other functions in the complex of social production. Surplus-value, therefore, splits up into various parts.
Its fragments fall to various categories of persons and take various
forms independent of each other, such as profit, interest, merchants'
profit, rent, etc.

On the one hand, then, we assume that the capitalist sells at their
value the commodities he has produced without concerning ourselves either about the new forms that capital assumes while in the
sphere of circulation, or about the concrete conditions of reproduction hidden under these forms. On the other hand, we treat the
capitalist producer as owner of the entire surplus-value, or better
perhaps, as the representative of all the sharers with him in the
booty. We, therefore, first of all consider accumulation from an abstract point of view—i.e., as a mere phase in the actual process of
production.

So far as accumulation takes place, the capitalist must have succeeded in selling his commodities and in reconverting the sale-
money into capital. Moreover, the breaking-up of surplus-value
into fragments neither alters its nature nor the conditions under
which it becomes an element of accumulation. Whatever be the
proportion of surplus-value which the industrial capitalist retains for
himself or yields up to others, he is the one who, in the first instance, appropriates it. We, therefore, assume no more what actually takes place. On the other hand, the simple fundamental form
of the process of accumulation is obscured by the incident of the
circulation which brings it about, and by the splitting up of surplus-
value. An exact analysis of the process, therefore, demands that we
should, for a time, disregard all phenomena that hide the play of its
inner mechanism.

CHAPTER XXIII

SIMPLE REPRODUCTION

Whatever the form of the process of production in a society, it must be a continuous process, must continue to go periodically through the same phases. A society can no more cease to produce than it can cease to consume. When viewed, therefore, as a connected whole and as undergoing incessant renewal, every social process of production is, at the same time, a process of reproduction.

The conditions of production are also those of reproduction. No society can go on producing, in other words, no society can reproduce, unless it constantly reconverts a part of its products into means of production, or elements of fresh products. All other circumstances remaining the same, the only mode by which it can reproduce its wealth and maintain it at one level is by replacing the means of production—i.e., the instruments of labor, the raw material, and the auxiliary substances consumed in the course of the year—by an equal quantity of the same kind of articles; these must be separated from the mass of the yearly products and thrown afresh into the process of production. Hence, a definite portion of each year's product belongs to the domain of production. Destined for productive consumption from the very first, this portion exists, for the most part, in the shape of articles totally unfitted for individual consumption.

If production is capitalistic in form, so, too, will be reproduction. Just as in the former the labor-process figures but as a means towards the self-expansion of capital, so in the latter it figures but as a means of reproducing as capital—i.e., as self-expanding value—the value advanced. It is only because his money constantly functions as capital that the economical guise of a capitalist attaches to a man. If, for instance, a sum of £100 has this year been converted into capital, and produced a surplus-value of £20, it must continue during next year, and subsequent years, to repeat the same operation. As a periodic increment of the capital advanced, or periodic fruit of capital in process, surplus-value acquires the form of a revenue flowing out of capital.

If this revenue serves the capitalist only as a fund to provide for his consumption and is spent as periodically as it is gained, then, *coeteris paribus*, simple reproduction will take place. And although this reproduction is a mere repetition of the process of production on the old scale, this mere repetition, or continuity, gives a new character to the process, or rather causes the disappearance of some apparent characteristics which it possessed as an isolated discontinuous process.

The purchase of labor-power for a fixed period is the prelude to the process of production; and this prelude is constantly repeated when the stipulated term comes to an end, when a definite period of production, such as a week or a month, has elapsed. But the laborer is not paid until after he has expended his labor-power, and realized in commodities not only its value, but surplus-value. He has, therefore, produced not only surplus-value, which we for the present regard as a fund to meet the private consumption of the capitalist, but he has also produced, before it flows back to him in the shape of wages, the fund out of which he himself is paid the variable capital; and his employment lasts only so long as he continues to reproduce this fund. What flows back to the laborer in the shape of wages is a portion of the product that is continuously reproduced by him. The capitalist, it is true, pays him in money, but this money is merely the transmuted form of the product of his labor. While he is converting a portion of the means of production into products, a portion of his former product is being turned into money. It is his labor of last week, or of last year, that pays for his labor-power this week or this year. The illusion begotten by the intervention of money vanishes immediately if, instead of taking a single capitalist and a single laborer, we take the class of capitalists and the class of laborers as a whole. The capitalist class is constantly giving to the laboring class order-notes, in the form of money, on a portion of the commodities produced by the latter and appropriated by the former. The laborers give these order-notes back constantly to the capitalist class, and in this way get their share of their own product. The transaction is veiled by the commodity-form of the product and the money-form of the commodity.

Variable capital is therefore only a particular historical form of appearance of the fund for providing the necessities of life, or the labor-fund which the laborer requires for the maintenance of himself and family and which, whatever may be the system of social production, he must himself produce and reproduce. If the labor-fund constantly flows to him in the form of money that pays for his labor, it is because the product he has created moves constantly away from him in the form of capital. But all this does not alter the fact that it is the laborer's own labor, realized in a product, which is advanced to him by the capitalist. Let us take a peasant liable to do compulsory service for his lord. He works on his own land, with his own means of production, for, say, 3 days a week. The 3 other days he does forced work on the lord's domain. He constantly reproduces his own labor-fund, which never, in his case, takes the form of a money payment for his labor advanced by another person. But in return, his unpaid forced labor for the lord, on its side, never acquires the character of voluntary paid labor. If one fine morning the lord appropriates to himself the land, the cattle, the seed, in short, the means of production of this peasant, the latter will thenceforth be obliged to sell his labor-power to the lord. He will, *coeteris paribus*, labor 6 days a week as before, 3 for himself, 3 for his lord, who thenceforth becomes a wages-paying capitalist. As before, he will use up the means of production as means of production, and transfer their value to the product. As before, a definite portion of the product will be devoted to reproduction. But from the moment that the forced labor is changed into wage-labor, from that moment the labor-fund, which the peasant himself continues as before to produce and reproduce, takes the form of a capital advanced in the form of wages by the lord. The bourgeois economist, whose narrow mind is unable to separate the form of appearance from the thing that appears, shuts his eyes to the fact that it is but here and there on the face of the earth, that even now-a-days the labor-fund crops up in the form of capital.

Variable capital, it is true, only then loses its character of a value advanced out of the capitalist's funds, when we view the process of capitalist production in the flow of its constant renewal. But that process must have had a beginning of some kind. From our present standpoint it therefore seems likely that the capitalist, once upon a time, became possessed of money by some accumulation that took place independently of the unpaid labor of others, and that this was, therefore, how he was enabled to frequent the market as a buyer of labor-power. However this may be, the mere continuity of the process, the simple reproduction, brings about some other wonderful changes which affect not only the variable, but the total capital.

If a capital of £1000 beget yearly a surplus-value of £200, and if this surplus-value be consumed every year, it is clear that at the end of 5 years the surplus-value consumed will amount to 5 x £200 or the £1000 originally advanced. If only a part, say one-half, were consumed, the same result would follow at the end of 10 years, since 10 x £100=£1000. General Rule: The value of the capital advanced divided by the surplus-value annually consumed gives the number of years, or reproduction periods, at the expiration of which the capital originally advanced has been consumed by the capitalist and has disappeared. The capitalist thinks that he is consuming the produce of the unpaid labor of others, i.e., the surplus-value, and is keeping intact his original capital; but what he thinks cannot alter facts. After the lapse of a certain number of years the capital value he then possesses is equal to the sum total of the surplus-value appropriated by him during those years, and the total value he has consumed is equal to that of his original capital. It is true he has in hand a capital whose amount has not changed, and of which a part, *viz.*, the buildings, machinery, etc., were already there when the work of his business began. But what we have to deal with here is not the material elements, but the value, of that capital. When a person gets through all his property by taking upon himself debts equal to the value of that property, it is clear that his property represents nothing but the sum total of his debts. And so it is with the capitalist; when he has consumed the equivalent of his original capital, the value of his present capital represents nothing but the total amount of the surplus-value appropriated by him without payment. Not a single atom of the value of his old capital continues to exist.

Apart then from all accumulation, the mere continuity of the process of production, in other words simple reproduction, sooner or later, and of necessity, converts every capital into accumulated capital, or capitalized surplus-value. Even if that capital was originally acquired by the personal labor of its employer, it sooner or later becomes value appropriated without an equivalent, the unpaid labor of others materialized either in money or in some other object. The separation of labor from its product, of subjective labor-power from the objective conditions of labor, was therefore the real foundation in fact, and the starting point of capitalist production.

But that which at first was but a starting point becomes, by the mere continuity of the process, by simple reproduction, the peculiar result, constantly renewed and perpetuated, of capitalist production. On the one hand, the process of production incessantly converts material wealth into capital, into means of creating more wealth and means of enjoyment for the capitalist. On the other hand the laborer, on quitting the process, is what he was on entering it, a source of wealth, but devoid of all means of making that wealth his own. Since, before entering on the process, his own labor has already been alienated from himself by the sale of his labor-power, has been appropriated by the capitalist and incorporated with capital, it must during the process be realized in a product that does not belong to him. Since the process of production is also the process by which the capitalist consumes labor-power, the product of the laborer is incessantly converted not only into commodities, but into capital, into value that sucks up the value-creating power, into means of subsistence that buy the person of the laborer, into means of production that command the producers. The laborer therefore constantly produces material, objective wealth, but in the form of capital, of an alien power that dominates and exploits him; and the capitalist just as constantly produces labor-power, but in the form of a subjective source of wealth, separated from the objects in and by which it can alone be realized; in short he produces the laborer, but as a wage-laborer. This incessant production, this perpetuation of the laborer, is the *sine qua non* of capitalist production.

The laborer consumes in a twofold way. While producing he consumes by his labor the means of production, and converts them into products with a higher value than that of the capital advanced. This is his productive consumption. It is at the same time consumption of his labor-power by the capitalist who bought it. On the other hand, the laborer turns the money paid to him for his labor-power into means of subsistence: this is his individual consumption. The laborer's productive consumption and his individual consumption are therefore totally distinct. In the former, he acts as the motive power of capital, and belongs to the capitalist. In the latter, he belongs to himself, and performs his necessary vital functions outside the process of production. The result of the one is that the capitalist lives; of the other, that the laborer lives.

When considering the working-day, we saw that the laborer is often compelled to make his individual consumption a mere incident of production. In such a case, he supplies himself with necessities in order to maintain his labor-power, just as coal and water are supplied to the steam engine and oil to the wheel. His means of consumption, in that case, are the mere means of consumption required by a means of production; his individual consumption is directly productive consumption. This, however, appears to be an abuse not essentially pertaining to capitalist production.

The matter takes quite another aspect when we contemplate not the single capitalist and the single laborer, but the capitalist class and the laboring class, not as an isolated process of production, but capitalist production in full swing, and on its actual social scale. By converting part of his capital into labor-power, the capitalist augments the value of his entire capital. He kills two birds with one stone. He profits not only by what he receives from, but by what he gives to the laborer. The capital given in exchange for labor-power is converted into necessities, by the consumption of which the muscles, nerves, bones, and brains of existing laborers are reproduced and new laborers are begotten. Within the limits of what is strictly necessary, the individual consumption of the working-class is, therefore, the reconversion of the means of subsistence given by capital in exchange for labor-power into fresh labor-power at the disposal of capital for exploitation. It is the production and reproduction of that means of production so indispensable to the capitalist: the laborer himself. The individual consumption of the laborer, whether it proceed within the workshop or outside it, whether it be part of the process of production or not, forms therefore a factor of the production and reproduction of capital just as cleaning machinery does, whether it is done while the machinery is working or while it is standing. The fact that the laborer consumes his means of subsistence for his own purposes, and not to please the capitalist, has no bearing on the matter. The consumption of food by a beast of burden is nonetheless a necessary factor in the process of production, because the beast enjoys what it eats. The maintenance and reproduction of the working-class is, and must ever be, a necessary condition to the reproduction of capital. But the capitalist may safely leave its fulfillment to the laborer's instincts of self-preservation and of propagation. All the capitalist cares for is to reduce the laborer's individual consumption as far as possible to what is strictly necessary, and he is far away from imitating those brutal South Americans who force their laborers to take the more substantial, rather than the less substantial, kind of food.

Hence both the capitalist and his ideological representative, the political economist, consider that part alone of the laborer's individual consumption to be productive which is requisite for the perpetuation of the class, and which therefore must take place in order that the capitalist may have labor-power to consume; what the laborer consumes for his own pleasure beyond that part is unproductive consumption. If the accumulation of capital were to cause a rise of wages and an increase in the laborer's consumption unaccompanied by increase in the consumption of labor-power by capital, the additional capital would be consumed unproductively. In reality, the individual consumption of the laborer is unproductive as regards himself, for it reproduces nothing but the needy individual; it is productive to the capitalist and the State, since it is the production of the power that creates their wealth.

From a social point of view, therefore, the working-class, even when not directly engaged in the labor-process, is just as much an appendage of capital as the ordinary instruments of labor. Even its individual consumption is, within certain limits, a mere factor in the process of production. That process, however, takes good care to prevent these self-conscious instruments from leaving it in the lurch, for it removes their product, as fast as it is made, from their pole to the opposite pole of capital. Individual consumption provides, on the one hand, the means for their maintenance and reproduction: on the other hand, it secures by the annihilation of the necessities of life, the continued reappearance of the workman in the labor-market. The Roman slave was held by fetters: the wage-laborer is bound to his owner by invisible threads. The appearance of independence is kept up by means of a constant change of employers, and by the *fictio juris* of a contract.

★ ★ ★

Capitalist production, therefore, of itself reproduces the separation between labor-power and the means of labor. It thereby reproduces and perpetuates the condition for exploiting the laborer. It incessantly forces him to sell his labor-power in order to live, and enables the capitalist to purchase labor-power in order that he may enrich himself. It is no longer a mere accident that capitalist and laborer confront each other in the market as buyer and seller. It is the process itself that incessantly hurls back the laborer onto the market as a vendor of his labor-power, and that incessantly converts his own product into a means by which another man can purchase him. In reality, the laborer belongs to capital before he has sold himself to capital. His economical bondage is both brought about and concealed by the periodic sale of himself, by his change of masters, and by the oscillations in the market price of labor-power.

Capitalist production, therefore, under its aspect of a continuous connected process, of a process of reproduction, produces not only commodities, not only surplus-value, but it also produces and reproduces the capitalist relation; on the one side the capitalist, on the other the wage-laborer.

CHAPTER XXIV

CONVERSION OF SURPLUS-VALUE INTO CAPITAL

SECTION 1—CAPITALIST PRODUCTION ON A PROGRESSIVELY INCREASING SCALE. TRANSITION OF THE LAWS OF PROPERTY THAT CHARACTERIZE PRODUCTION OF COMMODITIES INTO LAWS OF CAPITALIST APPROPRIATION

Employing surplus-value as capital, reconverting it into capital, is called accumulation of capital.

First let us consider this transaction from the standpoint of the individual capitalist. Suppose a spinner has advanced a capital of £10,000, of which four-fifths (£8000) are laid out in cotton, machinery, etc., and one-fifth (£2000) in wages. Let him produce 240,000 lbs. of yarn annually, having a value of £12,000. The rate of surplus-value being 100%, the surplus-value lies in the surplus or net product of 40,000 lbs. of yarn, one-sixth of the gross product, with a value of £2000 which will be realized by a sale. £2000 is £2000. We can neither see nor smell in this sum of money a trace of surplus-value. When we know that a given value is surplus-value, we know how its owner came by it; but that does not alter the nature either of value or of money.

In order to convert this additional sum of £2000 into capital, the master spinner will, all circumstances remaining as before, advance four-fifths of it (£1600) in the purchase of cotton, etc., and one-fifth (£400) in the purchase of additional spinners, who will find in the market the necessities of life whose value the master has advanced to them. Then the new capital of £2000 functions in the spinning mill and brings in, in its turn, a surplus-value of 400.

The capital-value was originally advanced in the money form. The surplus-value on the contrary is, originally, the value of a definite portion of the gross product. If this gross product is sold, converted into money, the capital-value regains its original form. From this moment the capital-value and the surplus-value are both sums of money, and their reconversion into capital takes place in precisely the same way. The one as well as the other is laid out by the capitalist in the purchase of commodities that place him in a position to begin afresh the fabrication of his goods, and this time on an extended scale. But in order to be able to buy those commodities, he must find them ready in the market.

His own yarns circulate only because he brings his annual product to market, as all other capitalists likewise do with their commodities. But these commodities, before coming to market, were part of the general annual product, part of the total mass of objects of every kind, into which the sum of the individual capitals, i.e., the total capital of society, had been converted in the course of the year, and of which each capitalist had in hand only an aliquot part. The transactions in the market effectuate only the interchange of the individual components of this annual product, transfer them from one hand to another, but can neither augment the total annual production nor alter the nature of the objects produced. Hence the use that can be made of the total annual product depends entirely upon its own composition, but in no way upon circulation.

The annual production must in the first place furnish all those objects (use-values) from which the material components of capital, used up in the course of the year, have to be replaced. Deducting these there remains the net or surplus-product, in which the surplus-value lies. And of what does this surplus-product consist? Only of things destined to satisfy the wants and desires of the capitalist class, things which, consequently, enter into the consumption fund of the capitalists? Were that the case, the cup of surplus-value would be drained to the very dregs, and nothing but simple reproduction would ever take place.

To accumulate it is necessary to convert a portion of the surplus-product into capital. But we cannot, except by a miracle, convert into capital anything but such articles as can be employed in the labor-process (i.e., means of production), and such further articles as are suitable for the sustenance of the laborer, (i.e., means of subsistence). Consequently, a part of the annual surplus-labor must have been applied to the production of additional means of production and subsistence, over and above the quantity of these things required to replace the capital advanced. In one word, surplus-value is convertible into capital solely because the surplus-product, whose value it is, already comprises the material elements of new capital.

Now in order to allow these elements to actually function as capital, the capitalist class requires additional labor. If the exploitation of the laborers already employed does not increase, either extensively or intensively, then additional labor-power must be found. For this the mechanism of capitalist production provides beforehand, by converting the working class into a class dependent on wages, a class whose ordinary wages suffice not only for its maintenance, but for its increase. It is only necessary for capital to incorporate this additional labor-power, annually supplied by the working class in the shape of laborers of all ages, with the surplus means of production comprised in the annual produce, and the conversion of surplus-value into capital is complete. From a concrete point of view, accumulation resolves itself into the reproduction of capital on a progressively increasing scale—the circle in which simple reproduction moves, alters its form, and to use Sismondi's expression, changes into a spiral.

★ ★ ★

We here leave out of consideration the portion of the surplus-value consumed by the capitalist. Just as little does it concern us, for the moment, whether the additional capital is joined on to the original capital or is separated from it to function independently; whether the same capitalist who accumulated it employs it, or whether he hands it over to another. This only we must not forget, that by the side of the newly-formed capital, the original capital continues to reproduce itself and to produce surplus-value, and that this is also true of all accumulated capital, and the additional capital engendered by it.

The original capital was formed by the advance of £10,000. How did the owner become possessed of it? "By his own labor and that of his forefathers," answer unanimously the spokesmen of political economy. And, in fact, their supposition appears the only one consonant with the laws of the production of commodities.

But it is quite otherwise with regard to the additional capital of £2000. How that originated we know perfectly well. There is not one single atom of its value that does not owe its existence to unpaid labor. The means of production with which the additional labor-power is incorporated, as well as the necessities with which the laborers are sustained, are nothing but component parts of the surplus product, of the tribute annually exacted from the working class by the capitalist class. Though the latter with a portion of that tribute purchases the additional labor-power even at its full price, so that equivalent is exchanged for equivalent, yet the transaction is for all that only the old dodge of every conquerer who buys commodities from the conquered with the money he has robbed them of.

If the additional capital employs the person who produced it, this producer must not only continue to augment the value of the original capital, but must buy back the fruits of his previous labor with more labor than they cost. When viewed as a transaction between the capitalist class and the working class, it makes no difference that additional laborers are employed by means of the unpaid labor of the previously employed laborers. The capitalist may even convert the additional capital into a machine that throws the producers of that capital out of work, and that replaces them by a few children. In every case the working class creates by the surplus-labor of one year the capital destined to employ additional labor in the following year. And this is what is called: creating capital out of capital.

The accumulation of the first additional capital of £2000 presupposes a value of £10,000 belonging to the capitalist by virtue of his "primitive labor" and advanced by him. The second additional capital of £400 presupposes, on the contrary, only the previous accumulation of the £2000, of which the £400 is the surplus-value capitalized. The ownership of past unpaid labor is thenceforth the sole condition for the appropriation of living unpaid labor on a constantly increasing scale. The more the capitalist has accumulated, the more is he able to accumulate.

Insofar as the surplus-value, of which the additional capital, No. 1, consists, is the result of the purchase of labor-power with part of the original capital, a purchase that conformed to the laws of the exchange of commodities, and that from a legal standpoint presupposes nothing beyond the free disposal on the part of the laborer of his own capacities, and on the part of the owner of money or commodities, of the values that belong to him; insofar as the additional capital, No. 2, etc., is the mere result of No. 1 and therefore a consequence of the above condition; insofar as each single transaction invariably conforms to the laws of the exchange of commodities, the capitalist buying labor-power, the laborer selling it, and we will assume at its real value; insofar as all this is true, it is evident that the laws of appropriation or of private property, laws that are based on the production and circulation of commodities, become by their own inner and inexorable dialectic changed into their very opposite. The exchange of equivalents, the original operation with which we started, has now become turned round in such a way that there is only an apparent exchange. This is owing to the fact, first, that the capital which is exchanged for labor-power is itself but a portion of the product of others' labor appropriated without an equivalent; and, secondly, that this capital must not only be replaced by its producer, but replaced together with an added surplus. The relation of exchange subsisting between capitalist and laborer becomes a mere semblance pertaining to the process of circulation, a mere form, foreign to the real nature of the transaction, and only mystify it. The ever repeated purchase and sale of labor-power is now the mere form; what really takes place is this—the capitalist again and again appropriates, without equivalent, a portion of the previously materialized labor of others, and exchanges it for a greater quantity of living labor. At first the rights of property seemed to us to be based on a man's own labor. At least, some such assumption was necessary since only commodity owners with equal rights confronted each other, and the sole means by which a man could become possessed of the commodities of others was by alienating his own commodities; and these could be replaced by labor alone. Now, however, property turns out to be the right, on the part of the capitalist, to appropriate the unpaid labor of others or its product and to be the impossibility, on the part of the laborer, of appropriating his own product. The separation of property from labor has become the necessary consequence of a law that apparently originated in their identity.

No matter how severely the capitalist mode of appropriation may seem to slap the face of the fundamental laws of the production of commodities, it does not arise from a violation, but from an application of these laws. A brief retrospect upon the succession of phases, whose climax the capitalist accumulation is, may serve once more to make this clear.

We have seen, in the first place, that the original transformation of a certain quantity of values into capital proceeded strictly according to the laws of exchange. One of the contracting parties sells his labor-power, the other buys it. The first receives the exchange-value of his commodity while its use-value, labor, passes into the possession of the other. This second party then converts means of production belonging to him into a new product belonging to him by right through the instrumentality of labor also belonging to him.

The value of this product comprises, in the first place, the value of the consumed means of production. Useful labor cannot consume these means of production without transferring their value to the new product. But in order to be saleable labor-power must be able to furnish useful labor in that line of industry in which it is to be employed.

The value of the new product comprises, furthermore, the equivalent of the value of labor-power and a surplus-value. It does so for the reason that the labor-power sold for a certain length of time, such as a day, a week, etc., has less value than is produced by its employment during that time. The laborer, however, has received the exchange-value of his labor-power and given up its use-value in return, as happens in every sale and purchase.

The fact that this particular commodity, labor-power, has the peculiar use-value of supplying labor and creating value cannot affect the general law of the production of commodities. Hence, if the sum of values advanced in wages is not merely reproduced in the product but also increased by a surplus-value, this is not due to an advantage gained over the seller, who received the value of his commodity, but simply to the consumption of this commodity by the buyer.

The law of exchange requires equality only for the exchange-values of the commodities passed from hand to hand. But it requires at the outset a disparity of their use-values and has nothing to do with their consumption, which does not begin until after the trade has been made.

The original transformation of money into capital proceeds, therefore, in strict compliance with the economic laws of the production of commodities and with the property right derived therefrom. Nevertheless it has the following results:

(1) That the product belongs to the capitalist, not to the laborer.

(2) That the value of this product comprises a surplus-value over and above the value of the advanced capital. This surplus-value has cost the laborer labor, but the capitalist nothing, yet it becomes the lawful property of the capitalist.

(3) That the laborer has reproduced his labor-power and can sell it once more, if he finds a buyer for it.

Simple reproduction is but a periodical repetition of this first operation. Money is thereby transformed again and again into capital. The general law is not violated thereby, but rather finds an opportunity to manifest itself permanently.

★ ★ ★

It does not alter matters any if simple reproduction is replaced by reproduction on an enlarged scale, by accumulation. In the first instance the capitalist consumes the entire surplus-value, in the second he demonstrates his civic virtue by consuming only a part of it and converting the remainder into money.

The surplus-value is his property, it has never belonged to anybody else. If he advances it to production, he makes advances from his own funds just as he did on the day when he first came on the market. That this fund in the present case comes from the unpaid labor of his laborers does not alter the matter in the least. If laborer B is employed with surplus-values produced by laborer A, then in the first place, A supplied this surplus-value without having the just price of his commodity reduced by one farthing, and in the second place, this transaction is none of B's concern. What B demands and has a right to demand is that the capitalist should pay him the value of his labor-power. "Both sides are gainers; the laborer, by having the fruit of his labor advanced to him" (that is, the fruit of the unpaid labor of others) "before he has performed any labor" (that is, before his own labor has borne any fruit); "the master, because the labor of this laborer was worth more than his wages" (that is, produced a value greater than that of his wages). (Sismondi, I. c., p. 135.)

True, the matter assumes an entirely different aspect when we look upon capitalist production in the uninterrupted flow of its reproduction, and when we consider the capitalist class as a whole and its antagonist, the working class, instead of the individual capitalist and the individual laborer. But in so doing we should be applying a standard which is totally foreign to the production of commodities.

In the production of commodities only sellers and buyers, independent of one another, meet. Their mutual relations cease with the termination of their mutual contract. If the transaction is repeated, it is done by a new contract which has nothing to do with the former one, and only an accident brings the same seller once more together with the same buyer.

Hence, if the production of commodities, or a transaction belonging to it, is to be judged by its own economic laws, we must consider each act of exchange by itself, outside of all connection with the act of exchange preceding it and following it. And since purchases and sales are transacted between individuals, it will not do to seek therein relations between entire classes of society.

No matter how long may be the series of periodical reproductions and former accumulations through which the capital now invested may have passed, it always retains its primal virginity. So long as the laws of exchange are observed in every act of exchange, individually considered, the mode of appropriation may be completely revolutionized without in the least affecting the property right bestowed by the production of commodities. The same right remains in force, whether it is at a time when the product belonged to the producer and when this producer, exchanging equivalent for equivalent, could enrich himself only by his own labor, or whether it is under capitalism, where the social wealth becomes in an ever increasing degree the property of those who are in a position to appropriate to themselves again and again the unpaid labor of others.

This result becomes inevitable as soon as labor-power is sold as a commodity by the "free" laborer himself. It is from that time on that the production of commodities becomes universal and a typical form of production. Henceforth every product is intended at the outset for sale, and all produced wealth passes through the circulation. The production of commodities does not impose itself upon the whole society until wage-labor becomes its basis. And only then does it unfold all its powers. To say that the intervention of wage-labor adulterates the production of commodities means to say that the production of commodities must not develop, if it wishes to remain unadulterated. To the same extent that it continues to develop by its own inherent laws into a capitalist production, the property laws of the production of commodities are converted into the laws of capitalistic appropriation.

We have seen that even in the case of simple reproduction, all capital, whatever its original source, becomes converted into accumulated capital, capitalized surplus-value. But in the flood of production all the capital originally advanced becomes a vanishing quantity compared with the directly accumulated capital, i.e., with the surplus-value or surplus product that is reconverted into capital, whether it functions in the hands of its accumulator or in those of others. Hence, political economy describes capital in general as "accumulated wealth" (converted surplus-value or revenue) "that is employed over again in the production of surplus-value," and the capitalist as "the owner of surplus-value."

SECTION 3—SEPARATION OF SURPLUS-VALUE INTO CAPITAL AND REVENUE. THE ABSTINENCE THEORY

Except as personified capital, the capitalist has no historical value, and the necessity for his own transitory existence is only implied in the transitory necessity for the capitalist mode of production. But, so far as he is personified capital, it is not values in use and the enjoyment of them, but exchange-value and its augmentation that spur him into action. Fanatically bent on making value expand itself, he ruthlessly forces the human race to produce for production's sake; he thus forces the development of the productive powers of society and creates those material conditions which alone can form the real basis of a higher form of society, a society in which the full and free development of every individual forms the ruling principle. Only as personified capital is the capitalist respectable. As such, he shares with the miser the passion for wealth as wealth. But that which in the miser is a mere idiosyncrasy, is, in the capitalist, the effect of the social mechanism of which he is but one of the wheels. Moreover, the development of capitalist production makes it constantly necessary to keep increasing the amount of the capital laid out in a given industrial undertaking, and competition makes the inherent laws of capitalist production to be felt by each individual capitalist as external coercive laws. It compels him to keep constantly extending his capital in order to preserve it, but extend it he cannot except by means of progressive accumulation.

So far, therefore, as his actions are a mere function of capital—endowed as capital is in his person with consciousness and a will—his own private consumption is a robbery perpetrated on accumulation, just as in book-keeping by double entry, the private expenditure of the capitalist is placed on the debtor side of his account against his capital. To accumulate is to conquer the world of social wealth, to increase the mass of human beings exploited by him, and thus to extend both the direct and the indirect sway of the capitalist.

˙ But original sin is at work everywhere. As capitalist production, accumulation, and wealth become developed, the capitalist ceases to be the mere incarnation of capital. He has a fellow-feeling for his own Adam, and his education gradually enables him to smile at the rage for asceticism as a mere prejudice of the old-fashioned miser. While the capitalist of the classical type brands individual consumption as a sin against his function and as "abstinence" from accumulating, the modernized capitalist is capable of looking upon accumulation as "abstinence" from pleasure.

★ ★ ★

At the historical dawn of capitalist production—and every capitalist upstart has personally to go through this historical stage—avarice, and desire to get rich, are the ruling passions. But the progress of capitalist production not only creates a world of delights; it lays open, in speculation and the credit system, a thousand sources of sudden enrichment. When a certain stage of development has been reached, a conventional degree of prodigality, which is also an exhibition of wealth and consequently a source of credit, becomes a business necessity to the "unfortunate" capitalist. Luxury enters into capital's expenses of representation. Moreover, the capitalist gets rich not like the miser, in proportion to his personal labor and restricted consumption, but at the same rate as he squeezes out the labor-power of others, and enforces on the laborer abstinence from all life's enjoyments. Although, therefore, the prodigality of the capitalist never possesses the bona-fide character of the open-handed feudal lord's prodigality, but on the contrary, has always lurking behind it the most sordid avarice and the most anxious calculation, yet his expenditure grows with his accumulation without the one necessarily restricting the other. But along with this growth, there is at the same time developed in his breast a Faustian conflict between the passion for accumulation and the desire for enjoyment.

★ ★ ★

Accumulate, accumulate! That is Moses and the prophets! "Industry furnishes the material which saving accumulates." Therefore, save, save, i.e., reconvert the greatest possible portion of surplus-value or surplus-product into capital! Accumulation for accumulation's sake, production for production's sake: by this formula classical economy expressed the historical mission of the bourgeoisie, and did not for a single instant deceive itself over the birth-throes of wealth. But what avails lamentation in the face of historical necessity? If to classical economy, the proletarian is but a machine for the production of surplus-value; on the other hand, the capitalist is in its eyes only a machine for the conversion of this surplus-value into additional capital.

★ ★ ★

In economic forms of society of the most different kinds, there occurs not only simple reproduction, but in varying degrees, reproduction on a progressively increasing scale. By degrees more is produced and more consumed, and consequently more products have to be converted into means of production. This process, however, does not present itself as accumulation of capital, nor as the function of a capitalist, so long as the laborer's means of production, and with them his product and means of subsistence, do not confront him in the shape of capital.

SECTION 4—CIRCUMSTANCES THAT, INDEPENDENTLY OF THE PROPORTIONAL DIVISION OF SURPLUS-VALUE INTO CAPITAL AND REVENUE, DETERMINE THE AMOUNT OF ACCUMULATION. DEGREE OF EXPLOITATION OF LABOR-POWER. PRODUCTIVITY OF LABOR. GROWING DIFFERENCE IN AMOUNT BETWEEN CAPITAL EMPLOYED AND CAPITAL CONSUMED. MAGNITUDE OF CAPITAL ADVANCED

The proportion in which surplus-value breaks up into capital and revenue being given, the magnitude of the capital accumulated clearly depends on the absolute magnitude of the surplus-value. Suppose that 80 percent were capitalized and 20 percent eaten up, the accumulated capital will be £2,400 or £1,200, according as the total surplus-value has amounted to £3,000 or £1,500. Hence all the circumstances that determine the mass of surplus-value operate to determine the magnitude of the accumulation. We sum them up once again, but only insofar as they afford new points of view in regard to accumulation.

It will be remembered that the rate of surplus-value depends, in the first place, on the degree of exploitation of labor-power. Political economy values this fact so highly that it occasionally identifies the acceleration of accumulation due to increased productiveness of labor, with its acceleration due to increased exploitation of the laborer.

★ ★ ★

Although in all branches of industry that part of the constant capital consisting of instruments of labor must be sufficient for a certain number of laborers (determined by the magnitude of the undertaking), it by no means always increases in the same proportion as the quantity of labor employed. In a factory, suppose that 100 laborers working 8 hours a day yield 800 working-hours. If the capitalist wishes to raise this sum by one half, he can employ 50 more workers; but then he must also advance more capital, not merely for wages, but for instruments of labor. But he might also let the 100 laborers work 12 hours instead of 8, and then the instruments of labor already on hand would be enough. These would then simply be more rapidly consumed. Thus additional labor, begotten of the greater tension of labor-power, can augment surplus-product and surplus-value (i.e., the subject matter of accumulation), without corresponding augmentation in the constant part of capital.

★ ★ ★

General result: by incorporating with itself the two primary creators of wealth, labor-power and the land, capital acquires a power of expansion that permits it to augment the elements of its accumulation beyond the limits apparently fixed by its own magnitude, or by the value and the mass of the means of production already produced in which it has its being.

Another important factor in the accumulation of capital is the degree of productivity of social labor.

With the productive power of labor increases the mass of the products in which a certain value, and therefore, a surplus-value of a given magnitude, is embodied. The rate of surplus-value remaining the same or even falling, so long as it only falls more slowly, than the productive power of labor rises, the mass of the surplus-product increases. The division of this product into revenue and additional capital remaining the same, the consumption of the capitalist may, therefore, increase without any decrease in the fund of accumulation. The relative magnitude of the accumulation fund may even increase at the expense of the consumption fund, whilst the cheapening of commodities places at the disposal of the capitalist as many means of enjoyment as formerly, or even more than formerly. But hand-in-hand with the increasing productivity of labor goes, as we have seen, the cheapening of the laborer, and therefore a higher rate of surplus-value, even when the real wages are rising. The latter never rise proportionally to the productive power of labor. The same value in variable capital therefore sets in movement more labor-power and, therefore, more labor. The same value in constant capital is embodied in more means of production, i.e., in more instruments of labor, materials of labor and auxiliary materials; it therefore also supplies more elements for the production both of use-value and of value, and with these more absorbers of labor. The value of the additional capital, therefore, remaining the same or even diminishing, accelerated accumulation still takes place. Not only does the scale of reproduction materially extend, but the production of surplus-value increases more rapidly than the value of the additional capital.

The development of the productive power of labor reacts also on the original capital already engaged in the process of production. A part of the functioning constant capital consists of instruments of labor such as machinery, etc., which are not consumed, and therefore not reproduced or replaced by new ones of the same kind until after long periods of time. But every year a part of these instruments of labor perishes or reaches the limit of its productive function. It reaches, therefore, in that year, the time for its periodical reproduction, for its replacement by new ones of the same kind. If the productiveness of labor has, during the using up of these instruments of labor, increased (and it develops continually with the uninterrupted advance of science and technology), more efficient and (considering their increased efficiency) cheaper machines, tools, apparatus, etc., replace the old. The old capital is reproduced in a more productive form, apart from the constant detail improvements in the instruments of labor already in use. The other part of the constant capital, raw material and auxiliary substances, is constantly reproduced in less than a year; those produced by agriculture, for the most part annually. Every introduction of improved methods, therefore, works almost simultaneously on the new capital and on that already in action. Every advance in chemistry not only multiplies the number of useful materials and the useful applications of those already known, thus extending with the growth of capital its sphere of investment; it teaches at the same time how to throw the excrements of the processes of production and consumption back again into the circle of the process of reproduction and thus, without any previous outlay of capital, creates new matter for capital. Like the increased exploitation of natural wealth by the mere increase in the tension of labor-power, science and technology give capital a power of expansion independent of the given magnitude of the capital actually functioning. They react at the same time on that part of the original capital which has entered upon its stage of renewal. This, in passing into its new shape, incorporates *gratis* the social advance made while its old shape was being used up. Of course, this development of productive power is accompanied by a partial appreciation of functioning capital. So far as this depreciation makes itself acutely felt in competition, the burden falls on the laborer, in the increased exploitation of whom the capitalist looks for his indemnification.

Labor transmits to its product the value of the means of production consumed by it. On the other hand, the value and mass of the means of production set in motion by a given quantity of labor increase as the labor becomes more productive. Though the same quantity of labor adds always to its products only the same sum of new value, still the old capital-value, transmitted by the labor to the products, increases with the growing productivity of labor.

★ ★ ★

With the increase of capital, the difference between the capital employed and the capital consumed increases. In other words, there is an increase in the value and the material mass of the instruments of labor, such as buildings, machinery, drain-pipes, working-cattle, and apparatus of every kind that function for a longer or shorter time in processes of production constantly repeated, or that serve for the attainment of particular useful effects whilst they themselves only gradually wear out and only lose their value piecemeal, therefore transferring that value of the product only bit by bit. In the same proportion as these instruments of labor serve as product-formers without adding value to the product, i.e., in the same proportion as they are wholly employed but only partly consumed, they perform, as we saw earlier, the same gratuitous service as the natural forces, water, steam, air, electricity, etc. This gratuitous service of past labor, when seized and filled with a soul by living labor, increases with the advancing stages of accumulation.

Since past labor always disguises itself as capital, i.e., since the passive of the labor of A, B, C, etc., takes the form of the active of the non-laborer X, bourgeois and political economists are full of praise for the services of dead and gone labor which, according to the Scotch genius M'Culloch, ought to receive a special remuneration in the shape of interest, profit, etc. The powerful and ever-increasing assistance given by past labor to the living labor process under the form of means of production is therefore attributed to that form of past labor in which it is alienated as unpaid labor, from the worker himself, i.e., to its capitalistic form. The practical agents of capitalistic production and their pettifogging ideologists are as unable to think of the means of production as separate from the antagonistic social mask they wear today, as a slave-owner to think of the worker himself as distinct from his character as a slave.

With a given degree of exploitation of labor-power, the mass of the surplus-value produced is determined by the number of workers simultaneously exploited; and this corresponds, although in varying proportions, with the magnitude of the capital. The more, therefore, capital increases by means of successive accumulations, the more does the sum of the value increase that is divided into consumption-fund and accumulation-fund. The capitalist can, therefore, live a more jolly life and at the same time show more "abstinence." And finally, all the springs of production act with greater elasticity, the more its scale extends with the mass of the capital advanced.

CHAPTER XXV

THE GENERAL LAW OF
CAPITALIST ACCUMULATION

Growth of capital involves growth of its variable constituent or of the part invested in labor-power. A part of the surplus-value turned into additional capital must always be retransformed into variable capital, or additional labor-fund. If we suppose that, all other circumstances remaining the same, the composition of capital also remains constant (i.e., that a definite mass of means of production constantly needs the same mass of labor-power to set in motion), then the demand for labor and the subsistence-fund of the laborers clearly increase in the same proportion as the capital, and the more rapidly, the more rapidly the capital increases.

Since the capital produces yearly a surplus-value of which one part is yearly added to the original capital; since this increment itself grows yearly along with the augmentation of the capital already functioning; since lastly, under special stimulus to enrichment, such as the opening of new markets or of new spheres for the outlay of capital in consequence of newly developed social wants, etc., the scale of accumulation may be suddenly extended merely by a change in the division of the surplus-value or surplus-product into capital and revenue, the requirements of accumulating capital may exceed the increase of labor-power or of the number of laborers; the demand for laborers may exceed the supply and, therefore, wages may rise. This must, indeed, ultimately be the case if the conditions supposed above continue. For since in each year more laborers are employed than in its predecessor, sooner or later a point must be reached at which the requirements of accumulation begin to surpass the customary supply of labor and, therefore, a rise of wages takes place. The more or less favourable circumstances in which the wage-working class supports and multiplies itself in no way alter the fundamental character of capitalist production. As simple reproduction constantly reproduces the capital-relation itself, i.e., the relation of capitalists on the one hand and wage-workers on the other, so reproduction on a progressive scale, i.e., accumulation, reproduces the capital relation on a progressive scale, more capitalists or larger capitalists at this pole, more wage-workers at that. The reproduction of a mass of labor-power, which must incessantly re-incorporate itself with capital for that capital's self-expansion, which cannot get free from capital, and whose enslavement to capital is only concealed by the variety of individual capitalists to whom it sells itself, this reproduction of labor-power forms, in fact, an essential part of the reproduction of capital itself. Accumulation of capital is, therefore, increase of the proletariat.

★ ★ ★

The law of capitalist production that is at the bottom of the pretended "natural law of population" reduces itself simply to this: The correlation between accumulation of capital and rate of wages is nothing else than the correlation between the unpaid labor transformed into capital and the additional paid labor necessary for the setting in motion of this additional capital. It is therefore in no way a relation between two magnitudes independent of each other: on the one hand, the magnitude of the capital; on the other, the number of the laboring population; it is rather, at bottom, only the relation between the unpaid and the paid labor of the same laboring population. If the quantity of unpaid labor supplied by the working-class and accumulated by the capitalist class increases so rapidly that its conversion into capital requires an extraordinary addition of paid labor, then wages rise and, all other circumstances remaining equal, the unpaid labor diminishes in proportion. But as soon as this diminution touches the point at which the surplus-labor that nourishes capital is no longer supplied in normal quantity, a reaction sets in: a smaller part of revenue is capitalized, accumulation lags, and the movement in the rise in wages receives a check. The rise of wages therefore is confined within limits that not only leave intact the foundations of the capitalistic system, but also secure its reproduction on a progressive scale. The law of capitalistic accumulation, metamorphosed by economists into a pretended law of nature, in reality merely states that the very nature of accumulation excludes every diminution in the degree of exploitation of labor and every rise in the price of labor which could seriously imperil the continual reproduction, on an ever enlarging scale, of the capitalistic relation. It cannot be otherwise in a mode of production in which the laborer exists to satisfy the needs of self-expansion of existing values, instead of on the contrary, material wealth existing to satisfy the needs of development on the part of the laborer. As in religion man is governed by the products of his own brain, so in capitalistic production he is governed by the products of his own hand.

SECTION 2—RELATIVE DIMINUTION OF THE VARIABLE PART OF CAPITAL SIMULTANEOUSLY WITH THE PROGRESS OF ACCUMULATION AND OF THE CONCENTRATION THAT ACCOMPANIES IT

Once given the general basis of the capitalistic system, then in the course of accumulation, a point is reached at which the development of the productivity of social labor becomes the most powerful lever of accumulation.

★ ★ ★

Apart from natural conditions, such as fertility of the soil, etc., and from the skill of independent and isolated producers (shown rather qualitatively in the goodness than quantitatively in the mass of their products), the degree of productivity of labor in a given society is expressed in the relative extent of the means of production that one laborer, during a given time with the same tension of labor-power, turns into products. The mass of the means of production which he thus transforms increases with the productiveness of his labor. But those means of production play a double part. The increase of some is a consequence, that of the others a condition of the increasing productivity of labor, e.g., with the division of labor in manufacture and with the use of machinery, more raw material is worked up in the same time and, therefore, a greater mass of raw material and auxiliary substances enter into the labor-process. That is the consequence of the increasing productivity of labor. On the other hand, the mass of machinery, beasts of burden, mineral manures, drain-pipes, etc., is a condition of the increasing productivity of labor; so also is it with the means of production concentrated in buildings, furnaces, means of transport, etc. But whether condition or consequence, the growing extent of the means of production, as compared with the labor-power incorporated with them, is an expression of the growing productiveness of labor. The increase of the latter appears, therefore, in the diminution of the mass of labor in proportion to the mass of means of production moved by it, or in the diminution of the subjective factor of the labor process as compared with the objective factor.

This change in the technical composition of capital, this growth in the mass of means of production as compared with the mass of the labor-power that vivifies them, is reflected again in its value-composition by the increase of the constant constituent of capital at the expense of its variable constituent. There may be, e.g., originally 50 percent of a capital laid out in means of production, and 50 percent in the labor-power; later on, with the development of the productivity of labor, 80 percent in means of production, 20 percent in labor-power, and so on. This law of the progressive increase in constant capital in proportion to the variable is confirmed at every step (as already shown) by the comparative analysis of the prices of commodities, whether we compare different economic epochs or different nations in the same epoch. The relative magnitude of the element of price, which represents the value of the means of production only, or the constant part of capital consumed, is in direct proportion, and the relative magnitude of the other element of price that pays labor (the variable part of capital) is in inverse proportion, to the advance of accumulation.

This diminution in the variable part of capital as compared with the constant, or the altered, value-composition of the capital, however, only shows approximately the change in the composition of its material constituents. If, e.g., the capital-value employed today in spinning is 7/8 constant and 1/8 variable, whilst at the beginning of the eighteenth century it was 1/2 constant and 1/2 variable, on the other hand, the mass of raw material, instruments of labor, etc., that a certain quantity of spinning labor consumes productively today is many hundred times greater than at the beginning of the eighteenth century. The reason is simply that, with the increasing productivity of labor, not only does the mass of the means of production consumed by it increase, but their value compared with their mass diminishes. Their value therefore rises absolutely, but not in proportion to their mass. The increase of the difference between constant and variable capital is, therefore, much less than that of the difference between the mass of the means of production into which the constant, and the mass of the labor-power into which the variable, capital is converted. The former difference increases with the latter, but in a smaller degree.

But if the progress of accumulation lessens the relative magnitude of the variable part of capital, it by no means, in doing this, excludes the possibility of a rise in its absolute magnitude. Suppose that a capital-value at first is divided into 50 percent of constant and 50 percent of variable capital; later into 80 percent of constant and 20 percent of variable. If in the meantime the original capital, say £6,000, has increased to £18,000, its variable constituent has also increased. It was £3,000, it is now £3,600. But whereas formerly an increase of capital by 20 percent would have sufficed to raise the demand for labor 20 percent, now this latter rise requires a tripling of the original capital.

★ ★ ★

On the basis of the production of commodities where the means of production are the property of private persons, and where the artisan therefore either produces commodities isolated from and independent of others, or sells his labor-power as a commodity because he lacks the means for independent industry, cooperation on a large scale can realize itself only in the increase of individual capitals, only in production as the means of social production, and the means of subsistence are transformed into the private property of capitalists. The basis of the production of commodities can admit production on a large scale in the capitalistic form alone. A certain accumulation of capital in the hands of individual producers of commodities forms therefore the necessary preliminary of the specifically capitalistic mode of production. We had, therefore, to assume that this occurs during the transition from handicraft to capitalistic industry. It may be called primitive accumulation, because it is the historic basis instead of the historic result of specifically capitalist production. How it itself originates, we need not here inquire as yet. It is enough that it forms the starting-point. But all methods for raising the social productive power of labor that are developed on this basis are at the same times methods for the increased production of surplus-value or surplus-product, which in its turn is the formative element of accumulation. They are, therefore, at the same time methods of the production of capital by capital, or methods of its accelerated accumulation. The continual re-transformation of surplus-value into capital now appears in the shape of the increasing magnitude of the capital that enters into the process of production. This in turn is the basis of an extended scale of production, of the methods for raising the productive power of labor that accompany it, and of accelerated production of surplus-value. If, therefore, a certain degree of accumulation of capital appears as a condition of the specifically capitalist mode of production, the latter causes conversely an accelerated accumulation of capital. With the accumulation of capital, therefore, the specifically capitalistic mode of production develops, and with the capitalist mode of production the accumulation of capital. Both these economic factors bring about, in the compound ratio of the impulses they reciprocally give one another, that change in the technical composition of capital by which the variable constituent becomes always smaller and smaller as compared with the constant.

Every individual capital is a larger or smaller concentration of means of production, with a corresponding command over a larger or smaller labor-army. Every accumulation becomes the means of new accumulation. With the increasing mass of wealth which functions as capital, accumulation increases the concentration of that wealth in the hands of individual capitalists, and thereby widens the basis of production on a large scale and of the specific methods of capitalist production. The growth of social capital is effected by the growth of many individual capitals. All other circumstances remaining the same, individual capitals, and with them the concentration of the means of production, increases in such proportion as they form aliquot parts of the total social capital. At the same time portions of the original capitals disengage themselves and function as new independent capitals. Besides other causes, the division of property within capitalist families plays a great part of this. With the accumulation of capital, therefore, the number of capitalists grows to a greater or less extent. Two points characterize this kind of concentration which grows directly out of, or rather is identical with, accumulation. First: The increasing concentration of the social means of production in the hands of individual capitalists is, other things remaining equal, limited by the degree of increase of social wealth. Second: The part of social capital domiciled in each particular sphere of production is divided among many capitalists who face one another as independent commodity-producers competing with each other. Accumulation and the concentration accompanying it are, therefore, not only scattered over many points, but the increase of each functioning capital is thwarted by the formation of new and the subdivision of old capitals. Accumulation, therefore, presents itself on the one hand as increasing concentration of the means of production and of the command over labor; on the other, as repulsion of many individual capitals one from another.

This splitting-up of the total social capital into many individual capitals or the repulsion of its fractions one from another is counteracted by their attraction. The latter does not entail the simple concentration of the means of production and of the command over labor, which is identical with accumulation. It is the concentration of capitals already formed, destruction of their individual independence, expropriation of capitalist by capitalist, transformation of many small into a few large capitals. This process differs from the former in this, that it only presupposes a change in the distribution of capital already in hand and functioning; its field of action is therefore not limited by the absolute growth of social wealth, by the absolute limits of accumulation. Capital grows in one place to a huge mass in a single hand because it has in another place been lost by many. This is centralization proper, as distinct from accumulation and concentration.

The laws of this centralization of capitals, or of the attraction of capital by capital, cannot be developed here. A brief hint at a few facts must suffice. The battle of competition is fought by the cheapening of commodities. The cheapness of commodities depends, *coeteris paribus*, on the productiveness of labor, and this again on the scale of production. Therefore, the larger capitals beat the smaller. It will further be remembered that, with the development of the capitalist mode of production, there is an increase in the minimum amount of individual capital necessary to carry on a business under its normal conditions. The smaller capitals, therefore, crowd into spheres of production which Modern Industry has only sporadically or incompletely got hold of. Here competition rages in direct proportion to the number, and in inverse proportion to the magnitudes, of the antagonistic capitals. It always ends in the ruin of many small capitalists, whose capitals partly pass into the hand of their conquerors, partly vanish. Apart from this, with capitalist production an altogether new force comes into play—the credit system.

In its beginnings, the credit system sneaks in as a modest helper of accumulation and draws by invisible threads the money resources scattered all over the surface of society into the hands of individual or associated capitalists. But soon it becomes a new and formidable weapon in the competitive struggle, and finally it transforms itself into an immense social mechanism for the centralization of capitals.

Competition and credit, the two most powerful levers of centralization, develop in proportion as capitalist production and accumulation do. At the same time the progress of accumulation increases the matter subject to centralization, that is, the individual capitals, while the expansion of capitalist production creates the social demand here, the technical requirements there, for those gigantic industrial enterprises, which depend for their realization on a previous centralization of capitals. Nowadays, then, the mutual attraction of individual capitals and the tendency to centralization are stronger than ever before. However, while the relative expansion and energy of the centralization movement is determined to a certain degree by the superiority of the economic mechanism, the progress of centralization is by no means dependent upon the positive growth of the volume of social capital. This is the particular distinction between centralization and concentration, the latter being but another expression for reproduction on an enlarged scale. Centralization may take place by a mere change in the distribution of already existing capitals, a simple change in the quantitative arrangement of the components of social capital. Capital may in that case accumulate in one hand in large masses by withdrawing it from many individual hands. Centralization in a certain line of industry would have reached its extreme limit if all the individual capitals invested in it would have been amalgamated into one single capital.

This limit would not be reached in any particular society until the entire social capital would be united, either in the hands of one single capitalist or in those of one single corporation.

Centralization supplements the work of accumulation by enabling the industrial capitalists to expand the scale of their operations. The economic result remains the same whether this consummation is brought about by accumulation or centralization, whether centralization is accomplished by the violent means of annexation, by which some capitals become such overwhelming centers of gravitation for others as to break their individual cohesion and attracting the scattered fragments, or whether the amalgamation of a number of capitals which already exist or are in process of formation proceeds by the smoother road of forming stock companies. The increased volume of industrial establishments forms everywhere the point of departure for a more comprehensive organization of the cooperative labor of many, for a wider development of their material powers, that is, for the progressive transformation of isolated processes of production carried on in accustomed ways into socially combined and scientifically managed processes of production.

It is evident, however, that accumulation, the gradual propagation of capital by a reproduction passing from a circular into a spiral form, is a very slow process as compared with centralization, which needs but to alter the quantitative grouping of the integral parts of social capital. The world would still be without railroads if it had been obliged to wait until accumulation should have enabled a few individual capitals to undertake the construction of a railroad. Centralization, on the other hand, accomplished this by a turn of the hand through stock companies. Centralization, by thus accelerating and intensifying the effects of accumulation, extends and hastens at the same time the revolutions in the technical composition of capital, which increase its constant part at the expense of its variable part and thereby reduce the relative demand for labor.

The masses of capital amalgamated overnight by centralization reproduce and augment themselves like the others, only faster, and thus become new and powerful levers of social accumulation. Hence, if the progress of social accumulation is mentioned nowadays, it comprises as a matter of course the effects of centralization. The additional capitals formed in the course of normal accumulation serve mainly as vehicles for the exploitation of new inventions and discoveries, or of industrial improvements in general. However, the old capital likewise arrives in due time at the moment when it must renew its head and limbs, when it casts off its old skin and is likewise born again in its perfected industrial form in which a smaller quantity of labor suffices to set in motion a larger quantity of machinery and raw materials. The absolute decrease of the demand for labor necessarily following therefrom will naturally be so much greater, the more these capitals going through the process of rejuvenation have become accumulated in masses by means of the movement of centralization.

On the one hand, therefore, the additional capital formed in the course of accumulation attracts fewer and fewer laborers in proportion to its magnitude. On the other hand the old capital, periodically reproduced with change of composition, repels more and more of the laborers formerly employed by it.

SECTION 3—PROGRESSIVE PRODUCTION
OF A RELATIVE SURPLUS-POPULATION
OR INDUSTRIAL RESERVE ARMY

The accumulation of capital, though originally appearing as its quantitative extension only, is effected, as we have seen, under a progressive qualitative change in its composition under a constant increase of its constant, at the expense of its variable constituent.

The specifically capitalist mode of production, the development of the productive power of labor corresponding to it, and the change thence resulting in the organic composition of capital, do not merely keep pace with the advance of accumulation or with the growth of social wealth. They develop at a much quicker rate, because mere accumulation, the absolute increase of the total social capital, is accompanied by the centralization of the individual capitals of which that total is made up, and because the change in the technological composition of the additional capital goes hand in hand with a similar change in the technological composition of the original capital. With the advance of accumulation, therefore, the proportion of constant to variable capital changes. If it was originally say 1:1, it now becomes successively 2:1, 3:1, 4:1, 5:1, 7:1, etc., so that as the capital increases, instead of 1/2 of its total value, only 1/3, 1/4, 1/5, 1/6, 1/8, etc., is transformed into labor-power and, on the other hand, 2/3, 3/4, 4/7, 5/6, 7/8, into means of production. Since the demand for labor is determined not by the amount of capital as a whole, but by its variable constituent alone, that demand falls progressively with the increase of the total capital, instead of, as previously assumed, rising in proportion to it. It falls relative to the magnitude of the total capital and at an accelerated rate, as this magnitude increases. With the growth of the total capital, its variable constituent or the labor incorporated in it also increases, but in a constantly diminishing proportion. The intermediate pauses are shortened in which accumulation works as simple extension of production, on a given technical basis. It is not merely that an accelerated accumulation of total capital, accelerated in a constantly growing progression, is needed to absorb an additional number of laborers, or even, on account of the constant metamorphosis of old capital, to keep employed those already functioning. In its turn, this increasing accumulation and centralization becomes a source of new changes in the composition of capital, of a more accelerated diminution of its variable as compared with its constant constituent. This accelerated relative diminution of the variable constituent, that goes along with the accelerated increase of the total capital and moves more rapidly than this increase, takes the inverse form, at the other pole, of an apparently absolute increase of the laboring population, an increase always moving more rapidly than that of the variable capital or the means of employment. But in fact, it is capitalistic accumulation itself that constantly produces, and produces in the direct ratio of its own energy and extent, a relatively redundant population of laborers, i.e., a population of greater extent than suffices for the average needs of the self-expansion of capital, and therefore a surplus-population.

Considering the social capital in its totality, the movement of its accumulation now causes periodical changes affecting it more or less as a whole, and now distributes its various phases simultaneously over the different spheres of production. In some spheres a change in the composition of capital occurs without an increase of its absolute magnitude, as a consequence of simple centralization; in others the absolute growth of capital is connected with absolute diminution of its variable constituent, or of the labor-power absorbed by it; in others again, capital continues growing for a time on its given technical basis and attracts additional labor-power in proportion to its increase, while at other times it undergoes organic changes and lessens its variable constituent; in all spheres, the increase of the variable part of capital, and therefore of the number of laborers employed by it, is always connected with violent fluctuations and transitory production of surplus-population, whether this takes the more striking form of the repulsion of laborers already employed, or the less evident but not less real form of the more difficult absorption of the additional laboring population through the usual channels. With the magnitude of social capital already functioning and the degree of its increase, with the extension of the scale of production and the mass of the laborers set in motion, with the development of the productiveness of their labor, with the greater breadth and fulness of all sources of wealth, there is also an extension of the scale on which greater attraction of laborers by capital is accompanied by their greater repulsion; the rapidity of the change in the organic composition of capital and in its technical form increases, and an increasing number of spheres of production becomes involved in this change, now simultaneously, now alternately. The laboring population therefore produces, along with the accumulation of capital produced by it, the means by which itself is made relatively superfluous, is turned into a relative surplus population; and it does this to an always increasing extent. This is a law of population peculiar to the capitalist mode of production; and in fact every special historic mode of production has its own special laws of population, historically valid within its limits alone. An abstract law of population exists for plants and animals only, and only insofar as man has not interfered with them.

But if a surplus laboring population is a necessary product of accumulation or of the development of wealth on a capitalist basis, this surplus population becomes, conversely, the lever of capitalistic accumulation, nay, a condition of existence of the capitalist mode of production. It forms a disposable industrial reserve army that belongs to capital quite as absolutely as if the latter had bred it at its own cost. Independently of the limits of the actual increase of population, it creates, for the changing needs of the self-expansion of capital, a mass of human material always ready for exploitation. With accumulation and the development of the productiveness of labor that accompanies it, the power of sudden expansion of capital grows also; it grows not merely because the elasticity of the capital already functioning increases, not merely because the absolute wealth of society expands, of which capital only forms an elastic part, not merely because credit, under every special stimulus, at once places an unusual part of this wealth at the disposal of production in the form of additional capital; it grows also because the technical conditions of the process of production themselves—machinery, means of transport, etc.—now admit the rapidest transformation of masses of surplus product into additional means of production. The mass of social wealth, overflowing with the advance of accumulation and transformable into additional capital, thrusts itself frantically into old branches of production whose market suddenly expands, or into newly formed branches, such as railways, etc., the need for which grows out of the development of the old ones. In all such cases, there must be the possibility of throwing great masses of men suddenly on the decisive points without injury to the scale of production in other spheres. Overpopulation supplies these masses. The course characteristic of modern industry, viz., a decennial cycle (interrupted by smaller oscillations), of periods of average activity, production at high pressure, and crisis and stagnation, depends on the constant formation, the greater or less absorption, and the re-formation of the industrial reserve army of surplus population. In their turn, the varying phases of the industrial cycle recruit the surplus population and become one of the most energetic agents of its reproduction. This peculiar course of modern industry, which occurs in no earlier period of human history, was also impossible in the childhood of capitalist production. The composition of capital changed but very slowly. With its accumulation, therefore, there kept pace, on the whole, a corresponding growth in the demand for labor. Slow as was the advance of accumulation compared with that of more modern times, it found a check in the natural limits of the exploitable laboring population, limits which could only be got rid of by forcible means to be mentioned later. The expansion by fits and starts of the scale of production is the preliminary to its equally sudden contraction; the latter again evokes the former, but the former is impossible without disposable human material, without an increase in the number of laborers independently of the absolute growth of the population. This increase is effected by the simple process that constantly "sets free" a part of the laborers; by methods which lessen the number of laborers employed in proportion to the increased production. The whole form of the movement of modern industry depends, therefore, upon the constant transformation of a part of the laboring population into unemployed or half-employed hands.

★ ★ ★

Capitalist production can by no means content itself with the quantity of disposable labor-power which the natural increase of population yields. It requires for its free play an industrial reserve army independent of these natural limits.

Up to this point it has been assumed that the increase or diminution of the variable capital corresponds rigidly with the increase or diminution of the number of laborers employed.

The number of laborers commanded by capital may remain the same or even fall while the variable capital increases. This is the case if the individual laborer yields more labor and therefore his wages increase, and this although the price of labor remains the same or even falls, only more slowly than the mass of labor rises. Increase of variable capital, in this case, becomes an index of more labor, but not of more laborers employed. It is the absolute interest of every capitalist to press a given quantity of labor out of a smaller, rather than a greater number of laborers, if the cost is about the same. In the latter case, the outlay of constant capital increases in proportion to the mass of labor set in action; in the former that increase is much smaller. The more extended the scale of production, the stronger this motive. Its force increases with the accumulation of capital.

★ ★ ★

On the one hand, with the progress of accumulation, a larger variable capital sets more labor in action without enlisting more laborers; on the other, a variable capital of the same magnitude sets in action more labor with the same mass of labor-power; and finally, a greater number of inferior labor-power by displacement of higher.

The production of a relative surplus-population, or the setting free of laborers, goes on therefore yet more rapidly than the technical revolution of the process of production that accompanies, and is accelerated by, the advances of accumulation; and more rapidly than the corresponding diminution of the variable part of capital as compared with the constant. If the means of production, as they increase in extent and effective power, become to a lesser extent means of employment of laborers, this state of things is again modified by the fact that in proportion as the productiveness of labor increases, capital increases its supply of labor more quickly than its demand for laborers. The over-work of the employed part of the working class swells the ranks of the reserve, whilst conversely the greater pressure that the latter by its competition exerts on the former forces these to submit to over-work and to subjugation under the dictates of capital. The condemnation of one part of the working-class to enforced idleness by the over-work of the other part, and the converse, becomes a means of enriching the individual capitalists, and accelerates at the same time the introduction of the industrial reserve army on a scale corresponding with the advance of social accumulation.

★ ★ ★

Taking them as a whole, the general movements of wages are exclusively regulated by the expansion and contraction of the industrial reserve army, and these again correspond to the periodic changes of the industrial cycle. They are, therefore, not determined by the variations of the absolute number of the working population, but by the varying proportions in which the working class is divided into an active and reserve army, by the increase of diminution in the relative amount of the surplus-population, by the extent to which it is now absorbed, now set free. For Modern Industry, with its decennial cycles and periodic phases which, moreover, as accumulation advances are complicated by irregular oscillations following each other more and more quickly, that would indeed be a beautiful law which pretends to make the action of capital dependent on the absolute variation of the population, instead of regulating the demand and supply of labor by the alternate expansion and contraction of capital, the labor-market now appearing relatively under-full, because capital is expanding, now again over-full, because it is contracting. Yet this is the dogma of the economists. According to them, wages rise in consequence of accumulation of capital. The higher wages stimulate the working population to more rapid multiplication, and this goes on until the labor-market becomes too full, and therefore capital, relative to the supply of labor, becomes insufficient. Wages fall, and now we have the reverse of the medal. The working population is little by little decimated as the result of the fall in wages, so that capital is again in excess relative to them, or as others explain it, falling wages and the corresponding increase in the exploitation of the laborer again accelerates accumulation, whilst at the same time, the lower wages hold the increase of the working-class in check. Then comes again the time when the supply of labor is less than the demand, wages rise, and so on. A beautiful mode of motion for developed capitalist production! Before, in consequence of the rise of wages, any positive increase of the population really fit for work could occur, and the time would have been passed again and again during which the industrial campaign must have been carried through, the battle fought and won.

★ ★ ★

The industrial reserve army, during the periods of stagnation and average prosperity, weighs down the active labor-army; during the periods of over-production and paroxysm, it holds its pretensions in check. Relative surplus-population is therefore the pivot upon which the law of demand and supply of labor works. It confines the field of action of this law within the limits absolutely convenient to the activity of exploitation and to the domination of capital.

SECTION 4—DIFFERENT FORMS OF THE RELATIVE SURPLUS-POPULATION. THE GENERAL LAW OF CAPITALISTIC ACCUMULATION

The relative surplus population exists in every possible form. Every laborer belongs to it during the time when he is only partially employed or wholly unemployed. Not taking into account the great periodically recurring forms that the changing phases of the industrial cycle impress on it, now an acute form during the crisis, then again a chronic form during dull times—it has always three forms, the floating, the latent, the stagnant.

In the centers of modern industry—factories, manufacturers, ironworks, mines, etc.,—the laborers are sometimes repelled, sometimes attracted again in greater masses, the number of those employed increasing on the whole, although in a constantly decreasing proportion to the scale of production. Here the surplus population exists in the floating form.

In the automatic factories, as in all the great workshops where machinery enters as a factor or where only the modern divisions of labor are carried out, large numbers of boys are employed up to the age of maturity. When this term is once reached, only a very small number continue to find employment in the same branches of industry, whilst the majority are regularly discharged. This majority forms an element of the floating surplus-population, growing with the extension of those branches of industry. Part of them emigrates, following in fact capital that has emigrated. One consequence is that the female population grows more rapidly than the male, *teste* England. That the natural increase of the number of laborers does not satisfy the requirements of the accumulation of capital, and yet all the time is in excess of them, is a contradiction inherent to the movement of capital itself. It wants larger numbers of youthful laborers, a smaller number of adults. The contradiction is not more glaring than that other one—that there is a complaint of the want of hands, while at the same time many thousands are out of work because the division of labor chains them to a particular branch of industry. The consumption of labor-power by capital is, besides, so rapid that the laborer, half-way through his life, has already more or less completely lived himself out. He falls into the ranks of the supernumeraries, or is thrust down from a higher to a lower step in the scale. It is precisely among the work-people of modern industry that we meet with the shortest duration of life. In order to conform to these circumstances, the absolute increase of this section of the proletariat must take place under conditions that shall swell their numbers, although the individual elements are used up rapidly. Hence, the rapid renewal of the generations of laborers (this law does not hold for the other classes of the population). This social need is met by early marriages, a necessary consequence of the conditions in which the laborers of modern industry live, and by the premium that the exploitation of children sets on their production.

As soon as capitalist production takes possession of agriculture and in proportion to the extent to which it does so, the demand for an agricultural laboring population falls absolutely, while the accumulation of the capital employed in agriculture advances without this repulsion being, as in non-agricultural industries, compensated by a greater attraction. Part of the agriculture population is therefore constantly on the point of passing over into an urban or manufacturing proletariat, and on the look-out for circumstances favourable to this transformation. (Manufacture is used here in the sense of all non-agricultural industries.) This source of relative surplus-population is thus constantly flowing. But the constant flow towards the towns presupposes, in the country itself, a constant latent surplus-population, the extent of which becomes evident only when its channels of outlet open to exceptional width. The agricultural laborer is therefore reduced to the minimum of wages, and always stands with one foot already in the swamp of pauperism.

The third category of the relative surplus-population, the stagnant, forms a part of the active labor army, but with extremely irregular employment. Hence it furnishes to capital an inexhaustible reservoir of disposable labor-power. Its conditions of life sink below the average normal level of the working class; this makes it at once the broad basis of special branches of capitalist exploitation. It is characterized by the maximum of working time, and the minimum of wages. We have learnt to know its chief form under the rubric of "domestic industry." It recruits itself constantly from the supernumerary forces of modern industry and agriculture, and specially from those decaying branches of industry where handicraft is yielding to manufacture, manufacture to machinery. Its extent grows, as with the extent and energy of accumulation, and the creation of a surplus population advances. But it forms at the same time a self-reproducing and self-perpetuating element of the working class, taking a proportionally greater part in the general increase of that class than the other elements. In fact, not only the number of births and deaths, but the absolute size of the families stand in inverse proportion to the height of wages, and therefore, to the amount of means of subsistence of which the different categories of laborers dispose. This law of capitalistic society would sound absurd to savages, or even civilized colonists. It calls to mind the boundless reproduction of animals individually weak and constantly hunted down.

The lowest sediment of the relative surplus-population finally dwells in the sphere of pauperism. Exclusive of vagabonds, criminals, prostitutes, in a word, the "dangerous" classes, this layer of society consists of three categories. First, those able to work. Second, orphans and pauper children. Third, the demoralized and ragged, and those unable to work, chiefly people who succumb to their incapacity for adaptation due to the division of labor; people who have passed the normal age of the laborer; the victims of industry, whose number increases with the increase of dangerous machinery, of mines, chemical works, etc., the mutilated, the sickly, the widows, etc. Pauperism is the hospital of the active labor-army and the dead weight of the industrial reserve-army. Its production is included in that of the relative surplus-population, its necessity in theirs; along with the surplus-population, pauperism forms a condition of capitalist production and of the capitalist development of wealth. It enters into the *faux frais* of capitalist production; but capital knows how to throw these, for the most part, from its own shoulders onto those of the working-class and the lower middle class.

The greater the social wealth, the functioning capital, the extent and energy of its growth, and therefore, also the absolute mass of the proletariat and the productiveness of its labor, the greater is the industrial reserve-army. The same causes which develop the expansive power of capital, develops also the labor-power at its disposal. The relative mass of the industrial reserve-army increases therefore with the potential energy of wealth. But the greater this reserve-army in proportion to the active labor-army, the greater is the mass of a consolidated surplus-population, whose misery is in inverse ratio to its torment of labor. The more extensive, finally, the lazurus-layers of the working-class and the industrial reserve-army, the greater is official pauperism. *This is the absolute general law of capitalist accumulation.*

★ ★ ★

The law by which a constantly increasing quantity of means of production, thanks to the advance in the productiveness of social labor, may be set in movement by a progressively diminishing expenditure of human power, this law, in a capitalist society—where the laborer does not employ the means of production, but the means of production employ the laborer—undergoes a complete inversion and is expressed thus: the higher the productiveness of labor, the greater is the pressure of the laborers on the means of employment, the more precarious, therefore, becomes their condition of existence, viz., the sale of their own labor-power for the increasing of another's wealth or for the self-expansion of capital. The fact that the means of production and the productiveness of labor increase more rapidly than the productive population, expresses itself, therefore, capitalistically in the inverse form that the laboring population always increases more rapidly than the conditions under which capital can employ this increase for its own self-expansion.

PART VIII

The So-Called
Primitive Accumulation

CHAPTER XXVI

THE SECRET OF
PRIMITIVE ACCUMULATION

We have seen how money is changed into capital; how through capital surplus-value is made, and from surplus-value more capital. But the accumulation of capital presupposes surplus-value; surplus-value presupposes capitalistic production; capitalistic production presupposes the pre-existence of considerable masses of capital and of labor-power in the hands of producers of commodities. The whole movement, therefore, seems to turn in a vicious circle, out of which we can only get by supposing a primitive accumulation (previous accumulation of Adam Smith) preceding capitalistic accumulation; an accumulation not the result of the capitalist mode of production, but its starting point.

* * *

In themselves, money and commodities are no more capital than are the means of production and of subsistence. They need to transform into capital. But this transformation itself can only take place under certain circumstances that center in this, *viz.*, that two very different kinds of commodity-possessors must come face to face and into contact; on the one hand, the owners of money, means of production, means of subsistence, who are eager to increase the sum of values they possess by buying other people's labor-power; on the other hand, free laborers, the sellers of their own labor-power, and therefore the sellers of labor. Free laborers, in the double sense that neither they themselves form part and parcel of the means of production, as in the case of slaves, bondsmen, etc., nor do the means of production belong to them, as in the case of peasant-proprietors; they are, therefore, free from, unencumbered by, any means of production of their own. With this polarization of the market for commodities, the fundamental conditions of capitalist production are given. The capitalist system presupposes the complete separation of the laborers from all property in the means by which they can realize their labor. As soon as capitalist production is once on its own legs, it not only maintains this separation, but reproduces it on a continually extending scale. The process, therefore, that clears the way for the capitalist system can be none other than the process which takes away from the laborer the possession of his means of production; a process that transforms, on the one hand, the social means of subsistence and of production into capital, on the other, the immediate producers into wage-laborers. The so-called primitive accumulation, therefore, is nothing else than the historical process of divorcing the producer from the means of production. It appears as primitive, because it forms the pre-historic stage of capital and of the mode of production corresponding with it.

The economic structure of capitalistic society has grown out of the economic structure of feudal society. The dissolution of the latter set free the elements of the former.

The immediate producer, the laborer, could only dispose of his own person after he had ceased to be attached to the soil and ceased to be the slave, serf, or bondman of another. To become a free seller of labor-power who carries his commodity wherever he finds a market, he must further have escaped from the regime of the guilds, their rules for apprentices and journeymen, and the impediments of their labor regulations. Hence, the historical movement which changes the producers into wage-workers appears, on the one hand, as their emancipation from serfdom and from the fetters of the guilds, and this side alone exists for our bourgeois historians. But, on the other hand, these new freedmen became sellers of themselves only after they had been robbed of all their own means of production, and of all the guarantees of existence afforded by the old feudal arrangements. And the history of this, their expropriation, is written in the annals of mankind in letters of blood and fire.

The industrial capitalists, these new potentates, had on their part not only to displace the guild masters of handicrafts, but also the feudal lords, the possessors of the sources of wealth. In this respect their conquest of social power appears as the fruit of a victorious struggle both against feudal lordship and its revolting prerogatives, and against the guilds and the fetters they laid on the free development of production and the free exploitation of man by man.

CHAPTER XXXII

HISTORICAL TENDENCY OF CAPITALIST ACCUMULATION

W hat does the primitive accumulation of capital, i.e., its historical genesis, resolve itself into? Insofar as it is not the immediate transformation of slaves and serfs into wage-laborers, and therefore a mere change of form, it only means the expropriation of the immediate producers, i.e., the dissolution of private property based on the labor of its owner. Private property, as the antithesis to social, collective property, exists only where the means of labor and the external conditions of labor belong to private individuals. But depending on whether these private individuals are laborers or not laborers, private property has a different character. The numberless shades, that it at first sight presents, correspond to the intermediate stages lying between these two extremes. The private property of the laborer in his means of production is the foundation of petty industry, whether agricultural, manufacturing or both; petty industry, again, is an essential condition for the development of social production and of the free individuality of the laborer himself. Of course, this petty mode of production exists also under slavery, serfdom, and other states of dependence. But it flourishes, it lets loose its whole energy, it attains its adequate classical form, only where the laborer is the private owner of his own means of labor set in action by himself: the peasant of the land which he cultivates, the artisan of the tool which he handles as a virtuoso. This mode of production pre-supposes parcelling of the soil and scattering of the other means of production. As it excludes the concentration of these means of production, so also it excludes cooperation, division of labor within each separate process of production, the control over and the productive application of the forces of nature by society, and the free development of the social productive powers. It is compatible only with a system of production and a society moving within narrow and more or less primitive bounds. At a certain stage of development it brings forth the material agencies for its own dissolution. From that movement new forces and new passions spring up in the bosom of society; but the old social organization fetters them and keeps them down. It must be annihilated; it is annihilated. Its annihilation, the transformation of the individualized and scattered means of production into socially concentrated ones, of the pigmy property of the many into the huge property of the few, the expropriation of the great mass of the people from the soil, from the means of subsistence, and from the means of labor, this fearful and painful expropriation of the mass of the people forms the prelude to the history of capital. It comprises a series of forcible methods of which we have passed in review only those that have been epoch-making as methods of the primitive accumulation of capital. The expropriation of the immediate producers was accomplished with merciless vandalism, and under the stimulus of passions the most infamous, the most sordid, the pettiest, the most meanly odious. Self-earned private property, that is based, so to say, on the fusing together of the isolated, independent laboring-individual with the conditions of his labor, is supplanted by capitalistic private property, which rests on exploitation of the nominally free labor of others, i.e., on wage-labor.

As soon as this process of transformation has sufficiently decomposed the old society from top to bottom, as soon as the laborers are turned into proletarians, their means of labor into capital, as soon as the capitalist mode of production stands on its own feet, then the further socialization of labor and further transformation of the land and other means of production into socially exploited and, therefore, common means of production, as well as the further expropriation of private proprietors, takes a new form. That which is now to be expropriated is no longer the laborer working for himself, but the capitalist exploiting many laborers. This expropriation is accomplished by the action of the inherent laws of capitalistic production itself, by the centralization of capital. One capitalist always kills many. Hand in hand with this centralization, or this expropriation of many capitalists by few, develop, on an ever extending scale, the cooperative form of the labor-process, the conscious technical application of science, the methodical cultivation of the soil, the transformation of the instruments of labor into instruments of labor only usable in common, the economizing of all means of production by their use as the means of production of combined, socialized labor, the entanglement of all peoples in the net of the world-market, and this, the international character of the capitalistic regime. Along with the constantly diminishing number of the magnates of capital, who usurp and monopolize all advantages of this process of transformation, grows the mass of misery, oppression, slavery, degradation, exploitation; but with this too grows the revolt of the working-class, a class always increasing in numbers, and disciplined, united, organized by the very mechanism of the process of capitalist production itself. The monopoly of capital becomes a fetter upon the mode of production which has sprung up and flourished along with and under it. Centralization of the means of production and socialization of labor at last reach a point where they become incompatible with their capitalist integument. This integument is burst asunder. The knell of capitalist private property sounds. The expropriators are expropriated.

The capitalist mode of appropriation, the result of the capitalist mode of production, produces capitalist private property. This is the first negation of individual private property, as founded on the labor of the proprietor. But capitalist production begets, with the inexorability of a law of nature, its own negation. It is the negation of negation. This does not re-establish private property for the producer, but gives him individual property based on the acquisitions of the capitalist era: i.e., on cooperation and the possession in common of the land and of the means of production.

The transformation of scattered private property, arising from individual labor, into capitalist private property is, naturally, a process incomparably more protracted, violent, and difficult than the transformation of capitalistic private property, already practically resting on socialized production, into socialized property. In the former case, we had the expropriation of the mass of the people by a few usurpers; in the latter, we have the expropriation of a few usurpers by the mass of the people.